PERSPECTIVE

DISCLAIMER: As an absolute condition of use you hereby agree to the conditions of the complete Disclaimer. The Disclaimer continues and can be found following this book's Endnotes and is, as this, equally binding. By reading this book in any/all forms, you accede to the nature of this book being a personal story written for your personal enrichment and edification. Except where provided within the full Disclaimer, you agree to hold harmless the author, the owner, the publisher, this book, and all entities affiliated with this work of art.

PERSPECTIVE

A flight to victory through relationship with a living Savior

PETER HOEWISCH

Dedicated to

my eternally faithful and loving Father
—and my relational Savior,
Lord, and Friend.

*With man this is impossible,
but with God all things are possible.*
—Matt. 19:26

CONTENTS

THE ROAD TO GOD'S FAITHFULNESS

A little over a decade ago I was mired neck deep in one of the biggest obligations I had yet to find myself. At least that is the way it seemed. I saw no way out of my commitments. I was in the crosshairs of something that would perplex anyone in his early twenties.

I was less than a month away from the end of my senior year of college. I had one more semester to follow in the fall, but threat loomed of buckling under the enormity of my situation. The temptation to doubt was chasing me, getting ever nearer. My first three years of school had been packed with affirmations of what I was doing. I had written numerous journal entries declaring my resolute spirit. My parents echoed my heart. Holding tightly to these immovable stones of belief had been easy at the start. That is, until the state of my existence began to morph from words into unchangeable reality.

I had come a long way, and I was too far into flight school to alter my course. The dollars had been spent. What could I do to change that?

By the time of my graduation I had accumulated school loans in excess of six figures. No doubt students now followed a similar road into aviation, facing even greater debt. If I was being led down a path of trust, then to what end? Whether God made provision for the debt would seriously influence my overall determination of whether my trust had been well placed. It would be years before I fully knew the answer.

Amazingly, God's perfect plan for my life would prove effective in concert with and outside the restraint of the unknowns. I would be unavoidably intertwined with God's infusion of life moments where I would be forced to trust Him implicitly—most often because I had no alternative. Trust would define my growth and the value in that journey would be dictated by the spiritual veracity of each moment.

God would stand powerfully and majestically above all the strain as His faithfulness bridged my weaknesses. In time I would become stronger as a result.

AN INTERACTIVE GOD

Some, perhaps even those who grew up in the church and learned of a faith in Christ, may argue that God doesn't exist—that any claim by a believer that He positively orchestrated or directed a specific event is, instead, pure coincidence. I concede when viewed in isolation or within narrow windows of time that it would appear each could exist apart from the Father's involvement. But as you walk with me through the remarkable encounters of my life, I believe you will be convinced, as I am, that none but a compassionate, involved Creator could have orchestrated these events.

People we encounter in day-to-day life may consider the Lord Jesus Christ impersonal, disconnected, and irrelevant. Many consider Him partially or perhaps completely out of touch with the world and our real lives. That view lends itself to the idea of a universal God, accessible by reason but inattentive to our personal dilemmas. But I have come to know Him as altogether different from that notion. I have experienced Him as personally relevant, even in the smallest affairs of life.

Beginning with my college search and continuing through today, the Lord has taken me down many roads of trial, excitement, and disappointment. This path was unmistakably His doing. In increasing measure, He unveiled before me a tangible faithfulness that impacted the way I handle every trial and event of life. He showed me how to achieve the victory of success. His faithfulness of the past motivated me to trust in the future. In fact, I would become so accustomed to His working presence that to push through this life with anything less would prove a waste of my full potential and cause me grief.

The Lord's intimacy through relationship would provide me experiences like those of Moses and Paul when He revealed Himself to them in personal ways. These amazing interactions would bring vividness to the Scriptures I already knew and show me how it applies to my life. Combine prayer and the encouragement of other believers, and each component would work in harmony to make Him ever more real to me.

In fact, these experiences have led me to believe in the Lord as the only viable answer to this life. His principles and guidelines I now realize are there for my protection. He's saving me *from* myself. He wants to work in me greater than the ramifications I'm otherwise hostage to in my own flawed ways. He would be an unloving Father if He did not guide me to achieve my greatest potential. Worse, any god without some principled standard of character would be uninvolved, dissociated from my life and this world. To see God as uninvolved yet seek Him in life's trials is like yelling in a room of other yelling voices. One won't be heard since his heart is not relationally connected to God. However, if the Lord knows me intimately and guides me through the unknowns, then there is neither limit to what He can do nor to my potential.

WHAT'S IN IT FOR YOU?

If I can demonstrate my examples of following the Lord as beneficial, then it should be taken as evidence by all that the Father can be trusted. I learned that I miss opportunities if I'm not listening to Him and obeying what I know He expects me to do. As with a human relationship between a parent and child, a lack of obedience interrupts communication and relationship.

I ponder the whole of my life like the ascent up a high, snow-capped mountain. Three hundred feet into the climb I look behind me. All I see is a brief portion of the trail I've journeyed as it disappears amid the thick grove of pine trees. I'm unable to see the peak as much as I've lost sight of the valley where I began. As I cross the tree line and approach the heights of the mountain I begin to see the panorama of where I've been as well as the unspoken wonders to come.

In the same way, overlooking the breadth and life history of God's involvement in the individual moments, seeing the whole of His plans, invokes a broader perspective. I find hope on the mountain heights. My desire is for you to be emboldened by seeing the Lord accomplish this work in me, to capture a glimpse, to experience the exhilaration in that life, and to watch *your* faith take to similar heights.

Stay with me now, as I take you back to my beginnings, to help you understand why these tests of my faith loomed large and impacted my journey so significantly. Perhaps a look into the earliest days will shed light on my adventurous search for life and how the Lord played a pivotal role at every turn.

One

EARLY ADVENTURES

It is in a boy's nature to search for adventure and bravery, sometimes even if he battles internal fears. It is here he begins to define himself. He must dare himself, build his courage, and then boast to his peers of the man he is becoming. I was an especially inquisitive little boy.

I loved life and soaked up every detail of my environment. From eating the living room plant to scoping out every last square inch of the white toddler blanket draped over my head, I always seemed to find more undiscovered realms. Curious George was not the only one who allowed his inquisitive nature to lead him astray.

The memories of my exuberance, daring, hesitance, and fear are still fresh. I recall playing with friends on a precarious ice-covered creek bed during a Michigan winter. The sense of accomplishment was palpable as a friend and I engineered and built an igloo on his front lawn. I also recall the feeling of danger as we sat inside hoping it wouldn't collapse.

Emotions of boyhood might and prowess intertwine with memories of snowball wars waged behind snow bunkers we built on either side of his driveway.

In those same years I would face isolating challenges—learning to jump off a diving board, for example. I stood at the edge looking into the deep, blue waters, frozen stiff. I wanted to show I had courage, but shame filled my conflicted spirit . . . until the day I finally achieved victory.

In later years I spent hours charting courses through the deepest woods while suffering the ill effects of my pioneering. Whether it was the agony of being covered in poison oak or coming face-to-face with a startled Water Moccasin, my eagerness for adventure seemed only a normal part of becoming a man. Gaining a bloody nose after a fall off a fence seemed somehow worthy of commemoration.

Yet, not every experience of my youth became a shining moment. I was often teased because of my accelerated growth and tall, slender stature. I repeatedly had stones thrown at me by my grade-school peers after stepping off the school bus. I was punched by someone who days before had called me *friend*. Bullying was common then, as now.

For me, their impacts reverberated deep into my search for belonging. Sometimes shameful reactions were my uncontrolled response, as when I hit a pre-Kindergarten classmate after becoming fed up by his teasing. Most of the time, however, I did nothing. More harmful was the catapult into a faltering self-confidence. I desperately wanted, no, *needed* identity.

Rather than finding many valuable connections to those my age, I regularly felt like an outcast or at least odd enough that I didn't fit in. I retreated, deducing I was better off alone. This wasn't altogether bad, as I'd always possessed an independent nature. My past only fed my tenacious and decisive search for meaning. In the years that followed I continued to strain to find the person I was supposed to be. Little could I have understood then that the Father would use this severe independence and isolation as a powerful instigator in my pursuit of Him.

This was me during my prime, receptive ages. There is a reason I remember those budding years. Those moments left an indelible mark. What I saw through the eyes of youthful imagination—later to be harnessed and played out on life's stage with vigorous invincibility—affected how I would engage my world.

I Was a Parenting Challenge

My parents were patient. They minimized the damage of my youth by always loving me and steering me in the direction of the Lord Jesus for the gentleness and truth He offered. They were careful to allow me to discover the world around me, yet help me comprehend and interpret it. Their aim was to allow for the development of God's wisdom so I would be spurred toward a personal conviction and walk with Christ. Thereafter I could behold my own spiritual growth and His power to stand above life's pain.

My father and mother were not able to protect me from all harm, but in the most crucial aspects they were supportive. They remain intentional in raising their children in the ways and character of the matchless Father. I now see their goals were being achieved in me early, because I *had* comprehended the Father's love for me. I often regret the challenge I was for my parents to raise. Though, I suppose I might not have otherwise known the depth of their love and the love of God, Whom they mirrored.

Family was a critical element in balancing and defining who I would become. They often initiated many of the adventures I harbor as fond memories. I spent countless enjoyable afternoons with my mom after being released from school. I'd ride along on her paper routes or share in the visits with her mother and others at the nursing home where my father worked. I remember my dad and me talking as we walked along the railroad tracks after he surprised me with a tour of the local train yard and a diesel engine locomotive. I savor the lasting memory of my dad sharing with me his enthusiasm for fishing while at a friend's shanty during the months of bitter cold and an ice-clogged river. He'd fish . . . while I nearly died in boredom! So, instead I matched the insignias of the passing ships with the chart posted inside . . . where it was pleasantly *warm*.

I am the youngest of three sons. Mark is the eldest by eleven years. I smile as I recall the time he'd sacrifice to join me in playing Hot

Wheels after he'd arrive home from school. Years later he'd spend hours taking me to the library and youth choir practice at church. Despite our difference in age, Mark never let me out of his sight.

Matthew has eight years on me. The memories remain fresh of playing "Garbage Truck" with him. Like Mark, Matt had his special place. He was the one to teach me to ride my first bike when I was seven. I remember him voluntarily standing up for me when other kids attacked or made fun of me. As we all grew older, these brotherly bonds matured into love and friendship.

INITIAL FAITH FORAYS

Matters of faith played into my earliest memories, as well. My parents recall me as an infant being rocked or fed. I would lock eyes on a Richard Hook portrait of Jesus we had hanging above our couch. Even then, it seemed, God was drawing me to Himself.

I hold vivid memories of church life, with all its culture and history. This was the existence I knew with the most clarity. I seemed to have an affinity for being there since the moment I was born. My mother would wheel me in by stroller to hear her lead children's worship before Sunday School.

I recall sitting in the pew as a toddler while eating my Cheerios. In later years, when my feet had full freedom to explore, my parents took me along while they had choir rehearsal or were printing the Sunday bulletins. While I waited I *had* to see if I had what it took to walk through the dark, cavernous-like realm of the basement under the sanctuary. It was usually only seconds before I'd run across its span, petrified someone was down there with me.

It was not long before I started to envision myself as having my own part to play in our church. After the sanctuary lights were extinguished, the organ stopped playing its reverberating melodies, and the choir departed, my father and mother attended to their voluntary duties. Meanwhile, I quietly and reverently proceeded to the altar and then the pulpit. With vivid imagination and a courageous eagerness to be older, I began to speak through the darkness to an imaginary crowd.

This role-playing neither stopped at the doors of our church. On more than one occasion at home I carefully picked up an ornate, green glass goblet stored in our house pantry. Finding myself once more in the limitless world of youthful reveries, I ushered in all my stuffed animals and worshipfully presented them on the shelves. Reiterating in the closest way I could the words spoken so many times by our pastor, I began to serve the Lutheran wafer and cup of wine to my own ceremonial congregation.

Every element of this reality was grabbing my attention, and most of the time I enjoyed being in church. Note, I said *most* of the time. I was not always amiable, namely when my feisty will created a grumpy demeanor that necessitated my parents to exercise their authority and require me to go to church. It would be more than a decade before I came to understand the true meaning in being there. Even during my middle school years I'd glance at my watch every five minutes, hoping somehow the sermon might conclude faster.

———

My dad was a Lay Minister in the Lutheran Church long before I was ever born. My parents' goal of laying a foundation was especially apparent as they taught me God's Word through memory cards and ensured my continual presence in church. By rule of my strong-willed nature and my incessant desire to chart my own course, I remained inquisitively open to discovering the Lord.

Being this stubborn and rebellious, I realized early on that I was not inherently good. This became personally evident at home. I readily perceived my innate human propensity to do wrong at a cost to others and the ease of surrendering to that controlling influence. I knew I was a sinner, and this became more apparent with every passing day. I wanted—*needed*—someone or something to fix what I, deep down, did *not* like.

My memory no longer serves the details, but I recall being younger than eight by the time I grasped the simple gospel of salvation. I understood Jesus Christ brought life, and His principles were designed to keep me from harm. I told the Father I realized how imperfect I was, and that His Son lived a perfect life and died in my place. Even though it might have only been verbalized within my heart, God knew I accepted that exchange on my behalf.

This grant of life from the loving Father would begin a new era of awe and wonder. In these early stages you would have found me praying with my parents or attempting to comfort them and others with the assurance that Christ would take care of their needs. I suppose this was where I began to flourish as an individual. I finally had a purpose and source for my steady aspirations to influence others' lives. I had begun to define who I was going to be and who I did not want to be. The more I learned about this faith called Christianity, the more I wanted to put it into practice and test the genuineness of the actual results. The more I tested the more I learned.

THE SISTER I NEVER MET

I would be seriously negligent, however, if I did not give light to one more facet of my childhood responsible for deeply influencing my early years and ultimately my view of faith. I would not be the same had I not witnessed the effects trying times had upon my family, and, yes, even my own life. One of these events would forever alter our family.

It was shortly before my birth that life hit the family with blunt force. A little more than five years prior to my unexpected birth, my sister Heidi entered their world. She was born three months premature. It was a trying time for my parents and brothers, so it has been explained to me. Heidi developed a common heart defect, which of itself would not have been so bad. What it did do was negatively impact her intestines and their ability to absorb needed nutrients. Eventually, combined with multiple other physical issues, and after countless surgeries, she passed away in my mother's arms after only ten months of life. It remains a sweet but tender topic in family memory. I never knew my sister. In fact, frustration over my parents and brothers being able to hold her while she lived has in the past been known to bring me to perplexing emotion. I miss her as though she was once a part of my life, and my many spilled tears reveal our unique bond.

Although I was the last in tow, I cannot point to any time when my parents and brothers did not love me unconditionally. I wonder, though, if I may have had more reason to believe I needed to know I belonged since I was unanticipated after a deep loss. A fear of being truly alone without family and love left me terrified early in life. This fear combined with my broad reach for acceptance catapulted me into a disorder long before the age of eight.

A Diagnosis and a Move

In the mid-1980s, Obsessive Compulsive Disorder was hardly a blip on the medical radar. It was barely understood. By the Lord's grace and my parents' attentive love, it was recognized early. Then, as surely by God's providence, my dad was relieved of his lengthy career as a controller and administrator in the nursing home industry. I had just had my eighth birthday. My dad was left with no choice but to look for solid employment in a hurting economy. Dallas was not the best city to find work, but it was the only home of the most renowned Christian counseling, particularly for childhood behavioral disorders.

My parents quickly realized it was no longer about the job. The Lord motioned in their hearts that where we moved was going to be necessitated by what was in my best interest. They pleaded with the Minirth-Meier clinic to counsel me. Despite the lack of a job or a place to live, in May 1988 we packed our belongings into a U-Haul and left everyone and everything we knew in Michigan bound for Dallas. Little did my parents know a letter had been in route to

Michigan officially rejecting their request for treatment and advisement not to come to Texas.

Through nothing shy of divine intervention, I was counseled for OCD. The transformation of my battling mind and tattered spirit began. It would be a long road to recovery. Would being raised and guided toward a focus on Christ and His offer of life be adequate to relieve me from years of oppressive, consuming patterns? Would I develop a faith to convey me out of OCD? Scientific data would not support those notions.

One thing remained unmistakable. The faith that was required of my father and mother to make this seemingly unwise decision to move on my account, gave me an enormous window into the reality of their belief in the Lord Jesus. It revealed the possibility that the Father was capable to supply every need for me, just as He had for them.

God would use these distressing difficulties that my family experienced to help me find my way. My parents maintain Heidi's brief physical life initiated a new phase in their spiritual walks as they realized the purposes and blessings from her life. Their faith and life was turned upside down and greatly tested, but in the end this only deepened them toward a stronger relationship with the Lord Jesus. The faith by which they have *all* handled that combined with the hard choices and faith necessary in my dad's joblessness . . . well, I could not ignore it. I witnessed the inexplicable. I was watching both my parents' perspectives and approaches to their troubles. There had to have been some measure of truth to my parents' faith.

A FAITH TO OWN

From the earliest defining evolutions of my life, I was maturing. I craved my own faith experience. In my own way I chose to be engaged in church and in challenging my own beliefs. After all, I was *born* an explorer. Adventurous curiosity was always my underlying driving force. I wanted to taste, smell, touch, listen and then come to my own conclusions.

This did not mean I was devoid of adolescent insecurities, particularly as I entered the common, self-defining teenage years. Though an adventurer at heart, I often outwardly revealed a mindset bound by caution. Whether flying on an airliner or riding a rollercoaster, I had internal, fear-filled limits to danger stashed somewhere. My strong independence only added to my complex nature. I did not mind going to church or sitting down as a family around the Word of God, but I loathed being told to do so. I found myself caught in the middle of my spiritual eagerness and my desire to define my manhood while trying to show my peers I had my own stake in life.

There was one problem. I had not yet conclusively resolved *who* this Person was into whom I had placed all my thoughts, feelings, and intentions. At this stage I had yet to taste a markedly close relationship with the Father as one that could radically change the way I behaved and engaged the world. Did I really have a faith of my own?

Then a transition occurred and I was surprisingly unprepared for it. The time arrived when I had to elect whether or not to take ownership of the foundations of the Christian faith. This was so true that I swiftly became individually firm in my own understandings of who Christ was. Concluding my high school years, I naturally cut the umbilical cord of my parent's faith and increasingly strove to define the independent relationship with Christ for which I was longing.

The Lord rapidly began to mold and shape. He built into me a growing confidence, a unique package of abilities, and the kernels of understanding His purpose for me. I began to find my identity in Him rather than from my peers and family. But this brought its own challenges, in discerning His direction. What was I going to college to learn? What should I do as a career? There was one thing I sensed for certain: the Lord was asking me to give my life in service to Him and to goals greater than anything I could attain apart from Him. That perception seemed genuine, but I wasn't sure. Was I actually about to witness the evolution of my independent faith?

That theory was going to be tested. Weeks prior to entering college I mustered the courage to do something extraordinary. While in an evening church service I felt His Spirit prompt me to pledge my life toward a ministry. I didn't know from Him what ministry that would be. Strikingly, this was my first, notable sense of God's power. It seemed I had been drawn near to the Lord, but had I if I wasn't sensing a leading to undertake formal education in ministry?

Doubts began to fill my heart and mind as to my own salvation. If I was saved and it was more than a childhood acquired confidence, then the Lord was going to have to reveal to me through His Word and relationship that proof of saving faith. It would need to come soon before I entered the real and expectedly harsh years of college life. All I really knew at the moment was that I arrived at a crossroads with *Indecision* being every street name on the signpost.

My faith was still in its infancy. It was as though I had learned how to put on my shoes, but hadn't yet learned how to tie them. I admit I was content to walk around with the laces loose and dragging on the ground. The Lord knew and appreciated the danger in doing this better than I. He knew I could never reach my full potential or realize the full life He wanted for me by maintaining the status quo. I was about to leave the roads of my past and board a one-way ship through rough seas and shallow waters that would challenge my beliefs and try my limits.

The hull of my ship would soon become riddled with holes. The inundating waters of coming trials would threaten to submerge my ship and plunge me along with it. These waters would at times have to be traveled in the pitch of night, leaving merely the assurance of His hand from behind with no guarantee of what was in front. Would I choose to navigate the more difficult, narrower waters? I asked every question I could *about* everything I could.

Amazingly, the Father responded, and the broader answer is found within His intimate orchestration of my life. It is in my story of redemption and relationship. It is there He used our encounters to captivate me to keep searching. It wasn't that a search was necessary to find Him. He already had found me. The Lord was the One Who grabbed *me*. He had His hand on me and never let go. He took hold of me when I was still lost trying to figure out who I was. Indisputably, the Lord used the influence of my parents' faith and my family. But, neither I nor anyone else initiated my Christian faith. Through Christ and His Holy Spirit, God the Father alone drew me to Himself. Only He knew how to perfectly orchestrate the affairs of this world to create the opportunity to reveal Himself to me, and invite me to join a friendship unlike anything I had experienced.

The *real* journey of my life was now setting sail. I was about to venture into entirely unexplored waters. Entering university life was when the Lord began to chart a new relationship with me, one that made my faith and trust challenging and powerful while thoroughly convincing me of the existence of both.

Every believer's relationship with the Father will be put to the test—where doubts and unanswered questions are exposed. It was my turn to be tested and to test—to see who the Lord was. All of me had become the springboard for what the Father was readying Himself to do in my vast world. My faith and trust in Him were about to be concretely defined and verified, and it was going to be on an accelerated learning curve. Life as I knew it was about to be strewn with questions, hurdles, complications, and conquests. Surrounded by a family and witnessing their faith holding true through sorrow and uncertainty, I was on course to learn, grow, and develop in Christ. I would discover exactly who this Jesus in whom I had come to believe proved to *really* be.

Two

A Proposal of the Impossible

So, how did I find the Lord to be relational? One of the ways was through watching Him do the impossible. Often, though, He waits for my own resourcefulness and logic to prove fruitless before He steps in and says, "You can't do it. But I can."

I saw Him work this way when I was seeking a college and a career path to follow. In January 1999 I was months from concluding my high school education as a home-schooled child from grades seven through twelve. Along with my parents, I began to explore possibilities. It became an intense time of praying and pursuing the Father's will and His best desire.

Meteorology captured my attention. I spent many hours closely watching severe Texas weather. I even wrote a high school research paper on tornadoes. I was engrossed *and* enthused in the science.

My home-school supervisor was quick to recommend a school deeply set in the green hills of southern Missouri, College of the Ozarks. It was also a tuition free, Christian institution designed as a work-study program. Ninety percent of the students who attend receive Federal financial aid. The other ten percent do not. I had no savings set aside. Additionally, my parents' ability to contribute was limited because my dad had been unemployed for two years. So, this school looked like quite the appealing and logical choice.

We took a several-day trip to Branson, Mo., to view the college.

Shortly after we began the tour of the campus the female guide asked my course interest. Without hesitation I enthusiastically answered, "Meteorology." Like a young boy watching his first bike demolished behind his parents' car, I was crushed when she told me they had no such program.

She then suggested we all go to a hilltop on their property. This became one of those God-moments when He intervened and unfolded His creative plan before my eyes. I can't describe the awe of the next few moments atop that plateau. The school had their own, functioning instructional airport. In an instant I was captivated by the notion of flying. I didn't know there were colleges with an instructional airport. This idea was such a foreign concept. I had come to appreciate flying, but for me to consider being in the *front seat* of those amazing machines had been beyond my imagination.

We stayed in the campus hotel that evening. Thoughts raced through my mind. I could apply myself to flying. I already had a love affair with the weather. Pilots need that. Mechanics had nearly formed an addiction as I maintained my parents' cars during high school. Check off another need. A personal inventory taken earlier had even recommended the field of aviation. How had I not made this connection before? Then, I remembered going forward in church to offer myself to ministry. God could answer that in being a missionary pilot. Aviation offered *all* of these facets—wrapped up in one amazing career.

As I prayed and deliberated more that night, I started wondering whether the Lord might be leading me into missionary aviation. In that capacity I could function as both mechanic and pilot. I was as pumped about this vision as a sports player is before a game. You know the final score is yet to be decided, but you have every expectation of winning.

With this newfound enthusiasm for the world of aviation and the financial needs that could be met through that school, I submitted an application to College of the Ozarks. But when I received a response, it was marked denied. I was disheartened. Wasn't it an obvious choice? How could the Lord disapprove of any of it?

WHAT COULD GOD HAVE IN MIND?

This was the season of my life where I learned a key truth that would become a refrain in later years: the Lord had better plans.

It was time to pray and search with more focus. A few months later my parents met with friends from church. When they learned of my innate hands-on inclination, they suggested we look at LeTourneau University in Longview. It was an easy two-hour drive, nestled in the heart of the piney woods of east Texas. I hadn't known of the school. But in May 1999 on a humid Texas day we ventured east for a campus visit.

The preview of LeTourneau was unlike my experience at College of the Ozarks. It wasn't the layout of the campus, the people, or what they had to offer. No, it was a sense of something inexplicably special. I still remember the feeling I had after arriving in the school's parking lot. I hadn't yet stepped foot out of the car and I could have sworn I had been there before. After inquiring of my parents, they said I had not.

Through some discussion, I came to identify this as one of my first, real encounters of His soothing peace. I couldn't explain this depth of rushing calm through any logic. On the contrary, my temperament typically is nervousness when considering anything new. There could be no other explanation but that I sensed the Lord's presence on that campus that day. He had gone ahead and was readying me to attend.

After touring the campus and the airport facility several miles south at East Texas Regional, it seemed the Lord was about to initiate the first challenge to my faith and trust. Everything about LeTourneau was great. The culture was instantly welcoming. Most appealing was their pure and humble focus on Christian values.

They didn't force students to accept Christianity, but they did intertwine faith with studies. This permitted an atmosphere conducive to spiritual and educational growth.

I stepped forward in faith and applied. I was ready to give my spiritual ship its first sea trials. We knew financial aid would be a significant hurdle; but, if this was the impossible task the Lord was accomplishing, He'd make a way. Tuition was in the neighborhood of $18,000 for a single, two-semester school year, and even more if I flew. We were discouraged by the cost. We didn't know where we would acquire that kind of money. Taking on debt was not our family way. Living within means exercises the stewardship the Lord desires. We believed He was aiming to enact a *greater* standard through asking us to trust Him.

COULD GOD OVERCOME THIS HURDLE?

Despite the prospect of loans, I still recall a personally specific directive from the Lord. He wanted me at LeTourneau. It was a peace that washed over me, as if He were saying, "Do what I have asked you to do. Do not worry about the debt. I *am* sufficient. I *am* more than able, and will take care of the debt in My way and in My time. I *am* going to prove Myself to you." I was blessed with more affirmation when my parents each felt a settled spirit about LeTourneau.

Weeks passed. Between excitement and fighting my human unsettledness, I was wondering what the holdup could be. Then the call came. The admissions office notified me that I had been awarded scholarships and grants in the neighborhood of $8,000. This cost reduction proved to be the glimmer of His promise we needed. My father, mother, and I had no question the Lord had confirmed our steps. Knowing He would go ahead of us we proceeded with the application process.

I opted to enter their flight program. Only later did I discover it was one of the most well-respected flight programs in the United

States. In fact, several years into my college education my brother, Mark, relayed to me a conversation between him and a Southwest Airlines pilot and coworker on a flight. Of all the pilots coming on board from the civilian sector, LeTourneau and Embry Riddle were the most appealing. LeTourneau had a rigorous flight program whose successful completion surpassed the FAA's high standards of excellence. I would be able to vouch for that in a few short years.

Even though I was only beginning to embrace this new, challenging relationship with my Father and Lord, I recall possessing a strong desire to be able to share with others what I had already learned about His active and faithful provision in my life.

I didn't see much of the "lessons learned" until months and years later, but as I witnessed about it, the clarity came as I pursued God continuously in prayer. My circumstances seemed impossible to overcome.

Even with the large grant and scholarships, the huge financial obligation that ensued seemed an impossible hurdle to me. I was confident God wanted me there. I wanted to believe He could do the impossible. That's why I kept seeking Him. I knew it was His voice and command, but I wanted to be sure I was hearing correctly and from the right source. My commitment to obey and follow His leading to LeTourneau was only the overture to my test, and it centered squarely on my trust. It was apparent to me I was supposed to be learning to fly at LeTourneau. What I had yet to discover was how far I would trust that "notion."

A whole new array of struggles coming in the years ahead would force my return to Him asking, "Are You *sure* this is what I'm supposed to be doing?" This question was quick to be asked in my first semester, Fall 1999. It was going to be a *big* one.

Three

A LEADING, A CALLING . . . AND A COMPLICATION

I enjoyed my first college experiences. I acclimatized smoothly and easily. What we had been told upon application was proving true. Those coming from the home-school background could find the transition into the demanding schedule to be astonishingly straightforward. I corresponded with my father by email. He and my mother became my sounding boards as I was feeling the intensity of my spiritual growth alongside my new educational experiences.

I did have my struggles, though. Almost immediately I experienced my first adrenaline hit. I overslept and was late to a core freshman class. Its purpose was to train a new student how to budget time and tailor study habits to one's own strengths. Evidently, I had not yet perfected its application.

One of the first email exchanges with my dad happened after a conversation with the instructor of that class. While admiring my yearning to follow the Lord anywhere I believed He was leading, the teacher affirmed that aviation, including missionary aviation, was a career field well-suited for my personality. I was fortified and bolstered. I began to see the Father at the ready not only to provide the capability to succeed, but also to bring immediate answers to my searching prayers for confirmation of the direction I believed He had given.

This transition into college made it evident that my desire was to be in the Lord's will. I was ascertaining that if I tried to go my own way or make decisions based on a gut feeling, I would more than likely not have happiness much less joy in my journey. I was learning that when I followed His will, no matter what I was led to do, the task would end up enjoyable and rewarding. When I knew I was *exactly* where I was supposed to be, the peace and delight that consumed me were worth any "sacrifice" in skipping out on my own desires. This view would continue to solidify as the years progressed. However, the real challenge to my faith was yet to take flight.

OFF MY MEDS

I was now twenty. I had been on various anti-depressant medications for OCD since age nine. Without delay upon entering LeTourneau the flight department made me aware that the FAA did not allow this medication for pilots. So, *now* what was I supposed to do? Almost instinctively, I did the only thing I knew to do—pray.

There was only one apparent and obvious conclusion when faced with the *inability* to fly while still possessing the belief I was *supposed* to fly. In Fall 1999 I came to believe the Father wanted me to permanently end my anti-depressant medication. I sensed He longed for me to trust He could forever deliver and actually *had* already delivered me from the earthly constraints of the past to which that childhood disorder had me bound. Through much advice from a caring flight instructor, Mr. Lauren Bitikofer, the steps to take were laid before me as I moved forward in this belief of deliverance.

I should tell you that after I turned sixteen, the counseling I had been receiving from Dr. Paul Warren had ceased. I was no longer qualified to be counseled due to the organization's age limits. So, I was teamed with another doctor for the purpose of monitoring my medication. His name was Dr. Darren Meyer. I did not know if he had ever experienced the far-reaching power of Almighty God, but both of us were soon to be given a wonderful opportunity to see science blown away.

The first step I had to take was to approach Dr. Meyer with my desire to discontinue the medication. As I was sitting in his office making this proposition he was quick to offer cautions. He wasn't opposed but was assuredly reluctant. He reminded me that most patients with OCD remain on medication for the rest of their lives. I told him I believed I was supposed to fly. I relayed my firm belief that the Father had delivered me from OCD's grip and the need to be medicated so that I *could* fly.

He agreed that we had not tried managing without medication for a number of years. So, we could attempt it again and weigh the outcome. Over the remainder of that opening semester at LeTourneau, I followed his weaning schedule. I eagerly pressed on toward the tangible deliverance I believed was inevitable. I reached the conclusion of this process on December 30. Taking pills for eleven years was finally a memory. It was over, and it was a relief.

I returned to Dr. Meyer's office for the scheduled follow up. He was pleasantly stunned I was doing so well off the medication. I found I agreed with him on some medical points, and he likewise found common ground with my beliefs. First, he believed addressing my OCD at so early an age when my brain was still rapidly growing contributed to this outcome. This, in essence, enabled my brain to rewire itself. Even then, I have to face the truth the Lord had moved my parents to treat me. So, it's not as if this notion is entirely explainable aside from Him. Second, after I reiterated to the doctor that the Lord had delivered me and taught me how to deal with the OCD through my biblical, relational reliance on God, he agreed this had helped free me from its long history. He acknowledged it had been shown that dealing in a spiritual manner with disorders like OCD can open certain neuro pathways. It was an amazing result for both of us to behold, and God used Dr. Meyer to be a part of His plan for my life.

I was purely and enthusiastically convinced this success was nothing to be answered with science alone. It was the Lord's divine deliverance. To this day I believe He conveyed me out of the disorder's hold on my life, I dare say miraculously. I remain free of all medicine and captivity. Seeing with my eyes the Lord's powerful hand moving in my life accomplished several things. Most critically, He nailed a hook in my heart on which I could hang His faithfulness. This was the first, real and vivid lesson in trusting Him to get me through whatever roadblocks would attempt to keep me from doing what He asked me to do. I trusted to the extent He made me increasingly capable to trust Him, and I found I didn't fall flat. I was filled with a new sense of excitement about the now more real prospect of flying, and a humble intensity to move forward knowing He had reinforced my placement at LeTourneau.

Now, I Can Fly

With the first semester and its pivotal test behind me, the next step was to officially proceed into the flight program. I had been gearing for this through my course studies, but I had yet to be in the airplane with my hands on the controls. The first assignment would be to get my Private Pilot's license.

Mr. Bitikofer, who by this time had become to me a good friend and mentor, was Director of Flight at LeTourneau. In knowing the way I learned, he confidently stated it would be best for me to train during the summer. He noted I excelled better with harder courses when I could focus on one thing instead of conjoining the time constraints and pressures of flying with other curricular studies. After consulting as a family we concurred with his recommendation. It is still amazing how intuitively knowledgeable of me Mr. Bitikofer was so early in our acquaintance. I could not help but imagine how much more Christ, a perfect, all-knowing, and intimate Creator understands me. That discovery was made all the sweeter now that

I had something of which to look forward. Before long I would actually be *flying*.

I felt as if I was once again that giddy little kid jumping up and down in the K-Mart checkout line filled with an insatiable exuberance while waiting for my parents to gift me the next edition to my Matchbox car collection. I hadn't grown up with the idea of flying like some youth. It persisted to be a new and crazy dream, but it was suddenly that much closer to being realized. I could nearly touch it. I could *taste* it.

Missionary Flight Becomes a Real Possibility

My eagerness to take hold of the dream and press forward with flight training would be fueled by the intrigue of one day putting it to use while tackling many of my interests at once. I hadn't forgotten about the initiative toward ministry the Lord planted in my heart and mind on the campus of College of the Ozarks. No, I actually had all the more reason to embrace it. On February 7, 2000, just months after I received my freedom from OCD, LeTourneau hosted their annual missionary expo. Multiple missionary organizations would come and talk to the student body to describe missions and what it entailed.

I learned what the LeTourneau flight program offered these organizations. Missionary Aviation Fellowship (MAF) had a list of schools where they would send their students to be trained as pilots. LeTourneau University was the only one out of the two I had considered. My growing enthusiasm was bolstered further when the MAF representative assured me I would be fully qualified to work with them immediately upon rounding out my LeTourneau education.

Then I was slammed to the mat by several unexpected counterpunches. It was true I would be qualified in the sense of Federal licensing. Though, as I unearthed the flight hour minimums, I learned I would likely have to accrue more flight experience beyond my training. This left two logical alternatives in my mind. I would have to be a flight instructor or pay to build my time. Then I would be eligible to maneuver in the industry. In either event, this would forestall any wish of entering missions straightway.

The most blaring conflict to the prospect of ministry was financial. I was accustomed to the thought of working as a missionary by means of financial sponsorship, but I learned I also had to be debt free. Not only was I accruing debt from my regular academic expenses, but my fellow students informed me flight would add to this growing total to the tune of $34,000.

To my relief the Father quickly appeased my faltering spirit. The threat of anxiousness was deterred when the MAF recruiter confidently explained it was customary to face mounting debt learning to fly. He wasn't disturbed. Many came to them with school loans. No matter which school I would have attended, levying flight was at minimum an expected requirement. My feet became eager to engage the battle head-on the moment he said they were trying to form a solution to this hurdle to assist in recruiting desperately needed pilots.

Likewise, attending LeTourneau proved timely as the flight department prepared to launch a bridge program with American Eagle. If I enrolled I would be guaranteed a job interview upon graduation and likely go on to be hired. So, it seemed a viably inclusive solution was readily presented, perhaps even orchestrated by the Lord's plans. I told my parents in an email my worry over the loans was waning as long as the Lord kept opening the doors. Those surrounding me at LeTourneau reminded me He was doing so already, because I had been medically cleared to fly.

Missionary aviation was dawning as a clear and logical goal. In fact, it would be more than simply a job. One of the most convincing reasons was my emergent yearning to nurture others toward the discovery of everything I knew about the Father. Curiously, I hadn't thought of my Christian faith as adequate to equip me to show it to others *through* my life, despite being compelled in that direction. I felt the Lord nudging me saying, "In the mission field, Peter, you could fly, work on aircraft engines, negotiate weather, and do My work all at the same time."

Convincing as this leading was, it was ironic to me. Like the absence of any boyhood dream of flying, I not once relished going into the mission field. Frankly, the prospect frightened me. For one, I had the unfounded fear that to be a missionary meant certain death. Furthermore, I was afraid of ministering to people because I didn't see myself as socially engaging. For now I was satisfied with the concept of being a missionary pilot pouring into lives through less intimately interactive tasks.

The notion of missionary aviation began to sound like something befitting of my personality. I became content to continue the immediate tasks of college while leaving an open mind to missions for what it offered in both the outreach to people and the exercise of my multifaceted interests.

FLYING DOUBTS

Frustratingly, new cracks of doubt would somehow reemerge to fracture the mental and spiritual clarity the Father had just mended. The contemplation of financial debt would rear its ugly head from time to time. It didn't help to later hear MAF warn against being lured away from an aspiring interest in missions by the "glitz and glamour" of other aeronautical pursuits. That risk would have to be addressed in the future. Meanwhile I began to ask: Was the mission field my own idea or God's? Would I be *unlike* my other enticed peers to instead be stubborn and focused enough on God's will not to let go of His leading?

I still recall the angst I felt in the fall and winter of that first year as I uncovered everything about aviation, the monster named *Debt*, the strong leading toward being a missionary pilot, and the many questions that arose. It could have consumed me, but I found the Lord was ever ready to console me in the stern way only a loving Father could. In one email to my parents I wrote, "I understand perfectly how scary this must be. I am in the middle of it myself. But, I trust Him to proceed here. Within the past couple of weeks I had been hearing Him say again, 'Who are you going to trust? Are you going to believe that I am bigger than money or are you going to rely on your strength only? I love you, but trust Me.'"

The Lord reminded me of how He had been faithful throughout the college search and the struggle of being permitted to fly. The more I kept my focus on trusting Him the more all the potential for failure and losing sight of His will washed away, to be replaced by eager anticipation. Putting the vacillation aside for a confidence in His faithfulness brought me peace and excitement. I concluded that email, "We'll see where He leads, but I *do* think that this is where I belong."

Emboldened, I continued to strain in pursuit of this course with all the focus and intent I could muster. Since those days, however, He would remain rather silent about the mission field. Instead, He would quietly confirm my path while calming my restless spirit by saying, "Peter, do what I brought you to LeTourneau to do. Then, after you are done I will tell you what I want you to do with that education. Do not worry about these other things." I am *still* blown away by His tenderness and love.

My most immediate task was to focus on my studies of that spring semester, and then take on flying in the summer. I was keenly, almost fanatically, looking forward to exploring the wide-open skies, especially having now witnessed the Lord's sovereign hand overcome such a critical road block as my OCD. Though it was *not* the last I would have to face that hurdle. Sadly, my history of OCD keeping me from flying was not over. It was just beginning.

Four

WHAT NEXT? I THOUGHT I PASSED THIS TEST

What was unthinkable became reality. Just when I had thought I was clear to move on to flying there arose a whole new set of complications linked to my OCD that would potentially keep me from tackling the course in early summer. A week after my intents toward missionary aviation found their real, firm beginnings, new information started bowling me over.

In the first of many frantic messages, an email to my dad dated February 16, 2000 revealed the impediment to flying. Mr. Bitikofer was promising to seek advice from an advocate. The Aircraft Owners and Pilots Association would be the best organization to clarify the FAA's stipulations pertaining to my OCD medication, a matter I thought was already concluded.

Here was the complication. I had to be medically cleared by the FAA to be a pilot. I had recently met with an FAA certified medical examiner near our home to obtain my first flight medical. The outcome of that examination was not what I expected. Instead of being cleared to fly, my application was submitted for review. Despite having been off medication the doctor stated I had a six month probationary period before I could start flying. The FAA needed to verify the absence of any adverse effects. Discouragement rapidly accumulated. Would I ultimately be disallowed from flying? At minimum it now appeared I would not begin my flight course that summer, as planned. In an anxious search for consolation I asked my dad's opinion, "I probably shouldn't take this as a definite 'no,' I suppose, do you? It just may not mean that I should fly right now."

Being the loving, caring father, my dad spoke with the medical examiner on my behalf since I was busy with school. My dad relayed the examiner's instructions to obtain a letter from my prescribing doctor stating how long I had been off of medication and the slim likelihood I would ever need to resume taking it. The examiner then supposed I would have to remain off the medication one to maybe as many as two years before I could be reexamined, suggesting we contact the FAA to be sure. To my emotional dismay my dad concluded his email: "It looks like the door is definitely closed for this summer."

Need I say this was a major blow? One to *two* years? This was *much* different from the doctor's previous statement of six months. Would all I had been through and all the lessons of trust only end up fruitless? I was *screaming* for an answer from the Lord. The door to flying might be just as quickly closing, at least into my junior year—which would seriously set me behind schedule.

I Reach the End of My Resources

My parents continued to be the source of experienced wisdom that I needed as I developed in my own relationship with the Lord. On February 25, they responded to an email I had sent discussing the struggles I was having with my grades and other affairs. Though it might not have pertained specifically to the situation, I found it to be applicable to the challenge of being approved to fly. They said:

> I think we both believe Satan is using fear as his weapon to make you scared. So number one, you'll have to arm yourself with Jesus' words because He says over and over again "fear not." Fear is not from Him, it is from Satan. Your mother said you have memorized Isaiah 41:10, so it would be a good

one to throw back at the enemy—he is your adversary. Peter, all through life, he's going to try to devour you. So stand firm on God's Word, whether it's spoken to you or whether you read it yourself, or hear it in a sermon in church or chapel. His Word is what counts. Your mom likes 41:10 in her Beck [AAT] translation: "Don't be afraid—I am with you. Don't look around anxiously—I am your God. I will strengthen you; Yes, I will help you. I will support you with My victorious right hand." That is going to mean times when you are screaming out to God for help and just maybe He'll let you fail. But you will still be growing. So, stay close to God even though you feel stretched to the limit. We are so proud of who you are and who God is making you to be, so hang in there and don't be afraid of tomorrow. God already has tomorrow planned out for you. We are praying on this end—always remember to be fortified by that knowledge.

A long, agonizing month dragged past before I heard any answer to my questions. One day while in a prerequisite ground class for the Private Pilot course, I was granted news from my professor, Mr. Bitikofer. It was true that I had to be off medication. He then added that I also had to have a letter from the FAA. What I still didn't know was the time required to be off the medication. Unfortunately, all I learned was that I now had *another* requirement before I could start flying.

The belief that the Lord had delivered me from OCD was holding rock solid. I knew ceasing the medication was something only *He* could have enabled and accomplished through His provisional strength. After hearing the statistics from Dr. Meyer, I knew I couldn't have made the conscious choice to decide to be done with OCD and its medications. It had all been so clear. God alone did this. I still believe this to be true.

Through this focused peace, however, there was rising an inward frustration. I had been through this test before; why did I need to go through it again? Didn't I already demonstrate I knew how to trust? I believe I possessed overconfidence. My impatience was growing, and it was about to be on the verge of interfering with the lesson the Father was aiming to teach me. Since I professed to know and trust God's direction for my life, it was time to learn to trust in His faithfulness to carry it through.

There was nothing I could do. It was out of my hands, and, in my humanness, I didn't like that feeling. Even the most immediate task of a phone call was not on my shoulders to complete. No one seemed to know for certain what the FAA's requirements were. That is why Mr. Bitikofer said he would clear up the confusion with the AOPA. I began to ask him every day whether he had received clarification, but he had just not had the opportunity. To his credit he was a busy professor, flight instructor, and director. So, my mental and spiritual anguish continued for two more tormenting weeks.

I wanted resolution now, even if I had to force it. For obvious reasons this usually doesn't get one far. Honestly, I wasn't doing well down this road of trust. That is when the Father lovingly grabbed hold of me. I remember that day clearly. I was exhausted from trying to obtain AOPA's answer as to how to acquire that elusive letter from the FAA.

I had reached my end and He was right there to hear me say, "Lord, this is out of my hands. There is nothing I can do. If this is not where You desire for me to be, I don't want to be here. I want Your will to be done. I don't want to put my hand in this situation only to become the one deciding whether I pursue flight or not. I want You to handle this and I want You to open the doors. I'm tired of trying to get an answer to this myself. I relinquish this to You."

Sometimes all He wants is for us to concede control to Him. To my embarrassment, this wasn't going to be the last time I'd have to learn to let go.

The next day I spoke to the Lord proclaiming my trust in Him. I had no choice but to recommit it to Him for a second time because I could sense I was trying to take back control. Well, get this: the following day I received an email from Mr. Bitikofer. Yes, he had finally called the AOPA and received a response.

Mr. Bitikofer's note was short, but sweet. I probably could have fallen over when he said I was only required to be ninety days removed from my medication. Afterward, my prescribing doctor had to write a letter to the FAA Airmen Certification branch giving the start and end dates for the medication, a reason it was prescribed, and a declaration that the condition which required its use has not relapsed after its discontinuance. The FAA would reevaluate and subsequently issue my medical certificate.

Any extended or multiple year evaluative period was now off the table. It had already been nearly ninety days. Flight for the summer was back on. I was encouraged and fortified in seeing the Lord not only reveal the next steps, but also bring me assurance He had heard my prayers and honored my submissive spirit.

New Intimacy with God

I couldn't keep this excitement all to myself. The next day I went into Mr. Bitikofer's office to tell him how I had relinquished the situation to the Lord knowing that I would not receive any answer until I did. I then shared with him my excitement in *being given* the answer the following day. Now, I must say this: Mr. Bitikofer was a pleasantly straightforward gentleman. He was technical in his thinking and uncontrolled by his emotions. Thus, I was all the more surprised when I noticed him looking at me with deep attentiveness as I told him of my encounter with the Father. It was as if I was sharing the news that he was a grandfather. I will never forget his face as he proclaimed out loud that he had experienced chills going down his back.

I couldn't resist calling my parents later that night. They also agreed in belief the Lord had been fully embedded in this course of events. So vivid was the Lord's hand that I was brought to tears because I loved Him for enabling me to observe and then comprehend His depth of love for me.

I wanted to do nothing but love Him right back. Consequently, I made a conscious choice to put down my homework and everything else I had to accomplish. With Bible in hand, I went to the center of our campus where Mr. and Mrs. R.G. LeTourneau were buried. It was a beautiful evening—crisp and cool. Alone, I started reading the Scriptures. I asked the Lord to guide me to see what He wanted me to see. I didn't even know what I needed to read. I was dumbfounded by the situation. All I wanted to do was glorify His name the way in which He wanted it glorified after He had been so good to me. As I looked in the concordance for a verse, He brought to my attention Psalm 3:

O LORD, how many are my foes!
    How many rise up against me!
Many are saying of me,
    "God will not deliver him." Selah

But you are a shield around me, O LORD;
    you bestow glory on me and lift up my head.
To the LORD I cry aloud,
    and he answers me from his holy hill. Selah

I lie down and sleep;
    I wake again, because the LORD sustains me.
I will not fear the tens of thousands
    drawn up against me on every side.
Arise, O LORD!
    Deliver me, O my God!
    Strike all my enemies on the jaw;
    break the teeth of the wicked.

From the LORD comes deliverance.
May your blessing be on your people. Selah

I was awestruck to have taken that time so naturally, so willingly, especially considering my studiousness. It was an equally remarkable moment as it represented a new phase in my relationship with the Father. It was now personal. Specifically, those verses spoke *such* truth to what He had just accomplished while also being used by Him to prepare me for what was next. This wasn't the last time I would have to apply this Scripture.

What Next?

No sooner had I put to rest the affairs of getting my flight medical that another road block was thrown across my path. Dare I even say Satan was trying to keep me from moving forward in what I remained convinced He was leading me to do? The Adversary either didn't want me to fly, or he was merely trying to keep me from drawing closer to the Lord. On my way to church two weeks later the car transmission clunked, causing the car to stall. Now that I was back on track to take my first piloting course in the summer, how would I transport myself between campus and the airport? I found myself again not knowing what to think. The Lord could have resolved the medical issues only to teach me trust. Maybe flight wasn't where He wanted me after all. I could not comprehend why the Lord would have escorted me through all that trouble when it appeared I now had no means to get to the airport.

Then one Friday afternoon I went to a lab Mr. Bitikofer was instructing to ask him what I should do. In a line that seemed as long as that of a department store's the day after Christmas, I stood waiting for him. This was good because it gave me a minute to think, *There is nothing I can do about the car, other than trying to get it fixed. So again, Lord, if this is not where You want me to be I ask that You will help me to trust You. Let Your will be done.* Had I finally come through this period of testing with the knowledge of how to trust His wisdom?

Encouragement rang clearly through my heart as Mr. Bitikofer told me summer flight was feasible without a car since, in the summer, you are teamed to fly in pairs, like high-school students taking drivers' education. One flies while the other observes from the back seat. Then you switch. Finding a ride was not going to be problematic. Had I flown during the semester, everyone's juggling of flight and academic schedules would have made it difficult. Summer flight was *not* going to pose that problem.

Most meaningfully, I was permitted to officially place my name on the list for summer flight school the following Monday morning. Everything was still a go. I couldn't do anything but praise God for His mercies. He had been gracious to me and clear about where He wanted me. As I shared these events in an email to my parents that Monday, the timeless song came rushing back, "'Praise Him, Praise Him, all ye little children.' I love Him for His love, Dad and Mom. He has shown His love to me and that it is always there. But, I will see it more vividly when I simply remain submissive to His leading and control."

It was decided. I was going to fly in only a few months. The academic school year would come to an end on May 5—not a day too soon. Flight wouldn't begin until May 16. I was going to be able to go home and relax before I had to return to start my Private Pilot course. Good thing, too. I needed to catch my breath.

THE BLESSING OF TAKING AFTER THE WRIGHT BROTHERS

The time to navigate the wild blue yonder arrived. The Lord had proven true, faithful, and most importantly, loving. He had brought me through the darkness of tumultuous obstacles and showed me there is no limit to what He is capable to accomplish. I was unreservedly stoked that my dream of controlling the flight of an airplane was on the verge of being realized. Adding to this growing wealth of blessings was the privilege of having Mr. Bitikofer—a venerated flight instructor and one who already knew me so well—as my Private instructor.

The Father had taken care of all the concerns, so exceptionally beyond what I could have envisioned. In concrete ways through witnessing the unimaginable He had argued the case that when my trust was anchored in Him then His care over any life situation would be assured. It was a lesson I could not move forward without. With it, though, I aimed to push forward by pursuing His will and straining to trust Him in the world of flight. Like most, though, even with that assurance, I would need Him to chasten me repeatedly to remember that lesson.

I took to the air for the first time on Monday, May 15, 2000. Let's say it was a good thing I was not blazing full throttle in a fighter jet. I must be honest. My stomach was not on board with the whole, new experience. I remember sitting in the confined back seat of that four-person Cessna on that hot Texas afternoon thinking, *Lord, maybe this isn't where You want me. I really can't fly if I'm going to get sick.* I was blindsided by how ill I became on that first flight. Eventually, after the turbulent thrashing in that tin can was over and my wobbling feet kissed the ground in awkward steadiness, I could hold in my spinning world no longer.

Doubts once suppressed came screaming back. The next day I emailed my parents begging them to pray for my next flight. I instinctively knew I was primarily reaping these physical consequences because I was not relaxed.

Mr. Bitikofer and I delved into my propensity to become nauseous. We concluded it was the new stress and stimuli of flying. He assured me the mind powerfully influences air sickness. A boost of encouragement was quick to follow when he noted that I became ill in the back seat because I was not engrossed with the task of flying. He doubted I'd have a similar queasiness in the pilot's seat. To my dismay my unsettling human physiology continued to pose a struggle. This evolved into deeper doubts as to whether the Lord meant for me to further pursue this course.

OUT OF THE WOODS?

Then came my third day of flying. It came too swiftly considering the physically draining days preceding it. When it was over, though, I couldn't hold back emailing my parents for an entirely opposite reason. "Well, praises are certainly due. . . . We had some light to moderate turbulence, including dropping and rising, and get this . . . *I didn't get sick...*"

I expressed to them my enthusiasm over feeling 90 percent better compared to the first day. I then added that Mr. Bitikofer wasn't surprised. Rather, with a certainty like my father had when trying to coax me onto a theme park ride when I was a child, my instructor knew I would get over the unwelcome feelings. He declared I was handling my queasiness better than some students from the prior summer. Combining my enthusiasm of the moment with a tidbit of sobriety I concluded the email, "So, just continue to pray. He is hearing."

The exhilaration of that day returned to me the smidgen of humor I previously possessed. I asked my dad to relay a message: "Let Mom know that the landing yesterday was okay. I'm talking, aren't I?" It probably didn't help her motherly concerns when I elaborated on the details *surrounding* that landing. "I was doing fine," I remarked. "I got about 200 feet off the ground, dropped, and Mr. Bitikofer had to pull up more than I was to flare. But, all is okay. He giggled at the land. But, hey, it was my first try." Besides manipulating the aircraft, there was often a large amount of flight information to relay to air traffic control. I was realizing I'd have to pick up the pace of multitasking.

You couldn't *buy* this much fun. Some of the most enjoyable flying was during those formative experiences. Where else can you intentionally repeat the sensation of free-fall except via the stalling of an aircraft? Undoubtedly Mr. Bitikofer took pleasure watching buckets of sweat pour off my face each time I practiced one of his many simulated engine failures over an empty East Texas pasture. Amidst the fun it was critical to acquire the skills necessary to make airmanship second nature. I look back on the newness of those times only to find myself smiling. My mind did not have the capacity to take in all there was to see and do. It's no wonder I miss those days.

EXHAUSTION AND MORE NAUSEA

Sadly, what I had hoped was a new trend of fun and successful adaptation did *not* persist. By the end of my second week of training my body continued to taunt me with air sickness. Nearly each new task came bonded with that undesirable threat, despite our attempts to suppress it. I then developed a problem of fixating on the aircraft instruments. I felt pressured by the challenges basic to my grueling fifteen-hour daily schedule. My character was being stretched. I allowed uncertainty to creep into my mind with each difficulty, "Awe, man, is this going to be *another* element that is going to keep me from flying?" Doubt was becoming my constant companion.

Even then, though, the Lord transformed each moment of question into a positive counterpoint so He could reveal and then perfect in me love and character. My dad kept offering bolstering assurances as he challenged me to consider the rewards of remaining humble.

The Lord also used Mr. Bitikofer's timely words to help me forge ahead. He was unwavering in his assurance I would soon excel in flying in the same manner he was convinced orderly radio communication and tireless dedication had shown great payoff in both of his apprentices. He even mentioned how tremendous an honor it was for him to have the two of us as students.

Then the loving Father bestowed upon me what to this day remains one of His paramount crowns of acclaim as an aviator. Mr. Bitikofer pointed out my conscientious nature, a trait which would go a long way to making me a good pilot. I was humbled to my core. How marvelous a display of His love it was hearing such penetrating words after so often being uncertain. I'm confident the Lord knew I needed this strategic confirmation. It empowered me to persevere in the task with the step-by-step assurance.

The Lord used every personally defying moment to reveal His love to me. He simultaneously used these challenges as a witness to those closest to me of His proven faithfulness. How could I complain? I was growing in skill and in spiritual relationship with the Lord. As my instruction continued, I found it increasingly easier to progress while resting in that knowledge.

FLYING SOLO

I kept plugging away in the Lord's strength. Sooner than I thought possible, it was time for me to venture courageously into the skies by myself. It was time for my first solo flight. It was May 31, two weeks into my training, and only my fifteenth flight.

I didn't write much that day. What I remember is the adventure of it. My body was overcome by adrenaline from all my muddled apprehension, vague uncertainty, and irritably eager expectation of commanding the ship. I am surprised my brain didn't explode trying to make sense of all the rushing emotions.

I called my mother and shared my exuberance. My dad later emailed noting he heard I had "made the grade" and informed me that my mother awakened at six that morning to spend an hour in prayer on my behalf. The Lord was undoubtedly proving Himself faithful to the task.

GOD'S HAND SO OBVIOUS

Mr. Bitikofer likewise genuinely believed the Father had His hand on my life and in my decision-making. Hindsight was making it abundantly apparent He was opening all the doors to flying. It was as though the more I progressed in time the less it mattered what discouragements, defeats, or failures came my way. On several occasions I remarked how the weather was more than cooperating and conducive to the training we needed to complete. The rain usually held off until the weekends when we weren't flying.

Now, before you claim this as an insignificant testament to my belief in the Lord's sovereign blessing, consider this. After I soloed, Mr. Bitikofer told of a female's first solo flight in the spring having been delayed five weeks as a result of weather and classes. That speaks more than coincidence. It attests to His hand of blessing and overall orchestration of events that placed me in the summer program.

The training regimen seemed to accelerate after my solo. Confidence in my Lord and His equipping of my abilities soon prepared me to broaden my repertoire of skill with night flying, including nighttime experience in blackout conditions. Next came my first solo day cross-country. It was an indescribably wonderful feeling taking on that level of responsibility and being so relaxed. Considering the consuming ill-effect of tension of those opening days of training, the nature of this long, challenging flight was uncanny. It couldn't have gone better. Instruction steadily progressed over the next several weeks. It appeared I was bound for a smooth sailing course to certification.

Stormy Weather

As I headed into the final week of the Private Pilot course, I found myself exhausted from pushing. After weeks of superb weather, this week reversed that stretch. Delays to finishing the course seemed inevitable. I was beaten, frustrated, and seconds shy of collapsing. I didn't feel like facing another trust challenge.

It was June 19. I wrote my parents about my fatigue and requested their prayers. I shared with them how I lacked my usual spiritual fervor even when reading tremendous Scripture verses. I maintained a strong desire to fly. More now than ever I sincerely believed I was following His leading. Yet, unless we had a string of good weather, my lingering weariness would be prolonged for another week. I saw the end, but that accentuated how hard it was to reach.

I was beginning to trust in my capabilities instead of trusting His endowed talents, as if I could have somehow mentally engineered my flying skill. It was time for me to be chastened by the Father again and remember not merely my place, but Who was responsible for granting the aptitude.

My dad responded the next day,

> I'm praying for good weather, but more, that the Lord will

have His way. He can move every cloud out of your way if He chooses and I've asked for that. However, He may bring clouds because He sees things we don't even understand; and, because we love Him and He loves us, we surrender to His superior ways. We don't always understand it. We don't always agree with it. We don't always appreciate it. But, if we could see what He sees, we wouldn't have it any other way. So I ask for spiritual eyes that we see with eyes of faith to accept each day as a special day prepared just for us by our God Who loves us even more than we are able to understand. Either He's in control, or we are—we both can't be. Pray for *EXACTLY* what you desire, but accept what He gives. . . . Be encouraged, my son. God has you in His hand. Don't strive to be anywhere else. It's the best place you could be.

I vaguely recall being in a state of frayed, teary-eyed emotions when I read this. My parents have been such a wealth of wisdom and understanding about my relationship with the Lord Almighty. What he shared was what my heart believed but was too tired to confess.

I identified with everything he said. I needed to trust the Father, and I *wanted* it no other way because I had never before seen the Lord work in my life in the ways He had in the previous year. My dad's statements were a fresh and timely reminder to keep my focus where I *intuitively knew* it belonged.

My final flight with Mr. Bitikofer should have been completed by this time, but I continued to have difficulties with short-field landings. My flying partner surged ahead of me. Competition may be normal. Unfortunately, it was proving to be a distraction. Yet again, though, these mental conflictions drove me back to the Lord. I needed to have Him reaffirm my steps, and I knew He wanted me to ask Him to do just that.

As Monday morphed into Wednesday, I faced the reality that I was going to have to fly with another flight instructor to iron out my shortcomings. If all went well, I'd have my final internal exam immediately prior to the official FAA check ride. Though these setbacks may have looked like unwanted complications, the delay served great purpose in aiding me to grab hold of a valuable understanding. I had come through the most ardent tutorial in persistence. I was forced to learn not to give up and instead fervently strive toward the goal that the Lord had set before me. At the outset I was unable to see I already possessed perseverance. I would not have recognized God's intervention had I not wrestled through the questions. Then and there He would harness and refine my perseverance.

CHECKED OUT BY THE FAA

With those delays I was amazed to realize I had completed all the required flights by that last week. More of a wonder was that I was able to have my FAA check before the week ended. Saturday, June 24, I went on my first critical examination. It couldn't have gone better!

For starters, I was awestruck by the most crystal-clear day since the second or third time I flew six weeks earlier. Smooth conditions would ease the inherently difficult test maneuvers—not to mention my nerves.

If that wasn't enough evidence of His love and blessing, here is just how first-rate the exam was. As the FAA examiner was leaving the airport, he commented to Mr. Bitikofer that I was a "good one." I am convinced the Lord had His hand on that day.

In my enthusiasm the following evening, I composed an email to all my family and friends saying,

I am now officially a pilot, by law, as of Saturday the twenty-fourth at 6:15 p.m. Let's see how long I remember *that*. I am excited not only to now be a pilot, but to see where He desires to take me next. I cannot describe the overwhelming excitement over seeing God's hand at work this entire summer and the things that He has taught me. I know some of you may think that I am excited because of what I have accomplished through Christ, and to some extent, yes. But, no, I am excited because I saw the Lord at work in my life this summer, not during the easy times but hard times—the times when He can be harder to see—and I saw Him.

I would be shirking my obligation if I did not reveal the most tangible proof of how directly involved God was in answering one exceptionally specific prayer pertaining to the acquisition of my pilot's license. The day before my check ride I had called my mother to inform her of the exam. By this point, she was understandably apprehensive after all the difficulties. We *all* had been, but we each had to address these reservations and fears with the Lord in our *own* ways. The Lord folded our two different requests into one vivid answer.

My mother read what the Lord had challenged her through her journal, "You want an answer, or you want direction for this? Well, that's easy. That's simple. Then ask Me to prevent his success, his obtaining certification. Then you'll know." How is *that* for straightforward? If it wasn't where the Lord wanted me, He would simply not let me get my Private Pilot's license. *Something* would go just wrong enough to let me fail the ride, cause me to spend more money than I could justify, or bring some comment or instruction from the FAA examiner or LeTourneau flight staff that would suggest this field didn't suit me after all. Think the latter of those couldn't happen so late in the game? Guess again. I witnessed it myself once.

Standing in the shower of the campus apartment the morning of the exam, I prayed with similar heartfelt intent. I remember it well, because it was the first notable (and hopefully repeatable) instance where my prayer was focused in genuine selflessness. I prayed that above everything else God alone would be glorified. Then, for His sake conjoined with the sake of my parents, I asked that the Father allow me to pass my FAA check ride the first time if I was squarely in His divine will. This would leave no room for confusion or second-guessing.

I remained convinced I was following His lead. He had opened far too many doors for me to come to any other conclusion but that He possessed sole control. Frankly, it was immaterial to me whether or not I passed the first time. Still, for the benefit of my parents, especially my mother, I sought an answer from the Lord. I think the Lord graciously understood. So, I beseeched Him that I would not merely pass it the first time, but that I would *more* than barely pass it.

The Lord heard and was at the ready to take the helm *that* day. You already know I passed it, but you didn't know I accomplished it while hardly suffering through two slight errors of execution. So, not only did He afford me the weather of my dreams, He did not simply grant me affirming comments from the federal examiner, but the Father saw fit to answer *all* of our family's prayers. We *all* were *thoroughly* convinced soaring through the skies by way of LeTourneau was precisely the course of the Lord.

FIRSTHAND KNOWLEDGE

Through this introductory flight course I had watched the Father stretch me in specific, *invaluable* areas. Amidst perseverance, He coached me in becoming more disciplined and more able to multitask. He taught me to hold captive my anxious thoughts while replacing them with His calm Spirit.

In the span of my first year in college I could authenticate the Lord's accomplishment of *all* this and more. I was fatigued from all the spiritual growth. I felt as pulled as taffy at the State Fair. In the end it was worth the drain because I had a *fresh* confidence I was being transformed into an improved child of God. What is more, I was positive this time I had acquired the growth rather than gleaning a form of it from anyone else.

I never sensed the loving Father looking down on me in condemnation despite my attempts to take matters into my own hands, worrying about my path, or exposing my lack of trust when I was frightened by the prospect of not flying even *after* His clarity to do so. Instead, He gently taught me that trust really means clinging to Him daily. It is defined by a ceaseless recommitment to His perfect will. The uncontrollable road blocks or mental battles are not relevant.

This divine instruction was *spectacular*.

Since that time I have prayed I would only grow more in every area of my character. I confess it's true. Persevering to the end of something regularly strewn with hardships and questions for the purpose of growing spiritually was not easy. It rarely is. If it had been, I might never have discerned the Lord's handiwork.

Freshman Year Lessons Learned

That was my first year at LeTourneau. It is *because* this spiritual growth occurred under austere conditions that I experienced His refining character. The implications of my OCD medication, the surprises with the car, repeatedly getting airsick, uncooperative weather, or trouble with my landings, all possessed one, underscoring purpose. I now had intimate knowledge through my *own relationship with the Lord; I knew* what it meant to trust Him.

I beheld the Lord's joyful faithfulness through it all. So, to Him is the thanks and glory. He is the most wondrous Father Who deeply loves me and desires to orchestrate His implanted dreams. They became my dreams. *Never* in my wildest dreams had I pictured myself as an aviator. How could I have ever envisioned partaking in so much fun in this vision apart from pursuing the Lord's will? It was simple. It was *breathtaking* doing something the Lord had designed for me. It was and will forever be far beyond what words can express.

Certainly, there is no other joy, no other overwhelming peace, no other refreshing happiness or reward than when any of us walks hand-in-hand with Him. If I am in His will, nothing is impossible.

Despite these early victories, many more trials were yet to develop and test my application of what I had learned. Still, something *had* changed forever: I knew there was no better place to be than in the hands of a loving Father. I was eager to see where He would lead me next. The good news was that this type of experience—this joy and peace that permeates the darkest of hours—had always been and continued to be accessible.

Now to him who is able to do immeasurably more
than all we ask or imagine, according to his power
that is at work within us
(Eph. 3:20).

Six

A Reprieve Through Confirmation

Navigating the manipulative air currents was in my blood. The sensations *and* the clear affirmations were irresistible. There was no questioning either the solidarity of relationship that was developing with the Lord Jesus or that He had paved my way.

I valued the University's solid education. More importantly it provided the safe, spiritual haven He chose to stimulate the growth of my faith and interpersonal relationships. It offered opportunities to engage my beliefs and connection with the Lord in chapel and in classes. I grabbed hold of each moment of safe harbor so I could focus on His interactions with me. Through my education, I found challenge to *own* my faith. I praise Him for holding me tightly while He nurtured my insufficient obedience into a yearning to be transformed in thinking and purpose.

We kept asking God whether it was His desire for me to carry on as I advanced through my tailwheel, multiengine, instrument, and eventually commercial pilot ratings. The farther I progressed in training, the more it became obvious to keep moving forward. Clearly, we would have squandered His money and time had we discontinued flight alone. He even enabled the incorporation of my parent's loan payments within my dad's salary, aside from his commissions. Pressing onward was not an easy task, but God came alongside every step to faithfully provide.

After a much-welcomed, yet short, reprieve I returned to the pilot's seat by November. I underwent a fast-paced crescendo of training thereafter. Stepping in our fabric-covered tailwheel aircraft was step one. It brought its own trials, but I completed that phase by March 2001.

A week later I moved into my multi-engine course. It was a hard-pressed goal to finish the course by the end of the semester. While still attacking demanding academic courses, I gave all the focus I could to flying, sometimes daily. By May 23, I had my multi-engine FAA check ride bringing my sophomore year to an official conclusion.

Flying would prove not to be the only challenging factor of the college experience. The Lord remained ready to send reinforcing successes and positive life changes. Looking back upon my heavy course load, I cannot help but reflect on the Lord's immense provision to sustain my energy, my wits, my spiritual fervor and my perspective.

BALANCING GRADES AND FLYING

Almighty God again *proved* faithful to be my one and only sustainer. My grades had become poor during the most difficult semester to date. So, I asked Him to help me attain a GPA above 3.5 and not fail any classes. He looked past my infantile faith with grace and fulfilled my request by enabling me to obtain a cumulative GPA of 3.53 and no failures. Again He was involved in equipping me to accomplish His task.

It was equally astonishing to watch the loving Father refine my reclusive, shy character that had been reinforced by my consuming course and flight schedule. I had no choice but to learn to reorganize my priorities and manage my time using self-discipline. This was necessary if my self-induced stress of personal achievement was to be relieved and counterbalanced by interpersonal relationships with my rapidly expanding circle of friends. I love remembering intramural and leisure sports because they offered camaraderie.

This character stretching was the Lord's way of convincing me that *He* was carrying me through. As long as I aimed to do my best in my studies, He would provide the grades. What He desired from sports and the other activities was to round out His child's life. Did I stop trying to achieve on my own? I wish I had. Nonetheless, the peace from this reformed life fed me with a steady flow of His love. That would help me shed my lack of trust more in the future.

I had one week to catch my breath between classes and my second summer of flight. I was entering the arena of instrument flight, albeit in the now less interesting single engine airplane. Tackling a summer flight course again provided an occasion to lean on God's wisdom. Little did I know at the outset that it would become my favorite method of flying, further motivating me. Not only did I complete the course in forty days, at theFAA's minimum flight hour-requirements, but the saved time resulted in financial savings. I felt blessed to have joined Him in being a steward of His resources.

COMMERCIAL PILOT

In the fall semester of my junior year, I began the first of three semesters working toward my Commercial Pilot license. This would equip me with the professional skills to acquire income in the flying industry, although not necessarily permitting me to step onboard any airliner and start flying. The course would incorporate all the previous knowledge and training into practical, real-world applications via cross-countries and scenario-based evolutions.

That semester would barely find traction before the world stopped on that horrific Tuesday, September 11, 2001. I was in one of my aviation maintenance labs testing aircraft engine igniters when Dean of Aeronautical Science Fred Ritchey hurriedly announced an aircraft had crashed into the World Trade Center. Not yet knowing the reality, we completed our lab, as required. We *all* rushed through our assignments and hustled back to our dorm rooms.

Sensing there was something more sinister taking place we turned on our televisions. We were acquainted with aviation rules, so it seemed odd such an event would occur by accident. With my heart already inching its way to my throat, I stood at the edge of my dorm loft frozen in time as I witnessed something I thought I would never see in real time. The video frames of the television seemed to slow as I watched the second aircraft menacingly and with vivid intention collide with the second tower. I was glued to the events and to my phone as I made calls of clouded desperation to my parents trying to make sense of what was happening.

I'll never forget the results of that crystal blue day. The lives of citizens as well as those of pilots would forever change. Security, though welcome and necessary, would require airline cockpit doors to remain locked during flight. For decades children and passengers shared interactions with pilots during flight. That was largely over, and with it much of the universal love of flying.

Though a pilot still learning to fly, I already felt cutoff from others in sharing my love of flying. Airports and flight schools were locked down and closely guarded. Each of us had to meet new and stringent TSA requirements to fly or even approach an aircraft. Freedom of movement once enjoyed by all who love aviation was quenched for some.

Years earlier I remember going with my parents to DFW Airport to await my brother's arrival. They knew I loved staring out the windows at the airliners coming and going, so we'd always arrive early. That was now a privilege future generations of non-ticketed children would never experience.

Aviation came to a standstill, and our flight operations were no exception. However, with the first of many new rules set in place, flight training quickly resumed—the memories of that day still fresh in our minds. By the end of that month my parents were on their way to a planned family reunion in my mom's hometown of Holland, Mich. My commercial instructor and I decided we could expeditiously meet the cross-country requirements if we flew to Holland in our twin engine Beechcraft Duchess.

It was one of my most prominent flying memories at LeTourneau as we traversed a large portion of the central United States. No longer did I cross the country as a passenger. I was now in the front seat of the airplane. This cross-country provided me the first, real opportunity to conduct a flight like a professional pilot. Our route covered expansive amounts of commercial airspace to include that of major cities. I recall keeping up my landing speed coming into St. Louis as several airliners were required to delay takeoff for us. Flying responsibly so soon after our country's disaster added even more reward.

Special Passengers Onboard

As the calendar rolled to 2002, I continued pushing through the smoothly progressing commercial flight studies as part of my average sixteen-credit-hour academic schedule. This semester my flying would entail applying instrument skills through cross-countries. Challenges and doubts of continuing to fly would try to nose their way into my busy life, but to no gain.

One such occasion was on a cross-country from Longview to Houston via Galveston. My instructor and I planned to integrate a real, corporate-style atmosphere to this flight. So, I invited my dad and mom to drive in from Dallas on Friday night, March 22. Leaving after my dad finished work, they drove to Longview, climbed aboard, and we were on our way. We landed at Houston Hobby airport and enjoyed dinner at Red Lobster.

It was an interesting evening. One of the first frontal systems of the spring season was moving through the state. By the time we left Longview, the route at our altitude was blanketed with multiple cloud layers driven by at least a fifty-knot north wind. Though uncomfortably bumpy, the flight proved one of the best I had ever conducted, with the two instrument approaches into Galveston and Houston being exceptional. In fact, the flight went so smoothly that my dad presumed the flight had been flown solely by autopilot. I hadn't engaged the autopilot at all. Through the turbulence I was piloting the aircraft. This was an invaluable and welcome compliment, as it not only gave evidence of a comfortable flight, but revealed to me the aptitudes with which the Lord had endowed me.

I would need this encouragement because the flight back was unidentifiably worse. Now we were head-on bucking the winds that had earlier been helping us. Darkness set in on our return and the aircraft was fiercely tossed. I found it increasingly difficult to keep my long-absent vertigo and queasiness under control. All I could do was eagerly long for Longview. Then, for the first legitimate time, I had to hold while an American Eagle regional flight passed underneath. To my great displeasure I had to do so in this turbulently cloudy, black abyss. After being released to proceed for the landing, I snaked my way down on the instrument approach. I wish it were not so, but "snaked" is nothing shy of the truth. My mind had fallen so far behind the flying curve that I overcorrected on my descending course while adjusting for the changing winds. It wasn't the brightest finish for which I might have hoped. Yet, the reinforcement from the flight down to Houston permitted the Lord to give me a suitably humble and non-discouraged outlook on the situation.

EXHAUSTED AGAIN, BUT NOT FOR LONG

The spring semester took top ranking among all the previous because it was the most exhausting. The physical and mental tolls upon my body had significantly affected my performance and alertness in flying. By April 29 I had completed the opening phase of my commercial flight syllabus. I also had received more academic Cs than ever before. I returned to a familiar place as the Lord met me in the midst of my need.

The day to perform my stage-check ride dawned. It was with one of the assistant chief flight instructors, Phil Rispin. He had given me my tailwheel check conducted over a year ago. Sadly, I had failed it. So, it should come as no surprise when I entered the exam being nervous as well as tired. Gratefully, the Father in His love and care exchanged these feelings. He bestowed a fresh measure of grace and mercy.

After the exam Mr. Rispin gave moving and memorable comments. During the flight and in post-brief he remarked that my steep turns were some of the most outstandingly proficient he had witnessed from flight students in a long time. With what I imagine was some humor and exaggeration, he added that he didn't even think he could have done them that expertly without practicing them first. He said it was one of the best final-stage checks *and* flights he had seen all semester. If this had been all Mr. Rispin said I would have been more than thankful to the Lord. But then he said he believed I would "make a good pilot."

How awesome is God's mercy and love! Sometimes it's especially evident. Most amazing to me was the timing. It had been a critical stage as in *any* flight syllabus, compounded with a check ride with an instructor who had the highest of standards. More profound was that despite a semester riddled with fatigue and academic struggle, my shortcomings of not being in communion with Him to the level I should have, and not living every day the kind of life to which He has called me, the Father had nevertheless demonstrated His unfailing love through a grant of flight success of this magnitude.

Mr. Rispin's observation about my future as a pilot granted me another booster shot of reassurance. The Lord again underscored His establishment of all the skills, talents, knowledge, and interest to effectively accomplish flying. I still had a lot to learn about flying techniques, and failures were certain to occur. Yet, the encouragement from those moments instilled within me a new motivation to press on.

Out of that rejoicing, I felt it only decent and right to thank Mr. Rispin for the compliments and the depth of meaning they had for me. I emphasized to him that the Lord had used his words to speak God's confirmation of my positioning as a pilot. His email reply was direct, "You deserved the pat on the back. You did well."

This became a marker stone in my life—one to which I could return when future doubts plagued me.

The Spring 2002 semester was complete, but the next semester would bring some of the most sobering questions to the future of my flying career since the barricades of OCD. The Lord knew I would have to return to this marker of encouragement sooner than I would have desired.

Seven

Just Another Day of Flying

*C*all me crazy, but I was learning to like having a versatile college life. My education could be accomplished as effectively with more on my plate as long as I was relying on His strength. It gave me cause to become more daringly ambitious. What I did not expect was for the challenge of college to intensify to a new and exciting level.

Entering the Fall 2002 semester I eagerly got chomping away at the academic routine. My recent, shining check flight with Mr. Rispin was fresh on my mind, but there remained one more evolution. The flight program's commercial syllabus required an End of Course Review with the Chief Flight Instructor, who at the time was Mr. Weldon Burnett. Only after this review would my tasks to be a multi-engine commercial pilot be complete. All that remained to become a fully certified Commercial pilot was to pass the FAA's add-on requirements in the single-engine aircraft. I expected to achieve this final step within the next few months.

My senior year at LeTourneau was off to a *great* start. I could smell the ripe scent of victory. Before I'd get there I would be presented with some honoring as well as not so pleasurable events. Little could I have known how *dramatic* this kickoff would be.

FLIGHT TEAM

On an inconspicuous fall evening near the end of September I received an invitation to an exclusive gathering of fellow flight students. The University was forming a collegiate flight team. It was the first time our school joined in friendly, flight-school rivalry under National Intercollegiate Flying Association (NIFA). We were briefed on the expectations and given the option of joining the team. I couldn't believe what I was hearing. I was like a giddy six-year-old on Christmas morning.

Unlike future teams, we had been hand selected. We had little time to organize or train to make the fall regional competition. I could not delay my decision. I had been handed a unique and tremendous honor.

Following a few enthusiastic and briefly inquisitive calls to my parents, I elected to accept the offer. How could I pass it up?

Short field landings was one of the events I was assigned. Setting a pace that would last through competition, those of us who consented finished our opening installment of practice on the last Saturday of September at a smaller airport south of Longview.

We trained constantly while pushing on in our regular courses and flying. My semester schedule rapidly compounded, but I was ready. I was multiplying time spent in airplanes and racking up landing experience, doing as many as twelve in one hour. Like the blur of a fighter jet being captured by a low-quality camera, in less than a month our LeTourneau NIFA team was off to Delta State University for our first competition.

We were geared, practiced, and eager to represent our university. We were stacked against some impressive flight schools; Delta State was paramount among them. It would prove a challenging week as we strove to make a respectable showing, and maybe even qualify for national competition. To get there, however, we had to rank overall as one of the top three regional schools. What were the odds a first-year school would outrank the established teams?

The last day of competition was on Friday, November 1. Later that evening in a grand dinner banquet on Delta State's campus we were shocked as we heard the news we had placed third overall and had secured a spot at nationals. In our enthusiasm I'm surprised we didn't just leave behind our trophies, walk out the door, and jump in the airplanes intent on heading straightway for that contest. Never mind it was an entire semester away. We were speechless, ecstatic, scarcely coherent, and yet bound by the glue of unified exertion and experiences.

We were humbled. Even our most challenging competitors applauded our performance. By stepping foot off the LeTourneau world we knew and away from the parent-like kudos of its faculty, we began to realize how blessed and fortunate we were. The affirmation from this competition carried intense meaning. It was an honor for me to have been a part of something that would lay the foundation for future NIFA team members to achieve even greater success. We were a blessed group, and I know I was giving God all the glory.

From Heights to Depths

Unbeknownst to me, though, all of my more than fifty specialty NIFA landings would prove counterproductive to the last phase of my commercial flight syllabus. The customary short-field landing I learned throughout flight training allowed me to add power at any time to land within the preselected portion of runway. However, with differing skill but similar form I had adapted to the routine of landing within NIFA rules. Under those guidelines I was restricted from coming out of idle power once I assured I could make the intended point of touchdown. My brain had been rewired, and this was to be my undoing.

To make matters worse, I had *one* flight after our NIFA competition to review and iron out kinks in my commercial single-engine maneuvers prior to my FAA check ride. Although I was focused on doing everything spot perfect on this final flight with my instructor, it would not be enough to rid me of this habit.

It was November 7, 2002. With what hindsight reveals as blind comfort, I climbed aboard the Cessna Skyhawk with the FAA examiner, Mr. Bryan Benson, and took to flight on my final commercial check ride. Every maneuver was textbook. Wrapping up the hour-long flight, I came in for my short field landing. Mr. Benson needed to see I exhibited the ability to positively and safely land the airplane within his simulated, several hundred foot runway. To land short would mean I ended up in the hypothetical water, field, or worse, the side of a mountain. It was a task that had to be mastered, and at this stage a skill that *should* have become second nature.

As I began my flare, I grasped the horror I was going to come up short of the imaginary end of the runway. My muscle memory was stuck, "*Don't add power.*" I landed twenty-five to fifty feet short. Game over. I failed the exam, due to my *last* maneuver. Because the error equated to a real world matter of flight safety, Mr. Benson had to sign my logbook, "Unsatisfactory."

It would have been one thing if I had failed an in-house LeTourneau check flight. Instead, I had biffed an *FAA check ride*. It was not only embarrassing, but after having represented the University at NIFA competition, I felt extra shame for missing something so fundamental. Had I conducted the landing as proficiently as I was capable to do during NIFA, this exam would be nothing but a welcome memory.

Tormenting me was *one* thought: all I would have had to do was add a little power to extend my float over the ground. This seemingly insignificant landing was the impediment to being certified as a Commercial pilot. Obtaining any less rating would make a flying career difficult, particularly since many initial jobs—*including* the missionary organizations—were in single-engine aircraft.

PRIDE GOES BEFORE . . .

The Father knew that in my heart I was hoping to be able to come back to campus that fall and tell all my "bros" that I was now a commercial pilot. I could see pride oozing out of my heart. What if this failure was similar to my inability to achieve great landings the day of NIFA regionals as compared to practice? Was it possible I *needed* to be humbled?

One more event, though, made this an excruciating failure. That morning I prayed what were now becoming common prayers of submission to His lead. "Lord, this is a crossroads and a crucial decision point in my flight training. I have been wondering with the past check ride weather cancellations if You may be prodding me to stop after getting my Commercial ticket. Well, I pray fervently right now that if it is within Your will for me to continue onward with flight instructing that You will allow me to pass this check ride today, and even with flying colors; and, if I don't pass it, then it will mean that perhaps I need to pray seriously as to whether or not I should go on."

I continued to ask the Lord to put so many road blocks in the way of my success that it would be more than obvious He was preventing me from continuing if He wished for me to enter the aviation industry with nothing more than my Commercial license.

I had grown so close to the Lord that I wanted Him to precisely know how serious and fervent I was in seeking His will. So, I prayed it twice.

This crossroads pointed to the following instructional stage when I would learn to impart the wonders of flying to others. It would require significantly more in financial commitment. I needed to know whether the Lord desired me to conclude with this phase, or if His design was for me to excel through LeTourneau's entire flight program and begin teaching other aspiring pilots.

The problem with this check ride failure was not that my future in flying was suddenly over. It is not uncommon to miss a task or two on an exam and have to fly the failed maneuver for the examiner again after some remedial review. There is no impact to one's ability to continue in aviation. My real difficulty was that I had arrived at an important intersection in my flight training. I needed to know whether or not I should continue. Now that I had failed the check ride, how was I to interpret that event? Was it simply time to pursue Him more definitively, or was I supposed to take these results as an indication to stop? I had asked God before going into the exam. I was starving for clarity.

THE WORDS OF A FRIEND

I had learned that as a Christian I was designed to seek not only the Father's will but also the advice of fellow Christians. So, I began by talking to my floor mate, Jason Bucher. In just one day, the Father was about to use him and a string of people to challenge my faith and answer my prayers. In all these interactions, my intention was not to place their counsel above that of God's. Yet, I also knew what the Word taught in seeking the advice of others. As Proverbs 13:10 says, "Pride only breeds quarrels, but wisdom is found in those who take advice."

Though Jason was several grades behind and several years younger, our mutual faith in Christ made those facts immaterial. This allowed for a strong and supportive friendship to blossom, just as it had with others who were already as close to my heart. In that spirit of caring friendship Jason quizzed me, "So, are you going to base your whole decision on this one prayer?" I flatly didn't know. I had said prayers like this in the past. However, I also recognized that I couldn't put God in a box and tell *Him* how to answer me. I did not like sensing this resurgence of weaker faith. So I acknowledged to myself (thanks to Jason) that the Lord had the right to answer as He saw fit.

Jason brought up another valid point. Did I have tunnel vision? I had been pondering my future so relentlessly that I began to assume my post-college route had been set. Could it be that I had become so dead set in the "plans" that the Father needed to lovingly prod my spirit to continue pursuing His leadership in my life? Had I forgotten how to remain open to looking to Him for direction?

Jason pierced my heart in the most unconditionally loving manner only a close friend could do. Could the Lord afford me several paths from which to make my own decision, while remaining in His will? It was a challenging question, and one I had faced several times. I already had begun to observe how His implanted desires matched my own when I walked with Him. The only thing of which I was certain was that I did not want to make my own decision, regardless if I possessed the freedom to do so. I wanted it to be His best will, and expressly His will.

Jason dug deeper by asking if I enjoyed flight instructing and teaching. My answer was a resounding yes. Tutoring DC electricity and giving a lesson to my Flight Instructor Theory class were rewarding. My parents observed my joy and success at teaching. Even the flight instructor responsible for preparing me to train others commented how my teaching was thorough and accomplished in a simple, understandable manner. He said he liked the way I taught.

Jason asked two follow-up questions. "Pete, do you believe the Lord can use you right now if you were to quit and not go on with flight instructing? Could He use you in the mission field?" I thought for a moment, and answered yes. Then he asked, "Pete, do you believe God could use you in flight instructing and in the airline industry?" To that I also answered yes. Ironic. Jason was spelling out that the Lord was capable of using me in either field.

Jason had one final remark: "From what I know of you and what I have seen in your life, I can see that you seek the Lord's will in everything you do. So, whatever you do, you will be in the Lord's will. I have faith in you, even if you don't."

Wow! My faith and trust were rather puny at the moment. I

was exhausted and feeble. Yet, the Lord brought me encouragement through Jason. The second of what would be a one-two punch came later during dinner when Jason said he didn't believe this one, little mess up implied I should call it quits on flight instructing. Curiously, it was almost the exact reiteration of Mr. Benson's post-flight ultimatum that I should not let this one error discourage me.

I know what you're thinking. The answer to my appeal of the Father was staring me in the face. Worst case, I needed to remain spiritually alert. Perhaps He had chosen not to answer *my* prayer and instead answer in a manner He knew would be best suited to me. As I reflect, it is a wonder I expected to receive *any* answer to that prayer when He had given so much confirmation in the past.

All I had wanted to know from the beginning was, "Lord, what do You want of me?" I would have been content whether He intended me to cease further flight training, to humble me, or to remind me to seek and rely on His plans. What I do remember adding as a caveat to my prayer was a promise that regardless of the outcome of the check ride I would give the Father the glory. It was conceivable He was waiting to see if I would fulfill that promise to honor while also humbling me from the pride of flying.

LESSON IN HOW TO PRAY

In a matter of hours, this had become a personally invoked disaster because of the way I mentally locked onto the details of that morning prayer. I had thrown myself more questions by believing a passing grade was the Father's only good answer rather than being content to trust in His previous directives. What I should have been doing amid this botch was continue stepping by faith in what I knew He had tasked me to do and waiting quietly for His confirmation. I had boldly applied this strong pursuit before this failure. Why of all times wasn't I now?

I was utterly confused, drowning in questions, stuck in turmoil, helpless to find my way out. All I knew that night was that I was capable of getting up again in His strength. It wasn't about passing the check ride. Rather, it was all about finding His continuing will for my life, experiencing His peace, and just knowing Him. I needed to be quiet . . . for once. I know. That is a gross understatement.

Though growing increasingly independent of my parents, I emailed my dad the night of my letdown. What college student *wouldn't* still talk to their parents after such a crisis? I poured my confusion before them.

Over the next day the Lord would restore my perspective, focus, and sanity. I needed it badly. Some spiritual honing was in store as the Lord continued to speak through those closest to me.

My dad wasted no time in coming alongside his son, just as the Father does for each of us. He conceded I might have failed the check ride because it was the Lord's way of preventing me from a future aviating mistake that might have cost lives. More importantly, it was his insight of knowing where I stood with our Father that enabled the Lord to center me back on Himself. It was clear I loved the Lord Jesus and wanted to follow Him. He already had my heart, and that was the most He could ever want. My dad echoed Jason's comment, "You are sensitive enough to His leading that when you make wrong choices, I'm confident He'll bring you back around where He wants you. Your willingness will enable Him to get you where He wants you."

My dad reminded me that I had to forgive myself as God does. Beyond that point I needed to move day to day patiently trusting in His guidance. Sometimes the Father can be specific and other times allow for several choices. Neither is it uncommon for the Lord to test our motivations. Whichever situation applied, my task was to consider but not live my tomorrows. Knock on the doors, but don't pound on them. I needed to do my best as the Father's child to follow Him, but then rest in the assurance He will be at my side always.

CHALLENGE FROM THE FAA EXAMINER

Mr. Benson, with whom I had drawn close due to knowing his son at my home church, also returned words of wisdom to my correspondence. He agreed I could not presume how God was going to answer my prayers. What I needed to admit to seeing was that the Lord used the "stumble" to hone my skillset and to shine as His servant. Mr. Benson guaranteed it would be years before I'd forget my mistake of landing short. He later told my instructor he wished he'd had his video camera with him on our flight.

Mr. Benson challenged me to pursue becoming a flight instructor. Doing so would be of value if I were to become a missionary aviator, because it would enable mission boards to use me as a check airman all for the glory of the Lord. Additionally, if I did not choose to instruct, how would I build the flight hours to meet the mission board minimums? It was an important question. Although I could walk into a missionary organization with only a Commercial certificate, a significant problem was my flight experience. Where *would* that come from?

Concluding his fatherly words of advice, Mr. Benson wrote,

Your CFI [Certified Flight Instructor] has been complimenting you on your developing CFI skills, the LETU flight program has observed your skills (both interpersonal and flight) and has offered hope for you to one day become an LETU instructor. On the commercial single engine add-on check ride I saw a man (you) fly all those maneuvers (save the short field landing) in a skillful, precise way. You possess the skills required of a CFI once you've fine-tuned the 'teaching skills.' Go for it!

Yes, I had been chided. Frankly, it was rather called for. I would have been remiss to ignore the Father's gentle hand of love as He renewed my focus and reinvigorated my drive to continue pressing through this disappointment.

While praying, the Lord brought to my thoughts that perhaps He wanted to check my *willingness* to change plans. I would be lying if I said I would never have desired to experience the excitement of flying an airliner. What if that was the route He deemed best to achieve my flight hours as opposed to flight instructing? Then again, who was I to say flight instructing at LeTourneau *wasn't* His idea?

Firmly, I concluded I could follow Him whichever way and trust Him to provide the financial means. I did not always see the big picture. Without question I could say yes to Him, leaving behind my desires. I was finally grasping this information in my mind and heart.

How could I have known the Father was field-testing my heart's willingness for something of *much* greater magnitude?

Dad's Counsel Rings True . . . Again

With a patience, wisdom, and love mirroring Christ, my dad came back with biblically sound counsel. He said it was not for insignificance the Lord had repeatedly confirmed for me that I was where He wanted me to be. If I allowed one failure to wipe away the Father's affirmations, I had to be careful it was not instead Satan who was trying to whisper a lie in my ear. Learning to discern the Father's voice is a crucial process. My dad concluded,

> I'm glad you are able to reap blessing even out of discouragement and I just want to say, "Don't give up the good fight." There will be discouragements and setbacks in life because that's the work of Satan. But, remain grounded and rooted in God and His Word, and He will always bring you through.

Friday turned out to be an exceptionally long day as I weeded through these perplexing questions. I stared at the "Unsatisfactory" in my logbook—an unchanged reality. I shared with my dad that I wanted nothing more than to make sure God, who loves me so much, had my heart so that I could hear Him calling me to go or to stop. Lovingly, Dad let me know he did not want this to become a Mount Saint Helens issue. He reminded me the Father doesn't wait for us to get it right prior to listening to our prayers, as Romans 5:8 clearly demonstrates.

There is peace in allowing the Lord to open or close doors as He knows best, even if a door might be unlocked but I have to open it. The challenge my dad left me with was to relax, take a deep breath, enjoy life, then trust Him to answer on His timetable. The Father loves us regardless if we get it right or not. The goal is to listen and let His Spirit lead through His Word.

OTHERS WEIGH IN

I also was in contact with other strong Christians who were part of the LeTourneau family—one of whom was the flight department secretary. In the motherly tenderness that made Mary Jackson special, she rejoiced in how sensitive I was to the Lord's will. She gave the solid reminder that the Father already possessed all He would require: my heart desire to follow Him. She said we aren't always immediately shown the correct life path to take, but she had the utmost confidence that I would not wonder long but would know which way to turn *because* I desired His will. The important thing was to remain in His Word and prayer.

How true these words were. For the second time I had been challenged to remain solid in the Word of God. Only then would I find solace. Had I forgotten this? It had been a couple of years since I went to the front of campus enthusiastically seeking to read His Word. Although my busy study schedule at times lent illegitimate excuse to forego studying His Word, I don't believe I had lost sight of its importance. These were reminders serving to draw my attention to the final source of authority, and that it was. God was not an author of confusion. The character of God is clearly delineated in 1 Corinthians 14:33 when it says, "For God is not a God of disorder but of peace."

Assuredly, one wouldn't biblically conceive a person could become so thoroughly beaten in one day. Between all the emails and introspections, my instructor and I found time to squeeze in seven practice landings in preparation for my retake the following day.

Saturday arrived and I again stepped on the airplane circumnavigating the pattern once with Mr. Benson. After one landing the flight was over as quickly as it had begun. I had passed. It was November 9, 2002. My eyes were fixed on his hand as Mr. Benson wrote in my logbook: "FAA Commercial Single-Engine Add-on Retest Satisfactory." I was a complete Commercial Pilot.

Just Like That

Confoundedly, all the fretting, worrying, and confusion washed away in that fraction of time. Was everything *I* had just put *myself* through a waste? Why hadn't I just brought to memory the success of the Commercial stage check only months prior?

Consider what Satan is capable to do in our lives if we allow him a foothold. As my dad aptly pointed out, we must be mindful to challenge from where we are sensing any perceived direction. First John 4:1-6 makes the responsibility of Christians quite clear when it says:

> Dear friends, do not believe every spirit, but test the spirits to see whether they are from God, because many false prophets have gone out into the world. This is how you can recognize the Spirit of God: Every spirit that acknowledges that Jesus Christ has come in the flesh is from God, but every spirit that does not acknowledge Jesus is not from God. This is

the spirit of the antichrist, which you have heard is coming and even now is already in the world. You, dear children, are from God and have overcome them, because the one who is in you is greater than the one who is in the world. They are from the world and therefore speak from the viewpoint of the world, and the world listens to them. We are from God, and whoever knows God listens to us; but whoever is not from God does not listen to us. This is how we recognize the Spirit of truth and the spirit of falsehood.

It had again become clear that the loving Father had and always will have my best interests in mind. After all the talking, searching, and praying, I had to grip the facts. He *had* confirmed my steps at many intervals. It was impossible for me to mess with His plan.

The most valuable takeaway from this experience is an epilogue of highest praise. The Lord Jesus had begun to nurture our relationship years before this setback. At no time could my relationship with Him be broken by anything I had done or might ever do in error. If it was true that I was in the quest of His will, then it seemed logical I was also His child. Why else would I care about His will?

My heart was filled with joy observing how tenderly the Father reassured me of our relationship. This could only have occurred through the tangible doubts, sweat, and mind-numbing striving to hear from the Lord and Savior in whom I had grown to love so much. I had merely been blinded to see the depth to which His firm and secure hand reached. It took me floundering around in frustration before I had the ears to hear His calm voice of love.

It wouldn't be the last time I would need to get rough-and-tumble with the Lord to grow deeper in my understanding of Who my Savior is. I pray you might see just how muddied even a believer's walk with Christ can become in just moments.

More critically, my prayer is that you would be encouraged by witnessing the Lord's tenderness through my lack of faith, His mighty hand upholding me in spiritual weakness, and His faithfulness carrying me through twists and turns to accomplish what He had begun. I want you to be encouraged that there is not only hope in knowing and accepting Him, but a reality that drives away doubts through trusting His perfectly spoken will and promise. My trust was still a work in progress.

Eight

KEEP PLUGGING AWAY . . . YOU'RE ALMOST THERE

Energized by newfound confidence and eager to see the culmination of my LeTourneau education, I proceeded with the work required to finish my schooling. Three remaining flight courses would usher the finale to my training, bringing with it the status of Certified Flight Instructor. The Lord was present through this stage, as well.

The extent of my financial outlay and the degree to which I had progressed gave the added nudge I needed to take the step of faith into flight instructing while waiting for His reinforcement. His preceding faithfulness was the energy fueling my perseverance.

Having wrapped up the Commercial course, I immediately assumed the role of teacher as I began the first and most extensive of three CFI courses. Within two days after the redo of my FAA exam, I was teaching *my instructor* how to perform maneuvers. The syllabus also required I take two non-aviation students for one-on-one training flights to put my instruction abilities to the test.

The Father encircled me with many close, solid, engaging friends throughout college. Beginning freshman year, I bonded with my roommate, Tim Singer. Other strong character friends were Adam Lewis and Micah Hollis, among many others in my valued inner circle. For these required flights Adam and Micah agreed to receive their first crash course.

Both of them thoroughly enjoyed the experience of flying. They offered honest evaluations, which to my amazement included shining compliments to the caring and thorough style of teaching I was displaying at this early stage. Early on, these flights showed me a glimpse of the aptitude the Lord gave me to become an effective educator. It was a timely realization and led me to meaningful introspection as the Fall 2002 semester drew to a close.

With a roaring energy spurred by holidays with family and the sugar of my favorite Gingerbread Christmas cookies, I charged into the hectic 2003 calendar year. I had the intense Multi-Engine Instructor [MEI] course to complete, preferably by the end of spring. Our NIFA team was destined for National Competition. With a lengthier time to prepare, my landing practice would accelerate. I also elected to obtain qualification in our Piper Lance, so I could fly more powerful aircraft once in the aviation industry. But, wait, I'm not finished. What would be the most time consuming task was a charge the Lord had given me to form, organize, and lead a small group of LeTourneau students on a spring break mission trip to Coshocton, Ohio. Tim and I would escort these students as they supported Missionary Maintenance Services and gained experience their degree mandated, as we had done during our internships.

The semester put out to sea with the ship's screws at full power. Curious how I thought I had seen my busiest days at LeTourneau. I don't want to lose you in the whirlwind of the semester, but I would be negligent not sharing the Father's continued nearness.

MORE UPS AND DOWNS

Two weeks into the year, my instructor gave a command to land the aircraft as smooth as silk during the most extreme crosswind I had experienced. Feeling intimidated that I would lack finesse, I wondered, *Why can't I just be an* average *pilot?*

I was speechless as I heard the elusive chirp of the tires greasing the concrete squares. My instructor couldn't restrain his enthusiasm as he applauded the landing to his peers. Again, the Lord used success to confirm I had the skills, talent, abilities, *and* the finesse necessary to make a good, safe pilot.

That was His grace calming the waters of discouragement rushing toward me the next day. The memories of my first flight flooded back. The nausea I'd thought gone for good returned as I recovered from aircraft spins in our cramped tailwheel aircraft. The FAA required this training for flight instructors, but I never imagined I could know such intense sensations of motion. Past successes, including from the prior day, left little room to dwell on failure this time.

These were foretastes of the calm *and* rough waters yet to be navigated. Amid my sporadic MEI training, NIFA practice would take precedence over the next month as our team focused on becoming the best in our various competitive trades.

As March came into view, I had the first of two flights in our Piper Lance. It was the prelude to receiving my High-Performance endorsement taught by Mr. Rispin. Though a brief, ad hoc course it wouldn't be completed until I returned from spring break.

After months of planning and coordination with the University Student Missions Board, what the Lord laid upon my heart became a reality. Shortly after Tim and I had visited MMS the previous summer I felt the Lord's command, "I want you to take a group of students to MMS over spring break to create a permanent LeTourneau mission trip for years to come." That direction was my heart burden. It was clear.

The inaugural MMS mission trip proved easy for that reason. It might have been tiring arranging all the details, since the university was unable to sponsor it the opening year, but I had no question the Lord had asked me to do this. I knew if the Lord was behind something, nothing could stand in my way. Since it happened during my senior year, I lost touch with what happened after Tim's and my second visit. Then, while I was writing this book, I learned the mission trips to MMS have continued. What marvelous reward it has been seeing the Father accomplish His objectives.

MORE REINFORCEMENT

I returned from that exhilarating spring break excursion to again find myself neck deep in the multi-faceted flight training schedule. I picked up where I had left off in the Piper Lance and success-fully completed the final flight. My High-Performance endorsement lacked nothing more than a signature. The unexpected came when Mr. Rispin said how comfortable and safe I had made him feel on the flight. How could this be? I had less than two hours in this type of airplane. I was hardly proficient. My experiences with Mr. Rispin attested he had a flight background that demanded exacting stan-dards. So, hearing this compliment from him carried considerable weight. It was another reminder I remained on the correct path.

Juggling an increasingly rigorous NIFA practice schedule over the next month, I had three weeks to prepare for the most significant flight-instructor check ride of my LeTourneau program. I would have two more, but if I made it through this initial phase of certifi-cation, the remainder would be on the downhill run to graduation.

It had been a long, rough road during those last few months of training toward the MEI rating. The financial tally escalated as it takes time for teaching to become second nature. It's not that I couldn't teach. But I had been largely stuck in the sheer performance of the maneuvers. About the time I obtained my High-Performance rating, it finally clicked. I could teach consistently at last. I can only wonder if this was a result of the Father's encouraging prompts that I had been bestowed with more value *and purpose* than I showed in my self-talk.

With my instructor and other flight-department faculty seeing I had acquired the most crucial skill, it was time to schedule my ini-tial flight instructor check ride. This was a *major* milestone. I had not planned to go this far in my flight training. This meant I would be departing LeTourneau with more debt than my parents or I had anticipated. So, I desired once again to sense the peace only the Lord could provide.

The weekend before my exam I prayed that the Lord would be gracious to grant me peace by enabling me to pass the check ride. In addition, I asked that He give my parents peace. Sounds familiar, doesn't it? That request is reminiscent of how I had prayed going into the Commercial Single-engine Add-on test.

I quickly realized the similarity. Consequently, I tweaked my prayer. I remembered what I had learned. The Lord could give me peace in more ways than just getting a passing grade. Instead, I prayed that He would simply, and with no strings attached, have *His* way. If it were in His will that I pass the check ride, then through that He was also free to bring peace. Above all, I wanted to sense His overwhelming presence. I didn't care whether it came through marvelous circumstances, or directly from His Holy Spirit. Knowing He was near would bring all the relational confidence I desired. This secondary prayer remained on my heart and lips for the duration of the weekend.

Having spent fifteen hours preparing the week before the MEI test, I wanted to conclude the week communing with God. The night before the exam, I knew I was not going to have the time or concentration to seek Him in the morning. I knew I needed to arrest my anxious thoughts, be reminded of His faithfulness, and be filled with a calm spirit. I turned to Psalm 103. I also read several Scripture passages my mother had relayed over the years, including:

> "For I know the plans I have for you," declares the LORD, "plans to prosper you and not to harm you, plans to give you hope and a future. Then you will call upon me and come and pray to me, and I will listen to you. You will seek me and find me when you seek me with all your heart. I will be found by you," declares the LORD, "and will bring you back from captivity" (Jer. 29:11-14).

Who can speak and have it happen if the Lord has not decreed it? Is it not from the mouth of the Most High that both calamities and good things come? (Lam. 3:37-38).

Your strength will equal your days. . . . The eternal God is your refuge, and underneath are the everlasting arms (Deut. 33:25-27).

I said, "You are my servant"; I have chosen you and have not rejected you. So do not fear, for I am with you; do not be dismayed, for I am your God. I will strengthen you and help you; I will uphold you with my righteous right hand (Isa. 41:9-10).

Jesus looked at them and said, "With man this is impossible, but with God all things are possible" (Matt. 19:26).

Moses answered the people, "Do not be afraid. Stand firm and you will see the deliverance the LORD will bring you today. The Egyptians you see today you will never see again. The LORD will fight for you; you need only to be still" (Exod. 14:13-14).

You will not have to fight this battle. Take up your positions; stand firm and see the deliverance the LORD will give you, O Judah and Jerusalem. Do not be afraid; do not be discouraged. Go out to face them tomorrow, and the LORD will be with you (2 Chron. 20:17).

In my quest for comfort, His Word was the prize. These verses reminded me God was going with me in this task. No matter the outcome, He would remain by my side. It was His battle.

Monday morning, April 14, came. The FAA examiner listened as I began teaching him flight concepts as part of the ground portion of the MEI test. I was amazed how relaxed I was. The tension rose slightly as I struggled in a few areas, and my concern grew. Would I pass? I wouldn't know until the flight portion was complete. To my relief with the ground portion now out of the way, the examiner instructed me to preflight the aircraft. He told me, "Take all the time you need." I did just that.

While I gave the airplane a drawn-out, thorough looking over, I begged the Lord again, solely for a quiet spirit. I told Him that I didn't know how I was going to remember all that was necessary unless He helped me. In a determined, submissive spirit I asked that He would have His way while calming my nerves.

Still uneasy, I climbed into the twin-engine aircraft with the FAA examiner. I decided to begin with prayer. Already knowing he was a former Methodist minister, I wasn't surprised when he obliged. I prayed, "Lord, thank You for such a beautiful afternoon to fly. Please keep us safe as we go. Lord, please calm my anxious thoughts and simply help me to remember what I have been trained to do and what You have called me to LeTourneau to do. Amen."

We were underway. The Father's peace was noticeable as it started to wash over me. Just as my teaching had clicked like second nature only a month before, so it did on this flight. No sooner did the wheels leave the runway and tuck tightly into their slots that I began to do what I had been trained to do—teach. For the duration of the flight *everything* flowed. I felt like I had been teaching the art of flying for years. The hour-long flight raced by in ease. After I landed and secured the aircraft, awestruck by the Lord's immediate response, I proceeded to thank Him.

I returned with praise to His throne of grace when I learned I had passed *both* parts of the check ride. God's swift and exacting intervention in this flight was proof enough that He had answered my prayer to the word. No one, except the examiner, could have possibly known the specificity of that asked and answered. I then thanked Him for answering Sunday night's prayer as well. Like whipping cream and a cherry on a sundae, He saw fit to use the passing of the exam as confirmation for my parents and me to continue. My praise seemed inadequate.

It was clear God had chosen to purpose me with a vast flying aptitude whose origin was found in Him. Sure, I did what I had been trained to do. Yet, He did the very thing I was incapable of attaining. He relieved my anxious thoughts, enabling me to be clear-headed to mentally and physically perform the flight *using* His endowed competencies. The fact I turned to Him authenticated He alone was my source of peace.

NIFA Nationals

There was no time to be dawdling over the amazing unfolding of events. NIFA Nationals were less than a month away. For the remnant of the spring semester I gave undivided focus to my short field landings. Throw in a cross-country over the rising plains of the Midwest to North Dakota, and the time to face off with the nation's best flight schools arrived.

We knew we were untested among this representation of schools. Yet, it was a week I will never forget. From the jaw-dropping size of the UND aircraft fleet, to flying in their CRJ simulator, to the energizing yet professional competition, I could not have been more thankful to the Lord to have been on the close-knit LeTourneau team. Considering we were surrounded by hundreds of excelling competitors from across the nation, we were not stunned to have finished without placing in the top three.

Yet, we walked away curiously strong. There was a humble pride knowing we had given it our best effort, and our observations showed us what adjustments would be necessary to make the NIFA team more viable in following years. Because this was my senior year, I would not participate in NIFA again. Despite that disappointment I was thankful for the added blessing of being able to handle it along with all my other tasks.

MY OTHER LIFE AS AN AVIATION MECHANIC

There is an important aspect of my college education that I haven't mentioned yet. It is regarding my aviation mechanic's license. It was one of my more routine daily academic exercises. It was not the leading focus of my degree, but it would reach its highpoint soon after NIFA.

To become a licensed aeronautical mechanic, I had to take several written tests, answer verbal questions, and tackle several hands-on projects. Attaining the status of mechanic may not have ranked as high on my list of desired achievements as did flight, but it still existed as a significant part of my education. It was just as important for me to pass this evolution.

Earlier in the Spring 2003 semester, I was expecting to take these exams and complete the course by the close of the same. After the mission trip and the major segment of my flight instructor training, personal concerns would mount as to whether it was going to be feasible to do the tests. I hadn't even had time to begin studying. Later there was a mix-up concerning one of my prerequisite technical courses. Although it was confirmed that I had met the testing requirements, that was known too late into the spring to schedule a test. All the slots had been filled.

Through what I believe was nothing short of intervention by the Lord, I ended up not taking them as planned. It did not take much of my brain matter to realize the Lord was standing in the midst of the confusion. I believe He prevented me from doing what He knew I was unable to do at the time. The simple solution resulted in my being scheduled to take the exams during the summer. Had I known how busy I would be that semester, I probably would have chosen to accomplish them in the summer anyway.

I had just returned from NIFA nationals as I cracked open the books to study for the exams that were spread over the next three weeks. The first week was a milestone. Passing the practice written exams allowed me to graduate from the FAA approved maintenance program. The four long years of studying late into the night and the days of being troubled about a test were over. By the second week I finished the FAA written exams. This granted me the keys to unlock the door to taking the orals and practicals June 13-14.

I bathed my upcoming exams in prayer as best I knew how. I prayed He would be personal to me, standing right by my side guiding my hands in what I did, my mouth in the answers, and my mind to retain the information I had gleaned over four years. I asked that His answers be revealed so I would know they could only be attributed to the ones I had specifically prayed. One might be inclined to say this was a vain request. It wasn't. I wanted to know He had *heard* me through our personal communion.

The grueling hours of testing began at 3:45 p.m. It wasn't until 9:15 that evening before I could breathe a partial sigh of relief, only to resume testing by 8:30 the following morning. By 2 p.m., I was spent. The hand on the clock ticked so slowly that I would have sworn the batteries were dying. I had three practical projects left to complete. Why was it taking me so long?

Finally, I was down to my last task. I had to find the top dead center of piston travel in the engine of what we liked to call the "Snow Goose." I couldn't *remember* the last time I had timed an engine, and by this point my brain was shot. I couldn't recall how to do it. I examined the textbooks and lab manuals that I hadn't opened since the first semester of my sophomore year. I began to think it was a procedure we had only been shown visually. Continuing to spend time contemplating, I eventually resolved the books contained no information that I could find. That was it. I had no clue. I couldn't think straight. There was no way I was going to figure it out, finish the testing, and pass the exam.

I brought what remained of my tattered mind to the Lord and pleaded with Him to help me recall how to do this last item. Within minutes the fundamentals came rushing back to me—*just like that*. Nothing external had triggered that memory.

I proceeded with that knowledge to take a stab at the assignment, but I could not completely summon up the *exact* procedure. So, my test administrator and academic advisor, Mr. David Scroggins, mentioned a few, subtle pieces of information to help my memory a little more. He could see I was near the point of falling flat on the floor.

Assignment complete. It only took that little, submissive cry for the Lord's help to jog my memory. He had answered *my* prayer *that* soon after praying. As I would step back viewing that moment, I realized progressively just how *personal* His answer was. No one else would have known to have been praying for that specific need. Only I knew the specific difficulty I was experiencing. Only the Father and I knew I had reached the end of myself, and His miraculous aid did not come until I asked for it. My exhaustion and His nudge, which was the key to my success, came before I approached my advisor. What is more, Mr. Scroggins told me his assistance, in and of itself, would have benefited me nothing if I hadn't already had some knowledge of what I had been aiming to accomplish. This was amazing.

It would be an injustice, though, to withhold how the Lord's hand continued to assist me through the duration of the exam. With the practical segment concluded, Mr. Scroggins examined my head knowledge. I felt like I had exhausted every last ounce of energy in my body's storehouse. Yet, an inexplicable strength gave me the fortitude to keep going.

I was asked four questions per section, not a remarkable amount. Yet, I didn't know them all. Within each section I could not recall at least two of them with any firm sense of certainty. If I didn't correctly answer 70 percent of his verbal questions, I would fail that section and the test. I sat making what seemed like incoherently educated answers. What other conclusion could I reach other than the Lord *must* have been guiding my thoughts?

The last agonizing question came. Would I strike out? I hit the ball back to Mr. Scroggins. "You passed!" he said. I couldn't believe my wearied ears. Could I trust what my mushy brain was telling me?

It *was* true. It was over. Four years of work culminating in nineteen excruciating hours of testing had come to an end.

I couldn't comprehend how the Father could continue to be so good to me when I so often had nothing more to offer Him than imperfection and disobedience. Why did I deserve His help? There was only one *real* answer. It was because He loved me just as I was. No strings attached. There was *no* other answer.

One More Semester

The long, arduous semester was nothing but a fond memory. It was time to take a break for the rest of the summer. I would require one more semester to complete my 150-credit-hour degree. Largely due to the addition of my ground and flight instructor courses, I was unable to graduate with the rest of my class. I wasn't demoralized over this. It was just four short months of classes. The most critical components were now behind me.

I pressed as hard as any into Fall 2003 with a boosted drive to wrap up my education and an eagerness to see what He had waiting beyond LeTourneau. All that remained of any real significance was the two closing phases of my flight instructor ticket. The MEI, though extensive, only permitted me to instruct in multi-engine aircraft. I still had to be qualified to teach in single-engine aircraft, much like the process of acquiring my Commercial license. I needed to first become a Certified Flight Instructor, and then be approved to train students in the art of instrument flying. This would then make me a CFII, or Certified Flight Instructor-Instrument.

After only six instructional and solo maneuver flights, I was ready to take the CFI check ride with the FAA. By October 4, I found myself facing Mr. Benson again. This time I *passed*. I could almost feel the fibers of my diploma between my fingers.

Less than a handful of flights teaching my instructor stood in the way of closing my flight training chapter. Couldn't we have just called it good already? I was eager to get done. Before I would be driven to insanity, the day of my CFII check ride finally arrived. It was the Friday before I was to walk across the stage with my remaining fellow peers. You guessed it, too. It was with Mr. Benson. I was beginning to think I had an FAA examiner in my own family. It was a pleasant reunion.

December 12. The final challenge was on. This FAA exam was the shortest, just a tenth under an hour. All I had to accomplish was to teach the student, Mr. Benson, how to fly the required instrument maneuvers. Then I would be *home free*.

HUMILITY AND CELEBRATION

If I hadn't been humbled enough or shown I needed to depend on the Lord, I was about to receive one final lesson before my days at LeTourneau were complete. I never wrote a journal from that day, or at least I don't know where it is if I did. I do, however, remember failing this ride. Best as I can discern from my pilot logbook, I was deficient with my approaches.

Sure, it happened the day before I put on the cap and gown. Strikingly, I wasn't all that disturbed by the failure this time. What had changed? Was it because I had reached the conclusion of my college experience? Maybe it was because I knew by now I would never do everything perfectly. Or, was it that I had finally learned how to rest in Him and trust His ability to carry me through to accomplish everything He would lead me to do? Probably all of the above. I would need to retest to obtain the pinnacle of LeTourneau's flight-training credentials. But, first, it was time to celebrate.

The culmination of all the joys and tears, progress and setbacks, and confirmations and doubts was bittersweet. It was the end of one of the most memorable periods of my life. It was the start of a future yet to be explored, and I was eager to get things rolling.

The festivities of graduation would begin the night of this second and last unsuccessful check ride. For now it was time to put that disappointment on the back burner. From the first opening moments of celebration I was finding myself covered in His honor and blessing. Not only did I see my oldest brother, Mark, at my graduation, but my last remaining grandparent as well. My parents had flown my dad's mother from her home in Wisconsin for this once-in-a-lifetime event. It became an all the more sobering honor as it would be the last time I would see her living. She would pass away eight months later. It was a blessed moment with her. I am eternally thankful to my parents and to the Lord for having provided me with this special gift. Though such a surprise was a challenge to top, the Almighty then bestowed upon me the reward of graduating with Cum Laude honors. It was a humbling and vivid testament to God's strength and His gift of perseverance throughout my LeTourneau experience. This was an unforgettable night indeed.

The long-awaited graduation ceremony came early the next morning. It was Saturday, December 13, 2003. With my family in their seats, joined by six other close family friends, my ceremonial rite of passage was underway. It all seemed to go in slow motion. It was surreal. A day that was once such a distant possibility had materialized. Unless you have experienced it yourself, it becomes impossible to explain the overwhelming sense of accomplishment, and in my case the ever-sweeter awareness of knowing He had caused it to come to pass.

It was a bright and sunny Wednesday. With three days of rest and my college diploma tightly in hand, I joined Mr. Benson on our final flight together. The retest of my CFII check ride was short and sweet. What made this flight especially memorable was that it was the day of the 100-year anniversary of the Wright brothers' first flight. On December 17, 1903, aviation was introduced to the world as an intriguing but distant concept that over the years has morphed into a safe and viable form of transport. Why had I been offered such an immense privilege? Achieving LeTourneau's last flight certificate on this occasion would forever sear the day into my memory. I believe God orchestrated all the events leading to this crossroad out of nothing but His good pleasure. He wished to express *to* me His intimate love *for* me. I had never imagined a *failure*, much less this one, could have been meant for *so great a blessing*.

THE REAL TEXTBOOK OF LETOURNEAU

The reality of the immense and personally focused depth of the Father's love was the primary lesson of LeTourneau. As I began my college studies, I had only begun to *intimately* comprehend God. Intimacy was the area of growth He desired. Just as it had been when I first came to accept Christ's beckoning call, He was the One Who initiated this relationally enlivening phase. These four years in college had ushered me into the first, real stages of a walk with Him as close Friend and King of the Universe. I began to build a relational repertoire of His faithfulness that would engage me in knowing Him on a greater personal level.

He enabled me to realize the kind of surpassingly meaningful connection He zealously desires to have with me. I obediently entered LeTourneau and aviation, and He actively convinced me of His provision and His personal plan for my life. Our relationship was now vibrant, growing at an accelerated rate. From the complications OCD had strewn across my path to the recurring questions arising out of failures, there remained *no* doubt this was real. It was tangible. I possessed an unadulterated view of *precisely* Who He was. He was my source of strength.

Looking back on my life, I had been led to believe that knowing the Lord relationally grew explicitly through the study of His Word, not out of an interpersonal dialogue. Appearances are deceiving. While I was joyfully discovering the Lord through this new and tender walk, His Word was no stranger to me. I had been exposed to it since before the time I could even utter the word "Jesus," and it continued to be emphasized to me through Bible study in church, the soul-piercing campus chapels, and the email correspondence. I was receiving and ingesting His Truth. I would be negligent not to take note of those times I had strongly desired to *pursue* Him through His inspired Word.

Though I may not have taken it upon myself to searchingly know Him through His Word as often as I should have, there remained a notable, increasing hunger to seek Him there. That craving would continue in the years that followed as He drew me ever closer to the Scriptures. You see, the story of my life was not over. It was only beginning. There lingered promises of the Lord that were yet to be seen.

The Tallest Hurdle Yet

The biggest uncertainty that remained after four and a half years was the indebtedness, well beyond six figures. The flight program alone had a tally of $30,000. The academic portion with its later accrued interest would exceed three times that amount. It was not easy watching debt grow, semester by semester. It was discouraging to see larger amounts added, especially when I expanded my major to include flight instructing. I had considered the notion of not proceeding with that just to reduce costs.

Neither my parents nor I possessed the funds to pay for my education. So, through prayer and contemplation, we set a course of action. I would take all the personal loans I could. My parents would take Parent Plus Loans to cover the majority of my education out of sharing the joy of pursuing the Lord. They were able to obtain lower interest rates, but at a cost of beginning repayment immediately when each loan was dispersed. Still, the Lord maintained His sovereign direction through those years of accumulating loans; we continued to be approved for each one against statistical opposition.

The Lord's promise of provision was revealed from the start. Though only drops in the bucket, I had been blessed by drawing $5,500 per school year in LeTourneau scholarships and grants due to my state residence and academic honors. By the end of the Spring

2002 semester as I achieved my Commercial license, I had saved $6,455.70 in flight costs. Yes, I *did* record the number. I'm glad I did. It was not uncommon for students to exceed standard minimums. I had *much* for which to be grateful to the Lord.

Don't think, however, that all these provisions enabled our trust in the Lord to evolve instinctively or without a little sweat. Yes, the Father *promised* He would take care of the finances. Yet, the responsibility would begin to weigh heavily upon me. I did not only have to pay back my own, but I had vowed to assume the remainder of my parent's loans, as well as every dime they had contributed.

The prospects of paying it down through the meager startup income of a fledgling aviator did not help in bringing much hope. Paying your dues for a year or two, like a doctor completing a residency, was normal. A pilot would do well to earn $20,000 the first year out of college. I was facing a daunting scenario if I were going to be a missionary pilot. I needed to acquire 700 to 1,000 flight hours to have a viable position in aviation. A pilot fresh out of training would be blessed to obtain 300. The more experience I got the better the pay, but substantial enough income to settle college loans would remain years away. Even if I could find a way to get the hours to become a missionary pilot, the college debt would impede that progress. Or, was the Lord going to find a way around this, too?

This equation of needing hours to get into the profession, the low pay, and the monster of debt chasing me seemed unfair. I felt like the school kid having my lunch snatched *and* my milk money stolen by the class bully. My flesh was screaming there was no possible human way out of this. Meanwhile, my faith was *beginning* to gain traction. When everything seemed against the ridding of this debt, God my Provider assumed His predetermined position.

I know how hard it is to conceive the Lord capable to *lead* someone into a task like this and not *give* a clear solution to the debt. I was living and breathing the experience. This then becomes the definition of trust, and I knew the Lord was growing it in my life through this debt. I didn't know how He was going to resolve it, but I had to keep trucking and keep trusting. The Father wanted all three of us to give Him our implicit faith in His original promise to pay off the debt in His way and timing.

The Father had shown me beyond a doubt that He had directed me. By now I was convinced I had been following His will as best I knew how, and He was filling in all my gaps. The spiritual peace from tucking my feet snuggly behind His was *indescribable*. It also felt down-right criminal possessing that peace while having *so* much fun soaring through the skies. Contrary to some beliefs, it wasn't cumbersome to seek His desires for my life. There was no way I could make an argument that my life was uneventful or unfulfilling. Now, that's amazing.

The unknowns related to being financially strapped, this massive debt, and the uncertainties of what I believed about debt were nothing but afterthoughts when God had already proven Himself capable. So, the majority of the time I had my eyes trained on Him. I never lost a wink of sleep worrying about how I was going to pay it all back. He would carry me through. He would then supply every need, including a sufficient job. I can't help myself but to even now *praise* Him for His simplicity in that design.

Seeing Him bring me deeper in the fold of relationship granted me the power of conviction, strength of encouragement, and undying motivation and fervent attitude that would propel me toward the personally unfathomable. Were the Lord to walk with me through the legitimate preparation, much less the rigorous tasks of qualifying, it would consequently prove to be my most challenging, life-altering, defining stage.

What would be the context of that defining period? Within that final fall semester I was seeing an unimaginable job offer materializing in the United States Navy. It would have the potential to forever define my spiritual walk *with* the Lord and initiate a permanent trend of changing who I was *in* Him. But, before that was even a remote idea, it would be preceded by my darkest, most gut-wrenching, and horrific hours.

Nine

DEATH: A PREPARATORY SPIRITUAL EXPERIENCE

My Lord had become the beaming light to my life in the years I attended LeTourneau. College was the first opportunity I had to live apart from my parent's faith, and what I had found changed me for the better. I never expected God to use that journey to transform my heart and life so radically.

The loving Father had initiated a lasting, growing, intimately personal relationship with me. The fascinating part was that He used my college and flight experiences to accomplish that goal while remaining true to His Word. He revealed His faithfulness. He introduced Himself as one possessing infinite capability to do all things, and I discovered I could look to Him to guide me through every success and trial.

Nevertheless, there was much more to come. He was more than Provider. He was determined to enter with me into something that was exponentially deeper than my earth-bound concerns. The God of the Universe loves *me*. I had an insatiable desire to love Him in return. This was the opening stage of my faith walk. Precious as the results of this college experience had been, I lacked equally important facets necessary to round out this relationship. Our fresh connection would not see maturity until I responded to this love with more than emotions.

I had only begun to visualize what it means to trust Him implicitly. He *needed* to bring more challenges into my life to stimulate a more meaningful, proper view of Him. Learning to trust Him would be a process.

The Father, in His love and sovereign awareness, knew that without trust I would not be able to step up to the looming mountain soon to come into view. It was my final summer at LeTourneau. In a few, short months God would propose the military to me. I would later consider entering the United States Navy Reserve, a challenge I perceived to be beyond my capabilities. I had yet to understand I would need to undergo a significant struggle of doubt if I was to simply be prepared for that notion, and I could not have perceived how that spiritual fight could play into that path.

Doubts and Fears

More crucial than the ability to survive the challenge of the military, I needed to trust Christ for my eternal salvation. Weeds of doubt about the willingness or ability of Jesus to eternally save me popped up. These doubts could keep me relationally chained and ineffective in my eternal concern for others. They could prevent me from doing *anything* the Lord desired.

I knew all the facts. I had come to believe I was inadequate to contribute anything to eternal life. I was aware of my lack of goodness. I had a faith in Christ alone. Still, despite His pronounced interaction and involvement with me during college, I doubted its genuineness and security. When I focused on what He had done, I was assured. Other times, though, I did not believe I was witnessing the outward actions and evidences of inward change I expected of a Christian who had experienced everything I had. I was looking for confirmation of what I knew and believed the Word of God to say about who I was.

The prospect of entering the military would require a refinement and nurturing of my simplistic understandings of my God and Savior. The loving Lord would *have* to do this. Through learning to trust Him for my salvation I would learn how to trust Him in life's hardest endeavors. Likewise, were I to see Him help me navigating an immense task such as the military, it would further invoke resoluteness of my relationship with Him. Therein He would reveal His indisputable presence in my life during a period in which the tide of my existence would forever change—a mountaintop experience that would certainly leave me staking claim on its precipice.

For there to be an experience of a deeper level of trust in Him would require me to first endure a trial of my faith. I would have to be taken through a dismal, perplexing moment to broaden my receptiveness in order to equip me to become bolder in my faith.

PROFESSOR DONNER'S LIFE LESSON

During the summer prior to my graduation God again used people close to me to accomplish His plan for my life. I had spent the last four years of my life getting to know the many great faculty and staff of LeTourneau. In particular I came to appreciate Marty Donner as both professor and beloved brother in Christ. I had many classes and labs with him. He had a way of making you feel like a member of his family from the moment he met you. So, I formed a unique level of closeness with him.

Marty had been a volunteer fireman, and had an extensive background in the realm of fire. I remember the summer he taught me how to extinguish blazingly hot fuel fires. Pardon the pun, but it was a blast. Seriously, what honest-to-goodness boy *wouldn't* enjoy experimenting with fire safely? He also was our aviation safety officer, so he kept me from enjoying fire too much.

I was envious when I then learned he had his hand in fireworks as well. Every summer, he would help assemble fireworks at a warehouse near Longview. My final summer at LeTourneau was no exception. Marty and a small team were preparing several firework shows that would enliven many Independence Day celebrations. For unknown reasons, a presumed static electric spark exploded the thousands of pounds of fireworks in the warehouse. It was so powerful it destroyed the building, broke windows of nearby homes and businesses, and took with it three lives, among them, Marty Donner.

Death had come unpleasantly close. We were in a state of shock. Marty was gone. I couldn't believe it. I didn't *want* to believe it. I fell to my knees and face in tearful disbelief. The darkest hour of my life to date had arrived, and it was about to turn my life upside down.

It was a moving time for the Donner family and the *entire* LeTourneau family. The host of people who attended the memorial service was testament to the love and care so many had for Marty Donner. The sweet comfort for all of us was the assurance he was a follower and lover of Jesus Christ. Knowing Marty was with our Lord eased the pain of his loss, but it didn't whisk away the confusion. To my dismay, his death was not where the confusion ended for me.

For the first time I had to face the fact that life can end in the most inconceivable ways. Now more than ever I understood the value of a person was incalculable, and I didn't appreciate it took this extreme event to get that through my head. I had taken Marty Donner for granted. Like a family member I expected to see him again, as I always had. How often does someone we care about leave for a short while, maybe only a few hours, yet we fail to tell them how much we love them? I would have given the best things of this life to have Marty back with us.

One thing is for certain: Life is *too* short. No one ever knows when our days will end. Marty's death left no room to doubt the crucial fact that we must know and believe in Christ today, not tomorrow. Had I been making the most of every opportunity to make my life count for Him and for others?

Deep Doubts

Driving back from the funeral I was listening to a Christian radio rebroadcast of memorable interviews, excerpts, and quotes from a well-known Christian who had died on July 4, one day after the explosion. I recall Larry Burkett, a Christian financial advisor and bestselling author, saying a person does not know what Christianity, grace, and living toward Christ entails unless they have come from a darker past. Moreover, there was never room for pride or conceitedness in the Lord's use of us. We're all part of His grand plan, not the plan itself.

Around the same time, I heard from my pastor about a pastor he had learned of who led a church for ten years. Only after those years of leadership did he finally understand grace and come to trust Christ for his own salvation. Both of these men understood the Christian faith, as Marty had understood it. But did I? The implications tied to this tragedy and these men, impaled me with doubts. I was in a weakened and vulnerable state. The ordeal was becoming one massive doubt, snowballing out of control.

Questions pummeled me.

Why was I only now grasping the brevity of life?

Wouldn't that have been a necessary premise when I came to Christ?

Why did the Father sometimes feel so distant and other times be intimately personal?

Was I saved?

Why was I struggling with an assurance of my salvation if I had truly beheld God's grace at the cross?

Had I rested satisfied with remarks from other believers that the light of Christ was present in my life?

What if, in reality, all I had possessed was a head rather than heart belief in Jesus and His gift?

Scripture was clear one could rationally know God and the Bible without receiving His free gift. I understood Christ was the spotless lamb, the sinless man, the *only* one by nature qualified to meet and pay the penalty demanded by my sin. Yet, did I have nothing but surface-layer knowledge?

The more I pondered Larry Burkett's words, the deeper these doubts seated themselves. Throughout the challenges at LeTourneau I staked claim the Lord had equipped me with everything I needed. I repeatedly attested *and believed* I had been following His will. My ongoing submission to Christ was authentic. There was evidence I had been following Him, He was working in me to will and to act according to His good purpose (Phil. 2:13). This meant I knew Him.

Yet, as I accomplished the goals, particularly within aviation, I felt pride. If I were a child of the King, how was it possible to think I had some special connection to the Father? Where would these feelings have root if I were truly dependent on the Lord to achieve these goals?

What so recently I concluded to be the powerful hand of a mighty God acting on my behalf to perform wondrous feats for His own child now appeared invalidated because it came attached with personal enjoyment. I was somehow misinterpreting my joy of existing in God's will for wrongful pride. Somehow I had forgotten about Christ's longing for me to possess fulfilling joy, for which I had given Him glory many times.

How could I belong to God and not have taken hold of so many fundamental certainties and attributes of His character? I couldn't, and I would soon take firm hold of that truth.

Deeper Still

I needed to recognize I was expecting comprehensive perfection of myself despite the reality of my rather young faith. It is a noble goal to strive to become like Christ, but I was missing the fact it is likewise unattainable this side of eternity. I was overlooking the truth of the relationship that already existed, as underdeveloped as it might have been.

Fact was I wanted to know *for myself* that I belonged to Jesus Christ. I *had* to know I was His child. Learning my life could be over at any moment made it imperative this ultimate question be answered conclusively. My own saving relationship with the Father became the chief focus of this struggle. I started caring nothing about life except my eternal state and the eternal status of the people around me. Right and good as that is, this persona was taking a toll spiritually, physically, and emotionally. It was draining the life out of me.

I could have only wished the Lord Jesus had stepped in at this point to say, "Enough. You have learned well." The Lord was patient, however, and through His Holy Spirit I began to experience peace. Unfortunately, my spirit's peace remained shakable.

The exhaustion of this grief-born lack of mature trust in His ability to save me finally wreaked havoc while I was working one afternoon. I saw a billboard that said, "We can save your car. Jesus can save your life." I *snickered* at the words. *Yeah? Well, if Jesus saves people's lives, then you sure wouldn't know it because I still don't have an assurance that I'm saved. So, what value is it to be saved if you don't know?*

Wait. *What?* Had I just smacked Christ in the face by denying His truth? What was going on? Greater waves of doubt swept over me as I wondered whether I had blasphemed or dishonored Almighty God by my embittered response. The Father was surely rejoicing because He had me where He wanted me. My shame made me capable to receive from Him a sane perspective on my heart. I was not thinking lightly of salvation at all. I was angry with God because I *didn't* know for sure whether I was saved during a time when I agreed with Him it was of highest importance. He understood my frustration and revealed with tenderness the truth present inside me. The fact I felt ashamed and *afraid* over my sharp response gave credence that I already possessed a right and healthy fear of the Lord. I held to an awe and respect toward God, which only a believer could possess. My *fear* was the *redemption.*

God had been trying to affirm His residence in my life and heart.

I had been refusing to believe the things I had known for certain.

Sadly, the struggle persisted because I was viewing even His most recent truths through *my* distorted lens. By my own allowance I chose to discount everything the Lord Jesus was showing me through His life-giving Word and Spirit, His character of love and faithfulness, and the help from the people around me. Even my heartfelt Bible reading seemed fruitless.

WISE COUNSEL

Then my parents wisely recommended I speak with my friend, mentor, and high-school youth minister, Scott Ward.

It had been two intense weeks to the day since Marty Donner's memorial service. In forty-five minutes on a Wednesday morning, I poured out my heart to Scott.

Scott's response echoed what my parents had been saying. I suppose I needed to hear them from someone on the outside.

Scott spoke Christ's love and truth to me. He said I was doing myself an injustice by ignoring the formerly retained peace, joy, and contentment flowing from an assurance of my standing in Jesus and the eagerness to see that relational journey nurtured. Prior to Marty's death I believed I was saved and was allowing Christ to direct my life paths. As Scott would later underscore, knowing *about* God but not *embracing* Him was the fundamental difference between a head and heart knowledge. My reliance upon the Father's guidance through LeTourneau and my walk with Him was evidence I had *embraced* the Lord Jesus.

Peace came rushing like a river into my soul when I heard this. I understood. Scott then reiterated one of my recent observations. An unbeliever doesn't have the capacity to comprehend concern about salvation and relationship with Jesus. The fact I was expressing these affirmed my salvation. I knew Christ *because* I held this understanding. I had been led astray by focusing on doubts. I should have been trusting God and His faithfulness to save me. After a long wait the simplicity of truth hit home. Doubts *are* feelings—not fact. After all, I cannot tangibly observe God with my human senses. The only alternative for the future was to trust His Word.

I could not remember when I first trusted my life to Him, but I had joyfully rededicated it to Him many times.

Scott said the crucial matter was to rely on the fruit of my life that existed out of a life *changed* by God rather than *when* I was saved. I had been transformed. I had come to unconditionally love a person because I understood the sinful, self-seeking nature in all humanity, including myself. I also relished the times God manifested His presence in a way I felt near enough to touch Him. Scott challenged me to focus on these.

Then he cautioned me. I needed to expect Satan to *prey* on me through the temptation of doubting my salvation, a susceptible area of attack compounded by my temperament. Even the feelings of shame and estrangement toward the Father, awkwardness when talking of Jesus, and hurt after spotting that billboard were emotions unreliably based. Somehow these had left me quivering in spiritual numbness.

It was all beginning to make sense. The self-imposed blinders were falling off. It was a blessing to be in the center of God's will. It was not cumbersome. I had witnessed His goodness to me all along. Enjoying being involved in His assignments was not wrong. If He's the author of them, there should be no guilt in being passionate in the effort.

As our conversation neared its end, it took an especially edifying turn. Scott read an excerpt out of Rick Warren's *The Purpose Driven Life*:

Character is both developed and revealed by tests, and *all* of life is a test. You are *always* being tested. God constantly watches your response to people, problems, success, conflict, illness, disappointment, and even the weather! He even watches the simplest actions such as when you open a door for others, when you pick up a piece of trash, or when you're polite toward a clerk or waitress.

We don't know all the tests God will give you, but we can predict some of them, based on the Bible. You will be tested by major changes, delayed promises, impossible problems, unanswered prayers, undeserved criticism, and even senseless tragedies. In my own life I have noticed that God tests my *faith* through problems, tests my *hope* by how I handle possessions, and tests my *love* through people.

A very important test is how you act when you can't *feel* God's presence in your life. Sometimes God intentionally draws back, and we don't sense his closeness. A king named Hezekiah experienced this test. The Bible says, *"God withdrew from Hezekiah in order to test him and to see what was really in his heart."* Hezekiah had enjoyed a close fellowship with God, but at a crucial point in his life God left him alone to test his character, to reveal a weakness, and to prepare him for more responsibility.

When you understand that life is a test, you realize that *nothing* is insignificant in your life. Even the smallest incident has significance for your character development. *Every* day is an important day, and every second is a growth opportunity to deepen your character, to demonstrate love, or to depend on God. Some tests seem overwhelming, while others you don't even notice. But all of them have eternal implications.[1]

Wow. That pinned me to the wall. I *was* witness to a senseless tragedy. The Father *had* seemed unusually quiet. Scott pointed these out to me but only to underscore that every test and all I encounter in my walk with Him is designed to deepen my relationship with Him as well as to refine and mature my character.

It was finally clicking. Just as Hezekiah had been walking in close fellowship with the Lord witnessing His miraculous wonders, so had I during college. Could there have been anything worse than the Father withdrawing His presence from me? However, as Scott pointed out, what if He had been testing my faith and faithfulness to Him? Perhaps God was observing if *I* was ready to move on. Little did I know that July day how true that statement would prove.

Scott and I closed our time by coming full circle. He interrupted my enthusiasm in understanding to tell me that evidence of the truth of God existing *in* my life had been at my fingertips the entire time, in the form of my journals. The Lord had granted me the unique privilege of having been through many events testifying to the Lord's presence, faithfulness, leading, and direction. I had ignored God's nudge to reread the testimonies. Scott and I agreed that I *needed* to now. I needed to focus on what the Father had accomplished and consider it a word picture of my saving faith.

Scott reminded me of 1 Corinthians 2:6-16. Here are a few of its highlights:

> We do, however, speak a message of wisdom among the mature . . . not in words taught us by human wisdom but in words taught by the Spirit, expressing spiritual truths in spiritual words. The man without the Spirit does not accept the things that come from the Spirit of God, for they are foolishness to him, and he cannot understand them because they are spiritually discerned. . . . But, we have the mind of Christ.

Scott reminded me that God's personal attention and divine leading are the identifying marks the Spirit used to validate the presence of God through Christ in my spirit. How could I have known the spiritual nature of God's thoughts except I possessed the Spirit of God? There was no question but that I had to be a Christian since I had been able to comprehend and testify of the ways He moved in my life. This was my *eureka* moment of understanding, comfort, and encouragement.

My devoted Father did not end the reinforcement there. My pastor preached a sermon about how happiness and joy are two separate realities: happiness depends on what happens *to* me within the material world—chance. The caveat is it only lasts for a short time. Joy is not an emotion but a *choice* to depend on an eternal source for my internal strength and needs—that God is in control for my personal good. It is available *only* for the believer, and it can *only* come through knowing Christ.

This morsel of reassurance meant joy was mine because I knew God was in control of my life. Nearly a month later, what I *knew* I once had was returned to me—peace, contentment, and joy.

TRUSTING GOD, NOT TRUSTING MYSELF

I came away with a crucial understanding that both I and my emotions can be untrustworthy. They ebb and flow. Sometimes they're genuine and affirming of God's truth. Other times they're flatly deceptive. God is the *only* perfect one. Therefore, He is the *only* trustworthy One. Had I relied on my understanding or trustworthiness, there would have been no hope.

I praise Him for His righteousness! Moreover, *praise* Him for His protection through the melee. I might have continued down dangerous roads. Out of His immense love, patience, and provision, He ultimately keeps me safe and secure. As a result I am stronger and more secure in my thinking. Scripture is more resident in my heart.

I'm amazed (but God isn't) that instead of the struggle tearing me apart, it brought about a renewed commitment and focus in my relationship with Christ. Not only do I *need* Christ, but I *want* Him in my life because of His love, grace, mercy, guidance, and generosity. I desire to give back my life to the One who first gave His life and love to me. It is how I felt then, and how I feel more now.

As even Scott had noted, the Father had transformed my faith from a need into a choice, the strongest assurance and the deepest trust I could possess. This is where I needed to be for what followed.

MORE TO COME

The Father was preparing me for a larger challenge—my most humbling yet. This latest trial caused my faith to grow, enabling me to entertain the prospect. I would shortly have to trust not only what He was going to ask me to do but also that He was commanding it. My next test would mean *trust* was compulsory. There was no room to doubt my eternal stance and relationship with Christ, and there would soon be no good reason to doubt again. His stake of possession would be indelibly clear.

The unprecedented ways in which the loving Savior would draw near to me would forever alter my course.

Ten

A Proposal of the Inconceivable

S ome of us enjoy a long heritage of military service members. Others have family members who serve. Still, others could put a finger on a friend or acquaintance who is in a branch of service. In my case, each of those applies. On my father's side, his father, Hans, and brother, Tim, served in the United States Army. On my mother's side, her father, Leonard, served during World War I. Two of her brothers, Gene and Stan, and one brother-in-law, Wayne, served in the United States Navy. My father served in the United States Air Force during the Cold War and Vietnam eras. Both my brother, Matthew, and my sister-in-law, Andrea, serve in the United States Army. My cousin Tina's husband, Ryan, and my friends, Micah, Jenn, and Elizabeth, also served or are serving in the United States military.

Prior to entering college I had been on seven military bases due to my brother's duties in the Army. The largest chunk of that time was at Fort Lewis, Wash., during my latter years in high school. I enjoyed visiting him there. I was familiar with the attitudes, lifestyles, language, mentality of achievement, honorable pride, and all that makes up the framework of the military. I looked up to my brother in pride and esteem over his commitment. I became wrapped up in this fascinating world of order, discipline, confidence, honor . . . and camouflage soldiers. It intrigued me. It filled me with awe.

I observed respect, courage, and decency through all the military graduations, award ceremonies, and changes of command. Outside the military routine, there was an evident regard for one another and for time spent with family and friends.

Nevertheless, watching the military environment that surrounded my brother did not encourage any of my thoughts toward joining. It seemed a distant, unlikely, undesirable, and inconceivable eventuality. Why?

Through the good experiences there lingered something subtly distasteful. For starters, the language and yelling that seemed to form the bedrock of communication did not appeal to me. There also remained some lacking aspect of the military life. I identified it as a consuming drive. In some, perhaps in many, their work and status defined them. The military life was who they were.

Having come to know Christ's sufficiency made it more difficult for me to appreciate the end game of such a human pursuit. What was the ultimate prize? Where was the fulfillment of achievement? Was there *anything* more to their lives? Assuredly, I'd discover such emptiness was possible anywhere and with any individual. Nonetheless, it was the lens through which I was then watching, and it looked largely empty.

Though I highly regarded the position, I wanted something more, something bigger than myself or anything I could achieve in this world. Frankly, that is in many respects a fact materializing most clearly to me right now. It was a subconscious hunger I had hidden in the recesses of my soul.

God already was molding and shaping my world view. Whether I realized it at every turn or not, it was still who I was becoming. Of a graver concern for me was the immorality I sometimes witnessed. The openness and flippancy with which immoral behavior was viewed among at least some who served caused fear to well up within me. What if my life would begin to be defined by such character? I *knew* that would be displeasing to the Lord. My heart's desire was to remain loyal and honor Him first.

I'm the first to admit that I wanted to remain sheltered. It is essential to remain guarded over a life commanded to be God-honoring and holy—even if it ultimately costs our lives. It was for those reasons I had become disinterested in that life path.

Not Me, Lord

Facing one, final semester before my graduation from LeTourneau I was resolute on never joining the military. My family and friends knew I was opposed to that route.

There the Lord stood, chipping away at my presuppositions and superimposed inadequacies and fears. Let me say this much: *never, ever say never* within earshot of God. He can assign the thing you never desired to do. It's almost comical. At the moment I think I'm least equipped, that's when the Father proves that notion correct. Then He steps in, equips me for the task, and provides the strength to carry me through.

Marty Donner's death caused me to revere the Lord more. Who could say, though, whether the eternal imperativeness I learned out of the passing of Marty Donner influenced me to begin offering glancing thoughts toward the military by the middle of that summer?

That spiritual revitalization had revealed God was bigger than me *or* my circumstances. He was capable to protect and safeguard me. This left no reason to think He couldn't protect me from any harm within the military. Did this mean it would be the last time I exhibited that fear? No. But, it was one of the critical obstacles to which the Lord dealt a blow so I could entertain the idea.

I wasn't entirely there in my thinking. Though, I was closer than I had ever been. His Spirit had already granted me peace in the direction of the mission field. If these changing inclinations were genuine, this would make me two for two in being wrong about my future.

I agreed to be my dorm floor's chaplain for that final semester. As part of the preparation for any student leadership position, I had to attend a leadership retreat the week prior to beginning the fall semester. There I again crossed paths with Luke Brown, a fellow student and leader. I had tutored him in his DC Electricity class during my sophomore year, but I hadn't had much interaction with him since.

It was at this retreat that I first contemplated the military, specifically the Navy, with any intention. I recall standing outside talking to Luke. I don't remember how the conversation started in the direction of the military that week. Perhaps it was out of deliberating what I was going to do when I graduated. All I know is my out-of-the-blue but clear focus on the military was sudden and unexpected. What once was the farthest thing from my mind had become a serious prospect. In any case, I shared with Luke I'd had passing thoughts of the military. He told me he had given oath to enter the United States Navy upon graduation. After the retreat, Luke and I continued to talk over my new interest in the military. We became good friends. I did not imagine this rediscovered acquaintance and common ground was soon to form a brotherly bond.

It never crossed my mind how much the military ponderings would become entrenched during that retreat. In increasing measure over the following days, they consumed me. Reasons why I should join, reflections on God's purposes behind joining, and questions as to my abilities to make it through the military increased. If I didn't have to focus on my academic studies, I was contemplating this once foreign and rejected future. I continued to pray and consider the direction I was sensing. Each day one or more thought, idea, or revelation would arrive.

Foremost among them was the faith struggle that transpired weeks earlier. Was it possible that the lowest of low points in my faith walk had been designed by the Lord to prepare me for the military? Could it be true there was a deeper purpose behind my becoming more confident of my identity in Christ? It would prove a necessity if I entered this spiritually challenging environment. Had both my parents and Scott been correct in echoing the notion that the Lord had been walking me through the event to prepare me for something harder?

I was desperate to find an answer from the Father. One afternoon I sat in conversation with Him as I pleaded for His guidance. In the midst of praying and thinking, past goals were exposing fresh perspectives. I persisted to firmly hold to the belief the Lord was leading me to the mission field. I likewise remembered my focused objectives of paying off the mounting debt. I intended to pursue commercial aviation as the means to that end. Perhaps the military could achieve the same. The debt was a serious issue, but I continued to trust the Lord's promise to remove it in His time and way.

My heart's desire was to allow my life to be an effective witness for Christ. The military could be one of the most morally vulnerable places where His love and truth could shine brightest. For example, I had a distaste for foul language. By my *not* succumbing to its use, could Christ show others it was unnecessary? Could God even use my times of questioning and faith-building to draw others to Himself?

The Father was also factoring in my temperament. The deeper I scrutinized this prospect, the more that became obvious. He knew self-discipline was not an inborn character trait. The Lord recognized that I tended to develop slowly spiritually and physically. It had taken years, but the near cessation of airsickness while flying and my newfound enjoyment of roller coasters indicated my tolerance for G-loading had improved. What would have become of my persistence had I gone straightway to the military and become ill as a result of more *extreme* motions?

Then practical thoughts randomly bubbled to the surface. It would only help that I had better than 20/20 vision. I always liked the water. I relished the idea of being on a ship. What if flying an aircraft onto the short and pitching deck of an aircraft carrier would prepare me for the short-field demands of mission flying? Who was I to say the Lord could not pay down my school loans, mature my spirit and discipline, and use my vested qualifications and interests? Could all of this actually have been His design? The Father knew me, and that was the most important note I was taking away from these self-analyses.

Then there were days I was sure this was not for me. What *about* my being protected, maybe even sheltered all my life? Would my tender and compassionate heart be destroyed? Was I going to lose everything that defined my spiritual character? This was my paramount fear of entering the military. However, through that week and the days preceding an unforgettable Sunday to come, He would dash that hesitance to pieces.

SCRIPTURE AFFIRMS THE DIRECTION

Dr. Scott Hummel, one of LeTourneau's Bible professors, had an extensive knowledge of Israelite, Jewish, and Old Testament history. I asked his biblical opinion one day, and he reinforced something already revealed to me by God's Spirit: knowing we're in God's will increases our faith, and knowing we're in His will enables us to keep going even if it's hard.

This statement had been *exactly* what had been on my mind days before. Then, if that weren't enough to convince me, the Father met me again when another university professor remarked that the Lord sometimes has us doing things we never wanted or never *thought* we could do. Sound familiar?

Was it my business to worry whether I was spiritually adept or mature enough, whether I could handle the difficulties of the military, or even about dying? Was it not in fact my simple duty to be obedient? Through the trust lessons of the previous four years, the Lord was beginning the process of having the final say as He revealed the truth of His Word to me.

The Lord worked through my search for His guidance by growing my desire to seek Him in His Word while affirming His words were reliable. One of the places my pursuit took me was in the second and third chapters of Proverbs. Here is some of what I read there:

> For He guards the course of the just and protects the way of His faithful ones. Then you will understand what is right and just and fair—every good path. For wisdom will enter your heart, and knowledge will be pleasant to your soul. Discretion will protect you, and understanding will guard you. Wisdom will save you from the ways of wicked men, from men whose words are perverse, who leave the straight paths to walk in dark ways, who delight in doing wrong and rejoice in the perverseness of evil, whose paths are crooked and who are devious in their ways (Prov. 2:8-15).

Then I read Proverbs 3, particularly verses 5–6, 23–26. I had learned the first two back in high school, but now I underlined them all in my Bible:

> Trust in the Lord with all your heart and lean not on your own understanding; in all your ways acknowledge Him, and He will make your paths straight. . . . Then you will go on your way in safety, and your foot will not stumble; when you lie down, you will not be afraid; when you lie down, your sleep will be sweet. Have no fear of sudden disaster or of the ruin that overtakes the wicked, for the LORD will be your confidence and will keep your foot from being snared.

After I had read this, I was stopped. I was brought to prayer, in a spirit of confession. I knew the Lord was speaking to me about not having fear over losing my spirituality, my tender heart, or my relationship with Christ. He had given me these things, along with His wisdom. Both 1 Corinthians and Psalm 119:98-102 affirm that truth. I had no cause to worry. God used His Word *and* His witnesses to further convince me He was behind the proposal.

Aside from that, the Lord was more than capable to provide means to assist me in remaining spiritually sound. He had provided Luke's friendship, possibly so we could motivate and encourage each other to remain spiritually strong. I would quickly discover God *had* strategically placed Luke for this purpose.

What other reason was there that would explain why my thoughts had changed in respect to the military? If I had been *so* opposed and obstinate to it previously, what else would have prompted *me* to choose to think any differently? I am confident the Lord had been changing my thoughts all along.

Eleven

My Lord, I Will Go . . . Are You Sure?

Trusting in God, in part due to the fact He is invisible to our human eyes, does not come easy as His child. It is arguably the most daunting and tedious lesson a believer will ever face. Anyone to suggest otherwise has not looked in the mirror lately. Trusting in Him is a growth process, and it cannot even exist devoid a relationship with Christ. It cannot develop in isolation.

Suppose *someone you had never met* asked you to consciously step into a fire hot enough it scorched people standing many feet away. You were assured of the goodness and honorableness of the person asking you. Yet, you received no cause and no promised result. That would be ludicrous, right? What purpose would there be in that? You'd burn to death for no good reason.

Now, suppose the person asking you to do this is God. Remember, this is the first time you met Him. Say He explains the purpose, "The reason I want you to do this is so that through you I can prove to your friends and the world that I exist. Others will come to know I am real and am able to meet their every need. Everyone will know of Me and My love for them from that point forward. No one will have to substantiate it ever again. However, it takes you dying before anyone is able to know of Me."

Would you be motivated to do it then? There would be a larger purpose behind doing it as it would benefit everyone else. What you don't understand is how His end result could be achieved by your death. Do you trust God to fulfill that purpose? Maybe you could, but it would be a blind stretch. That trust would have no basis to you. The benefit to others would not be enough to persuade you. *You* wouldn't have anything to gain.

So, He tells you He loves you. To do what He's asking would *require* a reciprocal act of love toward Him. But, what is there to motivate you to love Him? You have yet to experience for yourself proof of His love. If you're honest, you would at minimum be hesitant.

Let us now imagine you had known God for years. During that time, you spent hours with Him getting to know how He thinks, His likes, His dislikes. He reciprocates interest in knowing the same things about you. He helps you through hard times where you were ready to give up. He fends off people who would try to kill you. He even helps you understand the reasons behind what He does. He lavishes His love on you. You are convinced He has your best interests in mind. He loves you. All of who He is compels you to love Him in return. This time, God adds to His request, "I also have a plan and purpose for you if you do this. Trust Me. I will be glorified, and I want *you* to share in that glory with Me."

Isn't that what Scripture promises? Second Thessalonians 2:13–14 says, "From the beginning God chose you to be saved through the sanctifying work of the Spirit and through belief in the truth. He called you to this through our gospel, that *you might share in the glory of our Lord Jesus Christ*" (emphasis added). True, that would not make it your glory. Nevertheless, you receive an offer to enter into it with God, because He wants to relate to you on an intimate level.

Would that not then be incentive enough to oblige the request? This time there is a motivation out of relationship. The love was mutual. Though you had yet to discover everything about God, you had a foundation of love that would allow you to trust Him with your life. If you believed He was telling you the truth, you would have nothing to lose and everything to gain by stepping into the fire.

Can you note the progression? It is only when you step into a relationship with Jesus Christ that you understand the motives behind His requests. Then, you find the ability to trust what He says. You can truly appreciate the union you share in the outcome. What is fear if it isn't a lack of trust? Similarly, what is trust without relationship and love?

So, it comes back to the core issue. Trusting is a process, as is a relationship. The extent to which we trust Him correlates with the depth of relationship we have with Him. I had been rejoicing I *was* drawing nearer to my Jesus as He drew me to Himself. I had many reasons for being persuaded that He is fully capable. I was *learning* to depend on and trust in Him. Unfortunately, it was not a completed evolution. It never will be this side of eternity. My weak thinking would vie for my attention.

Though I sensed His leading to the military, lessons in trust would continue not only during these stages of consideration, but through the experience. I *didn't* see as reality what persisted as hypothetical. He was going to have to take me step by step. Through that progression the Father would draw me exponentially closer in relationship with Him.

ENTERING THE CROSSROADS OF DECISION

It would soon be vividly and powerfully evident that the Father was the one responsible to abruptly initiate my entry into the military. As my final semester launched, Luke and his friends invited me to attend his church in northern Longview. The first Sunday I interacted with the Crossroads Community Church members was on my twenty-fourth birthday. I enjoyed the time with these devoted, genuine, loving believers. It was easy to begin regularly attending and becoming part of that church family.

Luke's and my friendship flourished. As we discussed my possibility of entering the military, the prospect of choosing the same branch of service intrigued me. The challenge of flying an aircraft onto and off of an aircraft carrier deck was enticing. Three branches are widely known to operate aircraft on ships: Marines, Coast Guard, and Navy. The odds were in the Navy's favor if I wanted to get placed as aircrew on a fixed wing aircraft (rather than a helicopter) and operate on a ship instead of land.

In addition, Luke had already proven to be not only an accepting friend, but a living witness for Christ. This made the friendship personal, motivating, accountable, and encouraging. Beyond everything spiritual, I savored the camaraderie. For the moment Luke was the only close friend going into the Navy. For that reason he would be the one best able to provide spiritual support and comradeship. So, it made sense to join Luke in committing to the Navy. That became my desire, if I *did* enter service.

SURRENDER: A DECISION POINT

It did not cross my mind at the time that the Lord had placed Luke for the purpose of facilitating the vetting of my thoughts and inviting me to his church where the Lord had a word waiting for me. In the meantime I persisted to do the only thing I could do—pray. I had not yet concluded I was going to sign with any branch.

It was September 7, 2003. While in the dorm bathroom getting ready for church, I was moved by the Spirit to continue praying about the military. I brought the prospect before the Lord again, but I didn't give it much more thought.

Soon, I was walking into this new church for the second time. As was the custom, the church body participated in communion the first Sunday of every month. As I always did in reverently preparing my heart for communion, I confessed my shortcomings then rededicated and resubmitted my will to my loving Father. I told Him to use me however He wished. I just wanted Him to have *His* way in me. No doubt my heart was permeable to receive what would come next.

Immediately following communion the music team began to play a song that spoke directly to God's sovereignty and protection. The words of the music proclaimed that we have no reason to fear for God has planted our foot firmly upon the Rock, for He is our Shield. This was what I had been reading in His Word. Yet, my mind really was not thinking about the military.

Then, in sudden and unexpected clarity, all the ponderings, concerns, and reservations I had accumulated regarding the military came to a crescendo and climaxed in this one small, eternal second. It was as if the Lord were saying, "Peter, enough excuses. You know me! You know that I will keep you safe from the snares that may come in the military. You have nothing to fear. *NOW, GO.*"

In this one, solitary moment, the loving Father through His Spirit pierced me to the core of my being. I was convicted, and those words were the trigger. Despite my conjured excuses, He assured me I had nothing to fear. My obedience was all He wanted. I humbly fell down in my chair quivering and weeping for the rest of the song. With my head in my hands and out of the peace of relinquishment, I said, "Okay, Lord. If this is what *YOU* want, I will be obedient."

It was as if a burden I had been carrying was lifted in that instant. The thought *and* act of being obedient was strikingly simple. In that moment I felt closer to Him than I ever remembered. The interaction was so deeply personal that it literally felt like I was in a different place while I prayed. All my surroundings seemed to fade. I was conscious of things around me, but it felt like it was just the Lord and me in that room. Finally, my heart was at rest.

The peace to which I'm alluding is the indescribable assurance that God is in absolute control and I, therefore, have nothing to fear. Naturally, the prospect of what was going to be required of me, to include the physical challenges, would remain unsettling. The Lord's peace simply took its place as I leaned on the learned spiritual lessons, particularly from the recent summer's faith journey. He reminded me I *could not trust myself.* I am a frail human being who can *only* find true guidance through trusting in a perfect God Who knows all things.

If there was any emotional contemplation left, it was a sense of fearful awe and wonder. Oh, how I revered the sovereignty of an Almighty God Who would usher me into something of which I fearfully opposed. By what monumental things in the military would His strength be proven to me?

Affirmation and Confirmation

In the early days following that awe-inspiring, life-altering encounter, objections to obeying His command to go were more noticeable than they were before I said "I will go." Clearly, my sinful nature was ramping up the conflict with the Spirit, as Galatians 5:17 makes us aware. Every time I would even *think* of saying no to God's leading, I would feel a lack of peace. This temptation was even present while the Holy Spirit was convicting me during that church service.

I needed brotherly encouragement.

On the following evening, a floor mate who was serving in the United States Air Force approached me. He told me he had sensed the Lord instructing him to pray for me. He affirmed my concern about how military service would impact my spiritual condition, telling me there was no reason to worry when I was daily obeying God's leading.

Of course, I needed to speak with my parents about entering the military. Without delay I picked up the phone to call them that evening. During our talk, I asked whether they believed my reactions were solely based on feelings. They quickly said no. They said the military had never been an option in my mind, and now it was. For that to occur, it had to be largely from the Lord's moving through His Spirit.

That night I rested well.

I drew near to the Lord in prayer again the following night. I asked Him to continue to confirm for me the events of that Sunday. Just then, the comments from my parents came rushing back to me. The confirmation already existed. My parents had a peace about my proceeding. If they hadn't, it would have raised a red flag. Instead, they said they knew I was following the Lord. Wherever He took me, they believed I would follow. They had not *one* concern to share.

Truly, if there was anything I did not want, it was to be apart from the Father. Everything is better when my life runs His way. I didn't want to miss out on anything He had for me, nor did I want to be wasting time doing something I shouldn't. He was more than welcome to close the military door *any* time.

Perhaps the command to go was a test to see if I would be obedient. On the other hand, it all seemed too real to be merely a test. Strangely, since that Sunday I never once gave thought to the aspect of money. I *knew* the Lord would agree it unwise to go forward without any consideration regarding paying off my debt. The military could be the means by which He was intending to do so, but my focus didn't rest there. At last, after all the mental perspiration, I think I did feel prepared to follow in simple obedience.

The Lord would propel me further during one of my flight blocks that Thursday. My instructor and I began to discuss all that had happened. He shared his father and friend's insight learned during their time in the Air Force. The magnitude of flight experience I had acquired at LeTourneau put me in a prime position to have a significant head start on peers beginning their flight experience with the military. Flying in the military could foster jealous relationships with my fellow military pilots and instructors, in turn making it one of the hardest things for me. Conversely, the Lord could have strategically placed me in LeTourneau's flight program to help build confidence to deprive me of a reason to give up. I could not find anything but encouragement knowing I was already partially equipped.

Soon after all these week's events, I approached my friend, Jason

Bucher, and asked his thoughts about how I was processing all this information. Jason reminded me, as he had earlier, that regardless of where I ended up, I would be in the Lord's will since he could observe I was seeking after nothing but His will. Besides, he added that if my mother had not been concerned about my entering the military, then I really had no cause for worry.

Jason was also aware of the concern about the immoral atmosphere in the military and whether I was ready to deal with it. He challenged me in the loving way only a true brother in Christ can. I would see that environment wherever I went, and I would not be able to run from it. The truth of that statement pounded home. Somehow, out of that I drew a bold courage. Maybe the Lord had prepared me to handle it.

It was now September 18. The past three days had proven one thing. I was becoming increasingly thrilled and motivated about the military. This feeling brought back memories of what it was like when I entered LeTourneau with the purpose of learning to fly. I had been enthralled. His Spirit had indwelled me with boundless peace. Could the enthusiasm I felt in the past correlate to how I was now feeling? If so, then the excitement was that much more rewarding because it would be another confirmation. Funny thing, I had prayed that morning for more confirmation while I was in my quiet time. Then these thoughts came to mind. I can only deduce He gave them, because His wisdom and peace came along with them.

WHAT WAS TO BECOME OF MISSION AVIATION?

All this begged the question about the original leading toward the mission field. I was curious how a pause for the military, potentially the Navy, might play into His leading of being a missionary pilot. All that was necessary for me to know now was that the Lord was affirming I had the ability to join the military *and* still remain viable as a future missionary pilot.

That day I made a call to a Missionary Aviation Fellowship recruiter I had met several years before. I shared with him my aspirations for the mission field. At the same time, I knew the Lord was leading me into the military. In such a commitment, I could anticipate being 34 or 35 years old by the time I would be eligible to leave the service for missions.

Would that age inhibit a mission organization from obtaining the useful life out of me? The Lord dashed this concern through the MAF recruiter's reassurance, "The age won't really be an issue at all." What *enormous* relief. Had this not been the case I would have had confusion about joining the military. This confirmation made the command all the more clear.

The Adversary, I believe, wanted to try and overturn that verdict, however. Indeed, he would give it a noble try. The recruiter went on to express a word of caution. He said the conspicuously difficult aspect of going into the military while holding onto a desire of becoming a missionary would be in keeping my focus on that end goal. Suppose I got married, had children, and was offered a handsome retirement plan. Every one of these would offer incentives for me to remain in the military, and thereby distract me from my aim. MAF representatives often will hear wild enthusiasm from college freshman wanting to enter the mission field. When MAF comes back four years later, those same senior students will turn their eyes to the fame and riches of the airlines or other facets of aviation.

For a split second I hesitated, and Satan probably thought he had succeeded in causing me to doubt the Lord's call. But, wait. Not so fast. Oh, there was truth to the statement. I am never immune to the temptations and distractions. However, I *definitely* knew my own passion in becoming a missionary pilot and mechanic. Throughout my time at LeTourneau I had been growing *more* resolute in awareness and conviction in what the Father had commanded me to do. This made me increasingly certain God's Spirit was propelling me toward the military.

I would need to keep my eyes on missions. Yet, if my interest had not waned during my time at LeTourneau, it wouldn't wane in the military.

Instead, I relied on my passionate desire of incessantly pursuing God's will to keep me steadfast. So what if I married while in the military. Suppose I married someone who had as much passion about missions as I did. My focus would become all the more fixed. The reality was I believed in a sovereign God. If He had been, was currently, and would continue guiding my life, then my focus would *always,* yes, I say again, *ALWAYS* be precisely in line with His.

Confirmation From the Word

Several verses came to affirm this conclusion. Romans 12:2 says, "Do not conform any longer to the pattern of this world, but be transformed by the renewing of your mind. Then you will be able to test and approve what God's will is—His good, pleasing and perfect will."

Philippians 2:12-13 is even clearer: "Therefore, my dear friends, as you have always obeyed—not only in my presence, but now much more in my absence—continue to work out your salvation with fear and trembling, *for it is God who works in you to will and to act according to His good purpose.*" (emphasis added)

John 15:5-7 is most clear about our source for everything. Christ says,

I am the vine; you are the branches. If a man remains in Me and I in him, he will bear much fruit; apart from Me you can do nothing. If anyone does not remain in Me, he is like a branch that is thrown away and withers; such branches are picked up, thrown into the fire and burned. If you remain in Me and My words remain in you, ask whatever you wish, and it will be given you.

I was emboldened to continue striving forward with a focus on becoming an aviation missionary. I believed the Father retained a purpose in directing me toward the mission field. Yet, I didn't doubt His command to go into the service. Everything was going to play out differently.

HESITATION AND SELF-DOUBT

Despite all this affirmation and the authenticity of that Sunday encounter, I kept looking for more confirmation rather than obediently acting. It had been three weeks since the church service, yet I hadn't moved forward. I did not doubt what God decreed, but I *was* wrestling in self-doubt over my spiritual readiness in spite of His promises. The idea of the military was such a remarkably foreign concept that it caught me by surprise. The enormity of this assignment required a big step of trust. I *had* to be *positive* it was He speaking, just as did Gideon, an Old Testament judge. Nevertheless, it was causing me to drag my feet. Even Luke saw this. He was starting to get impatient with me, threatening to call the Navy recruiter himself.

The Lord was allowing me to sense His growing impatience by way of a lack of His Spirit's peace. I was enabling temptations to restrain me from obeying. In a tender yet tough love only God can show, the Father got stern with me. He convicted me that I had been procrastinating by not calling the recruiter. His call was not conditional on whether I got all my concerns resolved. It was a command. It was time to obey. I had no autonomous latitude remaining to do otherwise.

Was I sinning by not being obedient to doing those things that were required of me in following His decree? Yes, but not out of hostility toward God. I think that is an important distinction to make. Can one only partly sin? No. Either you do, or you don't. If your parents requested you undertake a chore immediately, but you did it two hours later, you still disobeyed. Likewise, to disobey the Lord was sin. It lacks love and respect. It pains Him just as it does any earthly parent. He had told me to enter the military. The disobedience was sin.

However, I did not delay out of malice. Gideon did the same thing after the Lord commanded him. He wanted to make sure it was truly the Lord he heard, *despite* the fact he had already known it. If this dishonored the Lord, I think Scripture would have shown the Lord getting more exasperated with Gideon instead of being patient and understanding like He was.

I think that speaks to His endearing nature. The Lord knew my heart. He understood I truly loved Him and was reaching out my hand to a loving Father to verify His nearness and instruction. I merely lacked a measure of faith that I didn't need to fret over things He already controlled. Like Gideon I yearned to obey even though I lacked the courage. My trust would grow as I drew closer to Him in relationship, and it was about to get a significant boost.

FORWARD, MARCH!

With this weighing heavy, I humbly yet boldly prayed again. My faith and trust were weak. I *needed* confirmation, without a shadow of doubt, it had been His command and not my incorrect perception. I needed God to be more real to me than He had ever been before. If I knew all that in utter clarity, I would follow in complete obedience.

So, I prayed, "Lord, alright. I confess that I have not been obedient, and worse than that, I have not trusted in You as I should. I have seen Your hand at work here at school these past four years. I have seen Your faithfulness. Forgive me for not continuing to trust You when things get harder. But, I need Your confirmation to Your call three weeks ago. If this is truly Your leading, and *Your leading alone*, I ask that You confirm it for me. In fact, even better, if this *IS* where You want me, then I ask that You would confirm it for me in church this Sunday. If it is reconfirmed [this was the real kicker], then I will take it as Your direction and confirmation *and I will say no more.* I will not be concerned anymore whether I will be strong enough spiritually. I will be obedient to You, and that *will be the end of the issue. It will be for certain—no questions asked.*"

Sunday came, September 28, 2003. The Lord would show me He had heard my humbly seeking prayer and prove to me it *was* He leading.

First, the worship team played the same song I had heard three weeks earlier—"Made Me Glad." God used the same words to confirm for me His will. *Knowing* I would be spiritually secure in the military was my highest concern; this song powerfully spoke to that truth. *How amazing is this God I serve that He would speak to me in such a clear manner? Again* He said to me through His assuring Spirit, "You have nothing to fear. You will not be moved. I, the Lord, will be your shield—your strong tower."

The interaction God was having with this sinner was, this time, immeasurably more personal. I was uncontrollably brought to my knees during the song. I remember where in the sanctuary I knelt. I was so overwhelmed by the presence of a Holy, *Almighty* God Who *demanded* my all and my obedience that I was unable to sing. You might say it was even Holy ground.

How *could* I now say no to going into the military? He answered my prayer completely. The answer could not have been more clear and concise. Now, I had told Him that if He answered, I would consider the matter of my going closed. He did answer. What *did* it mean to be in the presence of a God like this?

It was truly moving and *awesome* to encounter the living, personal God. I still cannot fully describe what His presence felt like. Surely, these two, key Sundays where He spoke to me through His Spirit were on the short list of special moments in His presence. He so lovingly met me, even though I had sinned by not obeying. Truly, it was a glimpse of what repentance leading to forgiveness and restoration looks like. When I confessed my failure and reaffirmed my trust in Him, He communicated with me in a powerful way. I was without excuse now.

But God wasn't through. As they ended the song, Pastor Bo Bolding asked if there was anyone who had not been relying fully on the promises outlined in the song. Was there anyone not trusting in the confidence of the Lord? *Whoa.*

I didn't raise my hand at first. Then, Pastor asked again. I can't help but laugh now. It was as if the Lord was waiting for *my* response. I felt as if the Lord were on stage pointing His divine finger directly at me. So, I raised my hand. People, including the friends who were with me, immediately came over to pray for me.

I knew then *this was* definitely *the Lord's call on my life.* How else could a prayer answered less than forty-eight hours later, confirmation by the same song, and the prompting by the pastor happen outside His precision? These *had* to have come about by God's divine direction and perfect orchestration. WOW, how real and personal He was and *is* to me! I was stoked and elated now that I *really* knew.

It had been confirmed. I was going into the military. I was going to join the United States Navy. I was 100 percent, unequivocally, positively, without a doubt sure. What true and immense peace it brings when you know you are in His will.

Twelve

ELIGIBILITY: FIRST OF MANY LESSONS IN TRUST

As I neared my last fall semester midterm at LeTourneau, I finally made initial contact with the United States Navy recruiters at Navy Recruiting District (NRD), Houston, Texas. Specifically, I connected with the same recruiters through whom Luke processed a few years earlier.

With nerves running amok, yet with a steady confidence, I picked up the phone and told the recruiting office, "I want to join the Navy to become a Naval Aviator." There was no turning back now. There was no time to waste. It is a long and arduous task to get accepted into an officer program.

The recruiters were cordial and honest men, the initial being Senior Chief Gary Cleaves. I began my inquiry process with him, then transitioned to work with other great recruiters, one of whom was Mr. Gauthier (he referred to himself as "Mr. G"). First we needed to verify I was technically qualified to be a Naval Aviator. Did I have the mental wherewithal and education required?

To accomplish this, I had to take the Navy/Marine Corp/Coast Guard ASTB, or Aviation Selection Test Battery. One most often hears of people taking the ASVAB, or Armed Services Vocational Aptitude Battery. My written exam was more specific to flying, and a bit more challenging. I had to travel to Houston to be tested by authorized proctors. This worked out well, so I could meet my recruiters and discuss the proposal in person.

I would be a liar to say I was not nervous. Luke loaned me the ASTB study books so I could do my best. It was a lot more studying to cram into three weeks of an already busy course of college work, but my enthusiastic confidence gave me an energy boost. I felt prepared.

THE TEST

It was Monday morning, October 20, 2003. I had driven home for the weekend so that my parents could join me on the trip to Houston. We piled in their car packed for one night's stay, eager to witness the Lord's first Navy confirmation. The test was scheduled for the following morning.

We arrived in the Houston area that Monday night in time to grab a quick bite to eat before I had to drop off my parents at the nearby Holiday Inn Express of Sugar Land. It was going to be a very early go for me in the morning, so I had no time to linger with them and chat. I took their car for about a thirty minute drive to the Crowne Plaza Hotel adjacent to downtown Houston where the Navy had made arrangements for me. To date, it had been the nicest hotel I had ever seen.

I didn't get much sleep that night as I brushed up on my study material one last time. I recall being roused around 4:30 via a wake-up call from the front desk. They had mistakenly grouped me with other military prospects who had also been staying in the hotel and had many more tasks to accomplish than did I, to include military physicals.

This would be the end of any rest. My alarm was set to wake me moments later as it was. My testing would begin early, and I would have to fight rush-hour traffic to get across town to the NRD office halfway back in the direction of Sugar Land.

My parents, Luke, and I, along with others to whom I had spoken, knew that I had received the command to go in the military. The Navy seemed the most logical choice. Granted, I did not perceive the Lord asking me to serve in any particular branch, but I believed He would assist me to pass these tests. I prayed that if this was the Father's true intentions for me, then He would not only allow me to pass the exam well enough to get the pilot's slot, but also make my scores *so* remarkable that the Navy would be duly impressed and accept me. My parents prayed the same. In fact, I told them that if I passed the test I was going to take them some place nice to eat dinner before heading back home.

I arrived in time at the recruiter's office. They escorted me down the hall to the testing room. I joined two girls and three guys. The test was in three parts. It would start with basic math and sciences. Then, we would take the aviation-specific portion. Finally, there was the dreaded personal inventory. Each section was tested and graded separately before continuing to the next.

After what seemed a moment, the first exam was complete. The test proctor gathered up our tests and graded them in front of us one at a time. We all eagerly awaited the results. One . . . then the two girls were notified they had failed to score high enough to qualify for anything. I really did feel bad for them. Frankly, the test had less to do with evaluating smarts than it did accomplishing the questions in a set time. My heart was pounding. Would I, too, come this far only to be disqualified so soon? I was up next for being graded. Would I pass? The Lord quietly said, "Trust Me." I passed.

With energy that was now at least half-zapped by counter-productive adrenaline, the remaining four of us continued to the aviation-specific portion. Our time was up in what seemed like the blink of an eye. To my assist, this one was a little easier for me. My training and knowledge from LeTourneau played a notable role.

The proctor again gathered our exams. The Lord must have been testing me to see how much I trusted Him, because my test was the last graded. Before he graded mine, two out of the four had failed to qualify as either a Naval Aviator (NA) or a Naval Flight Officer (NFO). They did qualify for other positions in the Navy, and they didn't appear too disappointed. There were only two left out of the initial six of us who might have the possibility to continue to the last part of the test. Would I be a wash? Sweating, I anxiously awaited. "Trust Me." the Father pleaded.

At last, mine had been graded. I couldn't believe my ears. I had done quite well on the aviation portion of the test. I had only missed *one* question in the spatial orientation bank of questions. I scored eight out of nine on the stanine grading scale in the spatial orientation subdivision, and seven out of nine on the entire Pilot Flight Aptitude Rating (PFAR) section.

This was huge. According to an ASTB overview sheet from the Navy this meant I would receive an Officer Aptitude Rating. In that rating were the individual scores of all the parts. Out of a normal group of people, roughly only *7 percent* achieve a stanine of 8. Granted, that score strictly applied to the spatial questions, but in light of the PFAR as a whole, only *12 percent* attain a stanine of 7 in any one category.[2] This was an enormous revelation. I was bearing witness to His confirmation already. I breathed a sigh of relief.

The test I had not been looking forward to was at last complete. I was escorted out of the testing room. As I proceeded down the hall into the common area, a gentleman approached to greet me. It was Senior Chief Cleaves. There was little time to savor my first occasion to meet him. It was time for lunch, and I had to pick up my parents from their hotel before checkout time. We parted and arranged to regroup after lunch.

I went to my parents' hotel and walked into their room beaming. I announced that I had not *only* passed, but from gauging Mr. Cleaves' reaction to my exam results, I had passed with flying colors. I knew this was true of the aviation section.

I recall seeing my mother's face. Tears rolled down her tender face because she knew the Lord had answered hers and *all* our prayers. I think what combined to cause my mother's tears was her equally keen awareness that at this moment a second son was going into the military. Her little boy whom she so long ago recognized as a leader was now also headed for the military.

After grabbing a quick bite, the three of us returned to the recruiter's office. I introduced my parents to Senior Chief Cleaves and the others. They waited outside while I went to meet with Senior Chief and discuss the details of what the Navy offered.

He reaffirmed his knowledge of the test scores, which had evidently impressed him. I had qualified for the Naval Aviator, Naval Flight Officer, *and* Intelligence Officer positions. I believed the Lord had prepared me to become a pilot. The NFO's duties were not primarily flying. I shared with Senior Chief that these factors insisted I target the Naval Aviator pipeline, and it was in my mind the first and *only* choice I would put on the application. *I was stepping out in faith, believing Naval Aviator would be the billet I would receive.*

I made three requests of Senior Chief Cleaves as a basis for joining. First, I would need to be guaranteed the Naval Aviator slot in writing. Second, I would request to receive financial assistance. I had the expectation I could since Luke had been compensated for his education. Third, and lastly, I wanted to go in with Luke.

He explained I would not be receiving any money from the Navy toward my education. Luke had entered early enough in his college experience to be accepted under the Baccalaureate Degree Completion Program. Such a program provided financial assistance to those who signed a post-graduation enlistment. Because I was due to graduate in less than two months, I was outside that offer window. Instead, I would enter as a "DEP'er," or into the Delayed Entry Program.

This was disappointing news to hear, but the Lord reminded me entering the military was beyond an issue of money. It was about obedience. So, I agreed to enlist believing the Lord insisted I trust

Him for the stack of loans I possessed. I was looking forward in expectant anticipation for Him to pay them off.

Senior Chief Cleaves directed me to Mr. Gauthier. I would work with him during the application sequence. Mr. G showed me an email he had just received from recruiting command. *All* Naval Aviator slots were *closed indefinitely*, and nothing would open until the class of 2004. He did offer encouragement, though. In the years he had spent working under such forecasts, he had learned it was never set in stone. When Luke applied, the board had only two Houston office slots. He was the fifth to receive one.

They promised to let me know as soon as one opened, but not before pushing strongly for me to accept the NFO billet. I kindly insisted I was supposed to fly. Inwardly, I simply *knew* the Lord was going to make a way. In the meantime, my next assignment was tendered. I needed to compile my life history so the required security background checks could be initiated.

After an emotionally rocked day, it was time to head back home. I had to be back at school the next day. On the drive home, we stopped to eat dinner at Outback Steakhouse. As was promised, I paid for dinner—well, attempted to do so. A tug-of-war between my dad and me ensued after the bill arrived. After my credit card was thieved and recovered several times, I had to finally submit to his paying the bill. But, I didn't go home defeated. We all witnessed the Father's confirmation. I knew my calling, and I would continue the long process of application.

One week later, I received an email and phone call from Senior Chief. He nearly yelled in my ear. They had received word that fifteen Naval Aviator slots had opened. This was more than remarkable as those were nationwide, not just Texas. We needed to move quickly on my paperwork to get it in for review by the Naval Board ahead of everyone else. I worked feverishly to assemble and send my personal background information to Houston.

This was surely the Lord's hand of divine intervention. I believed, and *still* believe there was no other way to explain it. There were tremendous odds in even being offered the Naval Aviator slot, much less having them come available just as I applied. The odds would become exponentially apparent and offer *much* sound truth to God's ability to defeat probabilities as the application process wore on. The Father most assuredly wanted me in this position, and He was *going* to see to it that I got placed in it.

OTHER CHRISTIANS WOULD BE THERE

Not long after I returned to LeTourneau, I gave what would become regular testimonies to the body of believers at Crossroads Church. In this service I shared my initial apprehensions relating to spiritual purity and then how the Lord led me to the Navy as well as opened the Naval Aviator slot. While Luke and I were still seated, a former Captain on a United States Navy ship came over to greet both of us. He said he had been a medical doctor in the Navy, and many of the crew had been Christians. This made his work all the more enjoyable. This Captain made it clear there were more Christians in the military, particularly the Navy, than we imagined. He bolstered us by underscoring the Navy needed strong, Christian young men to be leaders. As he and his wife parted, he told Luke and me, "Welcome aboard."

To say this was an encouragement would be an understatement. Pastor Bo later told me this man and his wife had been searching for a church. Just the night before (or possibly even that morning), the couple had been invited to worship that day. They had never been to the church, and I never remember hearing from or seeing them again. Was it coincidence? The depth of encouragement from this man's words—a reminder that the Lord would keep me spiritually secure—had to be more than coincidence. It *had* to be divine appointment.

Thirteen

APPLYING TO THE NAVY: ROADBLOCKS AND CONFIRMATIONS

I believed the Lord was going to bring me to the Navy. The recruiters were arranging for me to sync with Luke's class date in May. Spiritual partnership had been a desire of mine. The twist was that Luke was graduating in May, but I was graduating five months earlier. What job would even be available to me until we entered active duty training? Who would hire me for a few months?

Prior to considering the military, I had intended to flight instruct for LeTourneau University. Thereafter, I would likely venture into the airlines to begin paying off the school debt to become viable for the mission field. The University intended to hire me. Then the Navy changed everything. Since my anticipated time of departure to report for service was approaching, they had decided against hiring me. It did not behoove the University to standardize me for one semester, knowing I would not return.

The end of my final 2003 semester was approaching and there was much to accomplish. I never really had time to think about finding a job. The Lord had gone in advance, preparing an interim position that would financially provide for me until I entered training in Pensacola, Fla.

If you recall, I had to redo a check ride with Mr. Benson four days after my LeTourneau graduation. That retest entailed receiving my final flight rating on the 100th anniversary of the Wright brothers' first flight.

That day, after I passed the exam, Mr. Weldon Burnett, LeTourneau's Chief Flight Instructor asked about the test outcome and my Navy application status. I told him it was advancing well and that I had been informed by my recruiters I could anticipate a class date no sooner than May 15.

Mr. Burnett replied, "How would you like a flight instructing job until then?"

I couldn't believe my ears. "I thought that you had previously told me 'no' because I would only be here a semester?"

"We are losing three flight instructors, and we are in a bind to find more."

I sensed he needed an answer fairly immediately. I accepted. Sure, I sought the Lord's counsel on it. However, considering the way circumstances unfolded, I recognized the Father's handiwork. I had peace. This answer to a real problem unexpectedly and literally *plopped* in my lap. Again, the Lord proved He knew the future. I didn't. Trusting Him was becoming easier every day.

My flight instructing job would begin in January. Christmas break found Luke and me sharing our enthusiasm of entering the Navy. We agreed in Scripture's challenge to build one another up. As it says in Proverbs 27:17: "As iron sharpens iron, so one man sharpens another."

Luke and I were looking forward to going into the Navy together. For the moment, I had not been accepted, but I *did* now have a job to undertake while I waited.

CLAIMING SCRIPTURE'S PROMISES

The delay of being accepted into the Navy persisted as I began flight instructing. It had been rather quiet since the October trip to Houston. By mid-January, I had been told by my recruiters that the board of Navy Recruiting Command in Millington, Tenn., had my application and it was under review.

Senior Chief Cleaves did not see why it would take more than a couple of days to hear a verdict. If I was accepted as a prospect the next step was to be officially recommended. February 2004 came with no word. I was getting anxious. Yet, the Lord would prove faithful to the task of piloting me to the Navy.

It was the second or third week of February. Pastor Bo Bolding was speaking on scriptural instruction of how we are to pray for God's will for our lives. He explained how even when we feel certain about the Lord's guidance, it does not mean we should cease praying and seeking. I stood guilty amid this truth, and He let me know it through His Spirit. I had not been pursuing Him over the last few, quiet months like I should have.

Through pastor, the Father brought to my attention Scripture verses to embolden as well as persuade me to continue seeking Him. In Mark 11:24 it reads, "Therefore I tell you, whatever you ask for in prayer, believe that you have received it, and it will be yours." Granted, what one asks for must conform to His will. In this way, as I have come to understand the meaning, God is able to give you what you ask because it is already what He wants. In my case, I already knew His will in the matter of joining the Navy.

James 4:3 reaffirmed in me that the way I had been praying was congruent with a heart after His. My requests were never targeted in selfish human gain, but rather in spiritual, relational gains and in glory to His name. "When you ask, you do not receive, because you ask with wrong motives, that you may spend what you get on your pleasures." You surely would not find me calling the placement in the strenuous military environment as exactly a pleasure.

Matthew 7:7-8 rounded out the instruction, "Ask and it will be given to you; seek and you will find; knock and the door will be opened to you. For everyone who asks receives; he who seeks finds; and to him who knocks, the door will be opened."

With that knowledge firmly planted in my heart, I approached the Father through Christ Tuesday, February 24 at 9 p.m. *That date and time is integral to what happens next.*

It had almost been a month with no word. I decided to apply these Scriptures and pray in the manner they taught. I prayed in a confidence unlike I ever had previously. I asked, were it His will, that I would receive a call from the recruiter by the end of the week saying I had been "Officially Recommended." This would mean the next most crucial piece would be complete, and it would pave the way for my physical testing followed by my final selection.

Now, they *could* deny the application, and that would be the end.

I then asked the Lord to fulfill my prayer if for nothing else but that He would be glorified through a miraculous answer. Through His answer I would witness His faithfulness. Through the authenticity of His Word I would gain great confidence. I prayed in that strain the following day at 10 a.m.

I would be dishonest to say I didn't have a hint of a temptation to doubt. Yet, His Spirit gave me the faith I needed not to doubt and instead to *truly* believe He would answer and fulfill His promises. After all, *faith* comes from the Lord anyway. We are unable to do it in our own human strength.

At 3:07 p.m., my phone rang. It was Senior Chief Cleaves. I was already smiling. I knew before I answered what the message would entail. Sure enough, it was official. I *had been recommended.* Not only that, but my recommendation had come through the prior day.

I was speechless. I was astounded solely for the fact the Lord had been *so* evident in my life again. He went the extra length to prove faithful to His leading. If that weren't enough, He taught in vivid color the promise from Isaiah 65:24, "Before they call I will answer; while they are still speaking I will hear." The recommendation, thus the answer to my prayer, had come before I had even prayed Tuesday night. I hadn't known it, but *He* did. In the end, I was more blown away by the *reality* of the Lord answering my prayers (again) than by the fact I had been professionally and officially recommended.

I was taught a great deal witnessing Him bring everything together in perfect rhythm that day. So, it was imperative I keep trusting Him. I was growing in His wisdom and stature, and I was *loving* it. It was an *awesome* encounter with a real, personal, and living God. May He have the honor for it all!

PHYSICAL READINESS

After I spoke to Mr. Cleaves, I called and talked to Mr. G to get clarification about the significance of being professionally recommended. He explained to me that being recommended held a *lot* of weight. If they hadn't been interested in me, I would not have been endorsed. He said he once had three NASA applicants. Two never received a professional recommendation. According to Mr. G, I was a step ahead of them. The most poignant encouragement he shared was that the recommendation essentially implied I was nine tenths of the way toward being accepted. The *only* thing that could stand in my way was if there would be something negative revealed in my pre-entry physical or my Physical Readiness Test (PRT). Outside of those, I would be guaranteed the Naval Aviator position as long as I successfully advanced through training.

The application process was not yet complete, however. Remaining tasks would have to be accomplished in short order to retain my May class date. The next step would be to travel to Naval Air Station Corpus Christi, Texas, to complete the pre-entry, pre-OCS physical. It would test me to flight standards. Mr. G desired to go this more intensive route of examination to ensure nothing would disqualify me from flying in the future. The Navy board would review my package (including those medical results), and determine if I would make final selection.

It was off to Corpus Christi over spring break. I had a limited amount of time apart from my flight instructing duties. My friend Micah Hollis happened to be in town. I asked if he would help me drive down. It was a fun, laughter-filled drive. Making it to the NAS Corpus hotel we crashed in our room for the evening. It was a good thing I did.

It would be another early report the following morning. I should have been getting accustomed to the predawn wakeups. Shortly after sunrise, I had Micah drop me off at the Naval Air Station hospital. I spent several hours being tested. After having blood syphoned, my body measured to verify I would fit in Navy aircraft, my flexibility validated, my vision affirmed as superb, among a host of other exams, the rigors of the morning were complete. Everything from blood work to EKG registered as normal and was qualifying. The final step was to meet with one of the flight surgeons to review the test results. He liked everything he was seeing. *I was qualified for the flight position.*

JUST ONE EXCEPTION

But . . . *one* item caught his attention. On my medical questionnaire, which I had truthfully completed, he saw I reported my past with Obsessive Compulsive Disorder. Sudden doubts loomed. I explained that I had been medically cleared to fly by the Federal Aviation Administration, and I had been doing so without any negative effects for nearly three years. My heart was starting to race. Would something I had thought was once resolved come back to block me from entrance into the Navy? Was this as far as I was to go? How could this be the extent of God's leading?

I continued to express how well I had been doing since I was weaned off the medication. The flight surgeon said he understood my position, and even agreed that I exhibited no indications OCD was an issue. Nevertheless, he said he could not "qualify" me officially. I sat quietly.

Then, he added a sentence I was not expecting. He said the history with OCD should be nothing more than a matter of paperwork.

I thanked the doctor for his time and linked back up with Micah. Mr. Gauthier was already on top of the verdict. He soon informed me that the flight surgeon recommended a waiver. There *was* core purpose behind Mr. G sending me to NAS Corpus Christi. He said a waiver recommendation from an experienced Navy doctor would present well before the recruiting board. As long as the board concurred with the doctor, OCD would not stand in the way.

Breathing a sigh of relief, Micah and I spent the rest of the afternoon venturing around the local sights and taking a drive on Mustang Island Beach. I couldn't resist a swim in the chilly Gulf of Mexico. Micah declined, and in hindsight, he was probably the wiser man. With me in damp shorts sitting on a soggy towel, we drove through the night back to Longview.

PHYSICAL CHALLENGES

My next assignment was to take a Physical Readiness Test. Luke completed his prior to enlisting. Since he knew what to expect, he had been helping me get in shape. The first time he instructed me in push-ups I was unable to do even *five* on my knees. But I would grow stronger.

This challenge, too, was between the Lord and me. With Luke's bolstering words ringing in my head, I took my PRT the Thursday following spring break. I asked the Lord to grant me the best 1.5-mile run I had ever accomplished. I was weakest in my run. The best I had ever done was roughly eleven and a half minutes.

Before my run, I would first have to pass calisthenics.

I went to the local Navy recruiting office north of town. There, under the supervision of the test proctor, I achieved fifty-two push-ups and sixty-seven sit-ups. For me, that was good. I told him that I had been practicing my run on our college campus. So, we agreed to conduct it there.

As was typical in eastern Texas, it was a sunny, sultry day. I knew I didn't perform well under warm conditions, but I had no choice. After the proctor measured the distance, I received the command to begin. I began choking on the water in the air, gasping for each breath. I knew I had to keep plugging. The only words of self-motivation I could muster were, "Please, Lord. Please." I curved around the campus loop. I saw the proctor standing at the end of the last straight-away. In motivated energy, I pushed harder toward him.

He stopped his watch. I couldn't believe my ears. Run time: 10:27. I was floored the Lord had answered again. He enabled me to pass my PRT. According to the test proctor, I had done well. Now the only thing left was to await the letter of final selection.

WAITING AND SEEKING

The weeks that followed offered *more* than adequate time to think. I was about to commit my life, wishes, and future to the Navy. One event emboldened me. The Monday before Easter I learned Luke had been moved to an October OCS date. Until I was sworn in, I would be given no date or guarantee we would be in the same class.

Luke's new date gave me hope. The weight of the decision sometimes proved to be rather sobering, but I had no shadow of a doubt the Father was at the helm.

I drove home for Easter break. That Thursday night, our home church was sharing in Communion. The pastor was teaching from Exodus 33. He retold how the Lord had told Moses that He would not go into the new land with him or the Israelite people because of their sin and disobedience—lest He destroy the stiff-necked people. Nonetheless, the Lord promised He would provide them with all the power and strength they needed.

Moses cried out to God. If the Lord was not going to be with them, what point was there venturing into the land? Moses entreated God either go with them, or they would not go at all.

I readily attested to the same notion. What point was there in going forward in *anything* unless the Lord would go with *me?* The story ends with God promising Moses He would go with them.

On Easter, through a fresh reminder of the amazing gift of salvation Christ purchased for me through His death on the cross, the Lord's Spirit prompted me to recount the reason I was being asked to go into the Navy. I was to be a light of Christ and a servant in what really *is* a mission field.

I had become excited about flying in the Navy after manipulating a T-45 flight simulator during a recent tour of a Naval Air Station. I knew I was going to have fun, and I did not believe there was anything wrong with enthusiasm. Was I, however, becoming distracted? Flying was not the ultimate focus of the Lord's calling last fall. Neither should it be in the future.

I had heard little from the Navy since the previous month. I walked away from that Easter weekend *convinced* He was using the postponement to make certain my priorities were properly aligned so I would be in my right mind spiritually before swearing into the Navy.

Classes resumed after Easter, as did my instructing. So, I had to get back to Longview Sunday night. I sought the Lord before I returned to work the following morning. Regardless of what happened, I believed He would carry out His promises to me *as well as* remain true to His Word.

It was Monday, April 12. With the longing created in me that Easter weekend, I sought the Lord in an attitude of belief and humble fervency different than times past. I asked that above and beyond any other confirmation I had been given, if this was still the path He wanted me to take (even though I knew it was), then I *did not* want Him to allow me to hear final word from the Navy unless He promised to go with me. I did not want God to simply fulfill His promise of bringing me to the military. Like Moses, if He didn't go with me, *then why should I?* I wanted to receive a positive answer so that

I could swear into the Navy in the correct frame of mind thereby never losing sight of why I was being obedient to God's command. I was to be a witness and a servant. It would be a blessing being able to use flying to carry that out, but I wanted His presence with me.

I prayed that He would allow me to hear the final verdict by the end of the week. I then prayed that, were it His will, He would *send me word by that* very *day*. I figured, why not be specific in my prayer, and then trust and believe in Him to answer? I also asked that He enable Luke and me to enter the Navy together, hinging that request upon the claims of the Scripture verses onto which Luke and I had been holding: Proverbs 27:17, and Ecclesiastes 4:9-12. Finally, I expressed to the Lord that I would take His answer as the much needed confirmation that I should consent to the selection and swear in. If I accepted, I was permanently committed.

I *needed* and *wanted* the Lord. I recognized I would be unable to serve in the military on my own. I knew *that* much was true. By granting word of final selection, He would be affirming His presence moving forward. I also believed fulfillment of this prayer would be supernatural.

If you think the Lord had been prompt to answer before, then this is going to knock your socks off. That *same* afternoon, Monday, April 12, I received a voice message from Mr. G. My heart was pounding. Could it be that the Lord answered so immediately, *again?* It was. The answer did not come in the way I imagined. Mr. G said that he had good *and* bad news. First, the bad news was that I had to get another psychiatric evaluation from the doctor that had last treated my OCD. The good news was this: Since the Navy did not simply reply with a Disqualifying Letter, they remained interested in me. The last letter Doctor Meyer had written for the FAA was dated August 2000. It had been part of my packet the Navy board had reviewed. The Navy merely required confirmation that nothing had changed.

Initially I felt downtrodden because I didn't think my prayers had really been answered. Or, had they? I was looking at the situation from the perspective of what *I* wanted, rather than from God's viewpoint. He answered everything, just in His own unique way. What is "final selection" if it isn't the Navy wanting to perfect the paperwork to make it official? With the signature of the Navy's head doctor on my doctor's updated evaluation, the selection would be nearly inevitable. I knew what my doctor was going to say, and the recruiters and I already knew what the flight surgeon at NAS Corpus Christi recommended to the board. Practically speaking, it was a matter of semantics. This was final word in every sense.

The Father *had* answered my prayer. He *had* heard it, and the most convincing evidence was because He had not only assured the process continued by the end of the week, but by that very day—just as I had prayed.

I knew going into this prayer request that the Lord would answer as He saw fit. My responsibility was to be content in His response. Once I saw things from His vantage point, I believed He had answered it all. The only piece that had no answer was whether Luke and I would enter together.

The Thursday of that same week, I returned to Dallas to see Dr. Meyer and obtain the needed reevaluation. The doctor and I spent a mind-busting half an hour conversing, and even then, it was mostly me talking. In sheer amazement, Dr. Meyer remarked, "I believe this is probably the cleanest bill of mental health I have ever given someone, especially considering how many years you have been off the medication."

This brought tremendously refreshing encouragement to my heart. Though, I wasn't surprised because I had always known God had delivered me from OCD. He had done so not merely for the greater purpose of freeing me from the grip of such a lifestyle, but so I could fly. Dr. Meyer wrote a letter and faxed it to my recruiters before I left his office. The next day Mr. G forwarded it on to the Navy doctor to be signed.

This reevaluation was another reminder that God had truly relieved *and* delivered me from my past of OCD. This is clear testimony of His power to deliver from areas in our lives that restrain or impair us.

I anticipated hearing the announcement of official selection from the Navy and my OCS date by the following week. I believed the instant the board viewed Dr. Meyer's "clean bill of health," they would have no remaining hesitation in granting the waiver. I continued to wait with *more* resolve that the Navy was God's will. Little did I realize in the moment how dramatically this would conclude.

Fourteen

THE UNLIKELY
VS. REALITY

I was quickly learning the main thrust of this whole endeavor was designed to affirm my identity in the Lord, to know Who He is, and then to teach me to *trust* Him. To my amazement, He wasn't finished proving His presence. The capstone had yet to be placed.

I expected to receive the medical waiver as holistic completion to the Father's response. I continued forward trusting in Him and His timing all the more. Ten days passed since my recruiter forwarded my reevaluation to Navy Recruiting Command. I knew I was to continue praying.

It was Tuesday, April 27, 2004. The previous night I had returned home around 1 a.m. after a late session of flight instruction. As a result, I slept well into the day. That afternoon I sought the Lord on my knees as it was the only position in which I could forcibly stay awake. I pleaded He allow me to receive the Navy board's selection. The fervency with which I prayed was even more intense than in the days before.

A few hours later, while on LeTourneau's campus, I received a call from Mr. Gauthier. It was 2:30 p.m. He enthusiastically pronounced, despite all the bumpy roads getting my past history of OCD waived by the Navy doctor, *my waiver had been approved.* Additionally, I could anticipate an October 24 Officer Candidate School class date. I was so jubilant I had to restrain myself from running across campus announcing what had just happened.

In reality, this waiver was the first step of a two part process toward full-on selection by the Navy. The last piece was to be officially slotted as Naval Aviator. Getting into that pipeline was a sure thing at this point as Mr. G reassured as much a few days later. The Navy board was merely reviewing the paperwork one last time.

The actual waiver letter was dated *April 19*. Accounting for the weekend, my waiver was signed nearly as soon as the Navy board received Dr. Meyer's follow-up report from NRD Houston. This begs the apparent and now indisputable conclusion: *my* original prayer *had been answered*. It was purely procedural paperwork that delayed my waiver acceptance after April 12.

It is admittedly curious why there was another week delay before I found out. I make one reasonable guess. The Lord knew I was going to seek Him again in regard to my acceptance. Considering how He had already been communicating with me, why would He *not* want to again answer me in such intimate vividness? The delay was part of His perfect plan.

It was *such* an immense relief to have closure to the processes and tasks required in applying. It meant the Lord confirmed His leading and direction. The Lord also reassured me He was going with me into this new phase of my life. I believed these to be true then as I do today, because I believe He honors prayers driven out of a focus on Him, humbly submissive to His will, and congruent with His Word. I was now able to enter into the Navy with the peace and assurance He was going to be my guide and stay.

After I received the latest phone call, my thoughts were taken back to conversations I had with LeTourneau alumnus and Naval Aviator, Jonathan Slager. I remember his surprise that the Navy was offering me the Naval Aviator's slot because he was aware they literally did not *need* any more pilots. He reinforced that by noting the Navy was releasing Naval Aviators who couldn't make the cut, rather than requiring them to do something else. This left him no other conclusion than to verbally agree my acceptance into the Navy would undoubtedly substantiate God's leading.

Jonathan's comment delivered more indication God was behind it. I ended the day praying, "Please, Lord. Don't let me get wrapped up in the love of flying in the Navy, and instead to always keep You on the forefront of my mind so that what I do and what I say will lead others to Your Son, Jesus Christ." It was already my task to be a missionary: an ambassador and living example of our living Christ and God.

Several prayer-mustering weeks would pass before my packet was finalized. Then, on May 13 at 3 p.m., a day I again specifically sought the Lord, I received a call. The paperwork shuffle finally culminated in selection. I was *officially* offered the Naval Aviator's slot, designator 13950 – Naval Aviator/Pilot. It was finished at last. *I was going to enter the United States Navy Reserve.* I was assigned an Officer Candidate School class date of October 24. I would report to active duty training with Luke. The only thing left to accomplish would be to swear in one week later.

OPPOSITION FORCES

Of course, it would be correct to assume my proximity to the Lord in these moments would find me being opposed by the Adversary. This happened as the immensity of my decision to accept the offer sank in. I was committing to sign away at minimum the next ten years of my life. Six days later I discovered a former LeTourneau student was entering the Air Force with a pilot billet, and was going to receive remuneration for at least a reasonable portion of his school loans. This finding combined with comments from other people attempted to dissuade me from signing my enlistment papers and swearing in. In my mind I began to revisit formerly resolved questions.

Throughout these months I had sensed the Lord confirming, "Peter, this was never about the money, but only obedience. You are to enter the military. Trust Me for everything else."

Days prior to officially swearing in I had settled in my mind this was the direction I would take, but I had difficulty relinquishing the tension behind the fact there would be no monetary support. My momentary mental delusion subsiding, I resuscitated my confidence. If there had been any financial assistance available I know Mr. G. and Senior Chief Cleaves would have done everything possible to help me obtain it.

The Lord worked through all those involved in my recruitment to effect His plan for my life. This awareness enriched my heart. What Satan could have used to catapult me in the opposite direction was flipped on its head to be used by the Father to encourage and bolster me.

I consistently aim to be careful in crediting the Adversary when undesirable events occur, but the spiritual opposition I had sensed appeared to be Satan's signature handiwork. It was as if he had been attempting to impede me from going into the Navy. It was purely by resting in the convincing knowledge that God was leading all the way, I retained sanity and peace. As the Lord always has, He preserved me through it.

SIGN HERE!

The day of commitment came at last: May 20. In a small Navy recruiting office in a local shopping center in Nacogdoches, Texas, I sat with Lieutenant Boyanton to sign the many pages of my enlistment contract with the United States Navy.

I pledged I would commit to attending Officer Candidate School in Pensacola, Fla., on October 24, and I enthusiastically accepted the position in the Aviation Officer Candidate Program. I vowed that after I was commissioned as an Ensign and upon being designated as a Naval Aviator I would thereafter commit to eight years as a commissioned officer.

Since I was postponing my entry until October, I entered in the Delayed Entry/Enlistment Program.

Conditions understood and paperwork signed, I raised my right hand to promise to serve and protect my country. In the same stated manner as in my initial application, I did so based upon the principles on which this country was founded.

As of that day, I was no longer a civilian. The command by the Lord to go was followed. I was ecstatic and ready to not only serve my country, but more desirably, to serve my Lord and Savior. I was eager to see how the Lord Jesus was going to live through Luke and me.

The Father's divine hand of orchestration saw me beyond my oath. He strategically placed me in every moment, and I believe His specific intention for the United States Navy displayed that power. Three separate individuals told me I was "fortunate" to be offered a place in the Naval Aviator pipeline. It was said I would be the last for the next two years. Yet, it was *so* much more than coincidence. I had been provided, by an omniscient God, a specific window of opportunity. I believe He *wanted* to show me His intimate involvement by defying what was unlikely and nearly impossible. A Naval Aviator slot is one of the hardest positions to obtain.

With *everything* that had taken place to get me to this point, it was by *no* coincidence I was in the Navy. This was a time appointed for me by the *living God*. Many of my friends and family could attest to this conclusion today. Probably the best witness to this being God alone, *aside* from the Lord, was someone who had the greatest knowledge of my endeavor—my cohort, Luke.

Never before had I witnessed the Lord so mightily faithful to me. This intimately personal reality in my life is available to *all* who surrender to God, and I yearned for more of this close fellowship with Jesus. I am still blown away at His *majestic* threading of His will, and yet so humbled that He would do this for me. He loves me—and I love Him! I *knew* whose child I was—and I was entering the Navy with that knowledge firmly implanted.

To God be the glory!

O great and powerful God, whose name is the Lord Almighty, great are your purposes and mighty are your deeds (Jer. 32:18-19).

Call to me and I will answer you and tell you great and unsearchable things you do not know (Jer. 33:3).

Fifteen

THE RIGORS OF ACCOMPLISHMENT

My orders to report for active duty to the United States Navy were in hand. It was off to Naval Aviation Schools Command in Pensacola, Florida. The months of preparing and anxiously waiting were over. Filled with an uncertainty of what I could expect in Navy Officer Candidate School, I packed a handful of things into my car on the evening of Thursday, October 21, 2004 and began the two-day drive from home to Florida.

The first part of the drive would be short. Knowing I would not have contact with the outside world for a while, I elected to stay overnight with friends who were still attending LeTourneau.

I am not even sure how much sleep I logged that night, but I imagine it was not much. The next day, I composed one last email to all my family and friends.

I want all of you to know that the Lord has been more than abundantly clear with me that this *is* His calling on my life right now . . . perhaps I will just leave you with an "assurance note" in terms that anyone can understand. Two days ago I received a call from my recruiter in Houston. I was informed that not only are available pilot slots for the next year limited to ten slots *nationwide*, which by the way is typically how many are available to just *one* recruiting district of which there are several per state, [but also] the three of us from the Houston office that received the pilot seats in Officer Candidate School, which I'm off to now, are the very last ones until the class of October 2006. Now, if that isn't more evidence of His leading . . . well, then I can't help you. Please pray for me and my friend, Luke, who is going [in] with me. [Pray] that we will be given the strength, motivation, physical aptitude, and spiritual heart that will be needed to make it through training. But, please just pray that I, that we, will daily be focusing on the ultimate goal, and that is serving Christ with our lives and our career, and that we will look to Him and Him alone for strength every day, and that His strength will be abundantly overflowing.

In the largely vacant computer lab on the LeTourneau campus, I clicked the 'Send' button.

I was nervous about the unknowns. However, there remained a strong assurance. I embarked trusting I would soar on God's wings—and all things considered, I did—merely in a different way than I envisioned I would.

Friday afternoon I was on the road again. Making my way through Louisiana and then along the southern stretches of the United States on Interstate 10, which at times hugged the coast, I made it to Pensacola. To my chagrin I had a long night ahead. Weeks prior, Hurricane Ivan had slammed the southern U.S. coastline and impacted Pensacola. In fact, NAS Pensacola was devastated, losing the majority of its historical Naval District. Before leaving home, I was more than aware the storm had hit there, but I wanted to engage my sense of adventure and find a hotel upon arrival. I instead found one hotel after another booked full of recovery personnel. Some late-night help from my parents located an available hotel back to the west. Exhausted, I made it to my room—in Pascagoula, Mississippi.

The sun rose too early. I had only one more night before I was to report. I took time early that day to talk with the Father. Then Luke, who was already in Pensacola, called. We elected to tour Naval Air Station, Pensacola. It could not have turned out to be a more fun and relaxing occasion for Luke and me to hang out, share our wild expectations, and enjoy the remaining hours of our civilian friendship.

That night I traveled east to Destin where I spent a restless night at the Country Inn & Suites my parents had reserved. The alarm rang too soon that Sunday morning. My orders said I had to report by noon. It was a pensive few moments back to Pensacola. As I was blanketed in thunderous tropical downpours while driving, I, too, was washed in the Lord's peace. I thanked Him for what He had done and asked that He fulfill through me the purposes He had preordained.

ACTIVE DUTY IN OCS

I crossed the causeway that took me through the main gate of NAS Pensacola at 11 a.m. First stop was to get a parking pass for my vehicle. Tenseness grew as the minutes ticked by waiting to receive the permit. I couldn't be late. Pass finally in hand, and not knowing where I was supposed to report, I drove into the command complex. I gathered I probably did not belong there in my car. A sailor came up to me and asked what I needed. "I'm here to report to OCS." He pointed to a white van and instructed me to follow it.

I knew I only had moments of freedom remaining. I savored them as I followed in tow behind the military van to a remote parking lot by the main base red and white checkered water tower. I immediately noticed a line of unsuspecting young peers. Grabbing one small bag of personal items, I proceeded across the lot. My heart was really pounding now. I was asked my name and was handed a manila envelope containing all my documents for processing into the Navy.

We piled into the van. It was a quiet ride. Arriving back at the officer training complex, we climbed out and walked into a building to have our orders stamped to authenticate we reported for duty.

With a mandate of haste, our small group was whisked away to another building across the street. There on the blue veranda of this elegant, historic building outlined in white pillars standing boldly between waist-high fences, the barking from the upperclassmen Candidate Officers, or "Candios," began.

I would stand at attention with my classmates in the halls of the quarterdeck untying and retying my shoe laces in accordance with uniform standards while the upperclassmen yelled in my ear asking me to recite various items of required Navy knowledge. If I knew the information, they would comment to their fellow leadership that I was cocky. If I couldn't remember something, or got it partly wrong, I would be blasted for being unprepared. It was a game. All of the class was being taken down to a necessary and unifying core.

In the remaining hours of that day I would be hustled from chaotic meals in the galley to a barber that was strategically tucked away in a hidden corner of one of the main barracks. For the first time in my life, my head was shaved bald. I hated it then, and I hate the thought of it now. It was all part of the routine.

Thankful to see evening, I was escorted to the barracks where Luke, our other midshipmen classmates, and I would spend the next week as Indoctrination Candidates.

I was shown to my personal rack and locker filled with the skeleton gear from an equipment hold. This was all I needed for the coming days. There was no snazzy uniform yet. We all put on green jumpsuits fondly called Poopie Suits because it would be in these that weakness would be purged from our bodies. As a nice ensemble piece, we were also issued a silver spray-painted World War era helmet with our names written in black on a piece of masking tape. These were called "Chrome Domes." They would serve as our "covers" when outside.

It would be early-to-rise again on Monday, and it wasn't for physical training. We were bussed across NAS Pensacola to the main medical facility where we would be examined to ensure we were physically prepared. We each had EKG and other medical parameters checked. No issues were discovered. I had been cleared by the Flight Surgeon to continue.

Tuesday morning, it was time for our official Physical Readiness Test, the "In-PRT." It would be recorded on our personnel record; a negative outcome could be grave. The Lord strengthened my capabilities. I made it through the sit-ups and push-ups. Then, I was tasked with what I dreaded most—running. Spurred on by my fellow midshipmen, the Candidate Officers, *and* the goal the Lord set before me, I accomplished the 1.5 mile run. It was not one of my best runs, but neither did I finish last.

Those first few days we would learn many things including how to make our beds with appropriate hospital-grade corners. I think it was more difficult to execute the officially required alcohol and drug test. To maintain the integrity of these tests the Candidate Officers had to stand over our shoulders. Talk about uncomfortable. Good thing I had become largely accustomed to dormitory life at LeTourneau.

The physical rigor of those days was grueling. It always left such an impression that it had long ago earned the term *mashing*. I was the embodiment of that term. My sweat stripped the wax off the floor in front of my barrack rack as I performed repeated push-ups, sit-ups, and body-builders. The linoleum-tiled floor at the foot of each bed was marked with our individual signatures of sweat.

We were growing as a unit. Luke approached me that first or second night to ask, "How are you doing?" We kept the other in sight, supporting one another. It was bolstering knowing one of my best friends was going through the same thing I was. The camaraderie with Luke was immense.

By Wednesday that first week, the routine began to see normalcy.

We marched to a nearby military exchange. There we were each fitted for our working as well as dress uniforms to be received before Indoctrination week was complete.

Through the remainder of that week we were pushed to our limits. Were we capable of making the cut? At *any* time a midshipmen could declare, "DOR." This meant, "Drop On Request." If someone didn't want to go on, or they didn't think the Navy was for them, they could bow out. There was no turning back if you did. We lost several from our class that week.

BLACK SATURDAY

Then came *Black Saturday*. Black Saturday is the day of Physical Training (PT), and incessant, grueling mashing intertwined with introductory knowledge of our new home and life. It is the event known to cause a potentially large percentage of any given class to fall out due to injury, illness, or quitting. If one fell out due to medical reasons, then you would continue in OCS but would be placed in H-Class ("Holding") to sync up with the next class. It could turn out to be a repetitive nightmare. It was worse than throwing in the towel.

My Black Saturday was an early go in the darkness. The first assignment was to train at the track and field several blocks from the officer complex. I thanked the Lord that I had made it through one of my more difficult tasks—or so I thought. Famished, we received a hasty breakfast.

Shortly thereafter we were instructed to put on our working Navy khaki uniform and pack up all the other uniforms and gear into our single sea bag. We would be moving to our permanent barracks. One behind the other we hustled down the fire stairs into the stifling Florida sun.

To our shock, our crisply uniformed Marine Corps Drill Instructor halted our movement. He commanded us to step over to a sand pit that stood between us and our new home. With our sea bags by our side and our combination covers lying on top, we took an intense mashing. Time seemed to ebb.

Next, we followed the Drill Instructor for successive periods of instruction mixed with more PT. We had to leave our sea bags behind. Candidate Officers would deliver them later. If I had thought the chafing sand now embedded in my uniform was bad enough, then it could be labeled as sheer terror once I found out *all* the gear in our sea bags had been laced with sand after we left and we were going to have to clean it out.

For what felt like several hours, our Drill Instructor guided us through the halls of offices of the Navy and Marine Corp leadership. At each stop, we would be mashed. This was no easy task with the numbers of indocs we had and the narrow, cinder block halls. Grateful for the brevity of the session we were then commanded to line up single file and grab the pants waist of the person in front of us. In a motion of being pushed and yanked like a yo-yo, we ran as one line around the building to a secluded alcove.

Rounding the corner, my eyes quickly opened in a wide gaze. There's a *second* sand pit? With a running water hose in the Drill Instructor's hand, we were ordered to begin physical exercises in the pit. I knew what was coming. Sprayed with water, we strained to remain physically agile. The sand in our uniforms, now combined with the crusty sand on the outside, forming one congealed, abrasive mess. We would be led back and forth between this spot and more grand tours of the buildings as the day continued to tick away at an ever-slowing pace. That is, until we arrived in a foyer near a stairwell.

Worn and battered, we listened as the Drill Instructor sternly explained what was in store if we decided the Navy was the cup of Kool-Aid we would *choose* to drink. It was a parting challenge *and* "last chance out" offer. I had noticed that the doors to the foyer had already been opened and covered over with a white draping. I was *sure this* was the end of our day.

With a roar, the Drill Instructor commanded us to get out of his sight as he disappeared through the upstairs doorway. Relieved, we all turned around and ran out. Beaten, parched, and hungry we exited through the white into a boisterously cheering and enthusiastically clapping crowd comprised of senior classmates. Without delay, upperclassmen ran to give us a bottle of water and a candy bar. Ah, what a sweet reward *those* simple tokens were after a long week.

Full-Fledged OC

This was it. I had at last shed my status as an Indoctrination Candidate and put on the unified pride of becoming *an Officer Candidate*. The first week of training was complete, and I was fit to continue. The Lord had given me the strength to get through Black Saturday. The assurance I had what it took to become a member of the United States Navy coursed through my veins. For me, it was a colossal achievement. In this instant, any doubts I had of my capabilities were chased away.

With sighs of relief, our Candidate Officers informed us that we had the next few moments to ourselves in our new barracks prior to being ready for the evening meal. So, we all massed together in the showers spending a good part of our limited time getting the *sand* out of the soaked uniforms we were wearing.

We had become a cohesively bonded group of midshipmen that became like family. Or, had we? This new family felt incomplete. For one, where was my *closest brother*? Where was *Luke*? I became concerned. I knew he was not the type to DOR. In the personal confusion of the day's blurred activities I had failed to realize Luke, among others, had fallen out of our team during the morning run. In fact, he had been quietly transferred to H-Class. I bore some of his disappointment, but it was not needed. Luke wasn't demoralized or shaken. He knew he would continue.

Exhausted, I was all the more relieved that it was the night we gained an extra hour of sleep. The following morning, those of us who wanted to attend Navy chapel were escorted there in our pressed khaki uniforms and allowed to worship. I think nearly every one of us went just to get away from the training routine. In a thankful spirit, I began my week bathed in the presence of my Lord and Father.

The first half of the second week we moved from one evolution to another: class instruction, drilling, and gear maintenance in preparation for a quickly approaching Military Training Test (MTT). Then, on Thursday, we were taken to the indoor pool to be tested and approved in basic water skills. I was looking forward to this.

I'd had comfort and ability in the water since childhood. In the Navy, you need to add confidence in the water. Anything less could cost you your life. We watched our classmates be tested in shipboard water survival and confident swimming skills. Our first task was to simulate abandoning ship by jumping off a twelve-foot platform into the water. Challenge complete.

Next, we had to swim a combined fifty yards using our choice of strokes.

Down to our final two evaluations.

Then we jumped as a group into the pool as if we had abandoned ship. We had to prove we were capable to survive at sea under the weight of being fully clothed by performing a five-minute prone float and afterward *using* our pants and long-sleeve shirt to remain afloat through creating a makeshift life preserver.

Whatever it took to save our lives we had to show we could do it. Serious as this was, I enjoyed the few, relaxing moments—namely floating. I likewise embraced the results which revealed I had successfully passed the Navy's introductory swim tests. My motivation to plug forward received an encouraging boost.

Officer Candidate School in the Navy is a strenuous, seventeen-hour-a-day, six-day-a-week course in a stress pot that will change and refine a civilian into a tough, effective Naval Officer. In these first days and weeks, aside from all the tests, we spent every waking hour in academic or military instruction and assignments. I learned how to march as well as disassemble an M1 rifle and drill with it. I learned to salute, stand at attention, and keep my head locked on the person in front of me. I learned to reply to commands with the right amount of forceful volume: "Right . . . face . . . cock and drive," as our Candidate Officers marched us between evolutions. I learned to tend to a presentably shipshape uniform and dress in the ensemble according to exacting military protocol. I even survived one or two Personnel Inspections by this point.

Yet, there was always the need to prepare for another test.

I gained self-confidence, discipline, and a sense of unity in our joint accomplishments. The entire first three days of indoctrination could not have gone smoother. There was, however, a problem looming on the horizon by the time I made Officer Candidate. The fourth day into training, I started to experience erratic abdominal and digestive problems. Though, I was never unable to perform class requirements well into the second week despite the occasional discomfort.

At times the growing list of tasks in front of me would mount causing me to become apprehensive. How would it all get done in time? The only thing that seemed to keep me moving through training was courage and motivation rooted in honor. I confess it would have done me well during those foreboding moments to have sunk my anchor of trust in the Father deeper into His bedrock.

I think I was resting in the overall security that I was in the Lord's will but at the same time was losing that focus on the smaller-scale, day-to-day challenges. Despite that reality, there was something deeper going on than just this struggle to trust. My body was starting to do things it hadn't been, and it seemed to be resulting from something more than pressure.

I went to Branch Medical the ninth day of training. They believed it was nothing more than a viral illness and determined I was fit to continue. That was, until Thursday. Not too long after the swim test had been completed, my body hit a tipping point.

Sixteen

THE LONGEST 48 HOURS

Thursday November 4 after the swim test, my body began to feel peculiar. Later that evening we were bussed the short distance from NAS Pensacola to NAS Corry Station. It was time to acquire our Active Duty Navy Common Access Cards. One after another my fellow midshipmen obtained their CAC and were subsequently bussed to the barracks. I grew increasingly ill as I awaited my turn. I was one of the last to receive mine. By the time I had it in hand and we were heading back to our base, darkness had set in. I had begun to feel so poorly that I laid down in the van.

In my barrack room duties were in full swing. My classmates were cleaning gear and completing other tasks in preparation for our examinations. I attempted to begin my work. On several short-interval occasions I found myself standing against the wall slumped half over with incapacitating abdominal pain. It would come in waves, and each one seemed to grow worse. The pain was of such magnitude that I could not even stand erect. Taking a mere breath hurt tremendously. I had never before been so incapacitated by pain.

Members of my newfound family advised me to put down everything I was doing and try to rest. My misery simply grew as the hours grew late. Eventually the pain was more than I could tolerate. I became increasingly concerned that something in my body was going terribly, possibly *dangerously* wrong. I knew my appendix had never been removed. My older brother's had. I requested one of my fellow midshipmen locate and summon one of our Candidate Officers.

Several came without delay. They said I looked pale white and my fingertips were turning blue. I seem to remember being quite cold, too. I shared with them everything that had happened to this point. They informed me that I had one of two options. I could wait until morning and see the doctor at Branch Medical, or they could call for an ambulance to transport me to the Naval Hospital in Pensacola. Though, they quickly made me aware that if I chose the latter, I would forfeit the class I was in and be rolled to H-Class until I could rejoin at the same stage with a successive class.

This had progressed to a level that I knew required attention. I could *not* risk continuing if in fact it was a bursting, toxic appendix. Worse, what if it had *already* burst? So, I requested they call the medical professionals. I dare admit that as much pain as I had, I am not sure I could have made a choice *not* to go to the hospital. I doubt my leadership thought it wise to stay after seeing my symptoms. Little did I know how this small decision would so drastically alter my course.

The Candidate Officers, who had by now thrown off their teaching hats, waited with me as if they were exclusively my friends. Within what seemed like seconds I heard distant sounds of sirens. They grew louder. Thoughts rushed through my head as I considered the ramifications of my choice. The paramedics rushed to my room where I was lying on my bed. Knowing there were only narrow stairs available to descend to the first floor, they asked if I was at least able to walk down under my own strength. Understanding, I obliged. As I exited my room and proceeded down the halls, all the midship-men—my family—encircled me. They understood I would no longer be a member of their family unit. More than that, I sensed they were concerned about my well-being. In twelve days, I had become their brother.

With the support of the paramedics, I gently took one step at a time. I walked out the front doors of the barracks where I was greeted by flashing lights and more paramedics with a stretcher. Securely strapped, I was loaded into the back of the yellow ambulance. It was off to the Naval Hospital, a several minute drive across town. Soon, I saw the Emergency Room doors as we backed up to them. I was wheeled into the ER and the in-processing began.

During the next few hours of the night and then morning, they conducted a series of tests. Drawing my blood was one of the first things they did. They quickly discovered that my white blood count was high and well outside normal limits. Obviously, something internally was causing my body to fight back. I then had X-Rays of my abdominal area.

They transferred me to a room in the southwest corner of an upper hospital floor. I requested to contact my parents. Having spoken to my mom and dad, my IV tube inserted, and situated in my bed for the night, I was ready to sleep. My rest would prove to be limited, as the nurses continued to retrieve additional blood samples. There was nothing more they could do except ensure I remained stable.

The sun rose and the long day of doctor visits, tests, and probing questions began. The condition of my appendix could not be determined from the X-Rays. I presume this was what prompted the next test. After personally administering the required preparations, I was taken downstairs to have a CT scan.

Several times a team of doctors would enter my room to discuss my symptoms and outlook. To my initial relief, I was informed my appendix was fine. Much of the pain had subsided, even though I had not been given food or drink. Nonetheless, the doctors could not determine what was wrong with me. It was decided it was best to hold me over one more night for monitoring. Through the evening I strolled through the half-dark floor per request of the doctors and nurses. Time moved by *so* slowly during these excruciatingly lonely and isolating hours as I anxiously waited to discover my plight.

By morning I had another visit by one doctor. A final experiment was pursued. For the first time since arriving at the Naval Hospital I was given my first food and drink. No problems arose out of that test. So, I was told there was nothing more that could be done and I would be sent back to OCS shortly.

Obviously, I was thankful surgery was not required, but there remained no hint of an answer to what was happening. I *knew* the extreme pain was neither imagined nor exaggerated. I *knew* Thursday night that my body demanded immediate attention. How could there be no answer?

The last I had spoken to the surgeons I was told my painful symptoms could be caused by a number of things. The doctors and nurses understood my frustration and instructed me to go back to the doctors I had been seeing at Branch Medical on NAS Pensacola. In the interim I was given medical orders of SIQ, or Sick In Quarters, until I could see the doctors there. This meant I would not be allowed to leave my room except for bathroom needs, and all my food would be delivered. My primary task would be resting and recuperating.

It was only a matter of hours later that Saturday afternoon when one of the OCS cadre arrived at the hospital to transport me back to base. I knew I would not be returning to my familiar barracks. That wave of reality had already crashed over me. Instead, I was brought to my new room and rack in H-Class.

Then, for the first time in days I cracked a smile. There in the room to greet me was *Luke*. I hadn't seen him since Black Saturday. It was a welcomed sight to see him. Luke and I caught up on the events that had transpired for us both. It was a unique time for the two of us. The Lord again showed me His great blessing of being allowed to be fighting through OCS with such an irreplaceable friend, and all the more now that I was facing uncertain outcomes.

I was in literal limbo. There had been no conclusive medical determinations. My future in the Navy was anything but certain.

With nothing but time while confined SIQ, any misery of loneliness I had experienced in the hospital was perpetuated as I played out the possible eventualities of my decision. There was no semblance of informational continuity. The Candidate Officers keeping watch over me expected I would have a roughly three week delay in H-Class. I would sync with the newly inbound, ninth graduating class of 2005. I would pick up where I left off with my former class of 08-05. What we didn't grasp was the gravity of the medical decisions that were soon to take place. I *did*, though, possess inward stirrings of what was about to transpire.

Seventeen

FUTURE: UNCERTAIN

Over the next few weeks, I would continue light physical training and marching. In addition, I worked my way through course studies in Naval History and Engineering amid my assigned auxiliary duties of facility maintenance and watches on the Quarterdeck. Sometimes during a barracks watch I would be responsible to bring the daily weather and muster report to the Executive Officer of the OCS Command. More of an enjoyment was being recruited to sing in the Navy Chapel's Choir as well as being able to link up with Luke during Bible class and church on Sunday mornings. I had a full schedule, both good and bad. There was no down time. Instruction and training moved forward to prepare me for rejoining the next class. When not involved in my responsibilities, I was consumed in seeing doctors.

I would soon return to the medical doctors on our base as I had been instructed to do by the Naval Hospital. At NAS Pensacola, the leading route of medical treatment is Branch Medical; they're much like family doctors. Then, there are specialists who can make medical determinations within their fields of expertise. Lastly, Flight Surgeons are located on base to make ultimate, over-riding decisions as to the physical qualification of a person selected for any flight position, or in my case as a Naval Aviator.

When I went to Branch medical Monday, November 8, I was

hopeful I would receive a conclusive explanation. I was still having minor symptoms of pain and nausea. The doctor began by conducting more blood work. He would not get the results until the following day. Then, my ears heard what I would readily hold to be a forbiddingly reproachful condition. He went on to articulate the possibility of a number of issues including anything from a parasite to—Irritable Bowel Syndrome (IBS).

This news hit me hard. Such a prognosis could negatively affect my future as a Naval Aviator. It potentially meant I would be found Not Physically Qualified (NPQ) for a pilot position. To make this theory graver, I was informed that the Navy's attrition rate in flight school was 68 percent. The Navy *was* relieving flight students for lack of need, just as I had heard throughout my applying. That was especially true with those entering from the civilian sector. It was difficult to listen to this news. How could this be? I knew I was supposed to fly, and now it appeared I might be nearing a dead end.

A follow-up appointment was arranged for Tuesday to meet with the doctor and review my blood results. Until then, my mind was filled with a plethora of questions. What if the Lord had merely intended to show me He could do the impossible, and then test my trust and obedience? What if the Lord had designed something even *greater* than the Navy?

The simple truth is that the Lord was capable to use me whether I stayed in the Navy or not. As I expressed to my parents that night, I recalled how the Lord placed me in the Navy. He, more than anyone, knew what my future held. I was willingly becoming amiable to whatever that might be. I knew my purpose was to serve the Father, as was Luke's commitment. Though, surprisingly, even he was beginning to question whether he belonged there. In a spirit of prayer and a request of the same to my parents, I awaited the news that would come in the morning.

Hope Dwindles

Tuesday came and went. I recall having my appointment rescheduled. I did, however, record a meeting with another Branch Medical doctor the following day. The news of my future was about to take a solid turn for the worst.

Speaking strictly from the paperwork in my file this doctor slammed me with the devastating words: "You're gone." He had called me into his office so I would not be shocked if I was found NPQ. His compassion didn't help much. I went into shock anyway. Making the outlook more dismal, I was then advised a possible disqualification no longer revolved around the lone matter of my undiscovered illness. My past of OCD was combining to seal the lid on what was quickly becoming my Navy coffin. The doctor went on to say that my mind could handle the military, but my body was simply unable to physically cope with it. No one understood why not, while one thing *was* for certain on this Wednesday. Any determination leading to a finding of Not Physically Qualified would leave little room for redress in light of my history of OCD.

Finding myself in the crosshairs of *comprehensive* elimination thrust me begging for an answer to the next logical question. What about the waiver? I thought it was overarching to include flying. As it turned out, the waiver I had received for OCD was only for entrance into Officer Candidate School. The Navy had *not* granted a waiver for entry into the Naval Aviator program. To secure the aviation slot I would have to jump through the larger hoop of obtaining a specific waiver from the Flight Surgeon and Navy. Where I once rested in affirmation I was to fly, my heart and mind now absorbed the real possibility the Lord may have had different intentions for bringing me to the Navy.

This forced me to trust Him all the more given the wealth of uncertainty. This became increasingly necessary as I continued to be passed from one doctor to another.

By Thursday the truth was palpable. My H-Class president said her orthopedic surgeon relayed that the Navy doctors had been given instructions to NPQ whatever Naval Aviators *and* Naval Flight Officers they could. She had the NFO designator and was facing her own finding of NPQ. She observed *all* the NPQs had been on the Aviation side of the house during the preceding two months. I learned another student, while in the middle of his advanced flight training, was effectively told, "Well, thank you for your time. Don't worry about your contract. You don't have to fulfill it. See you." Evidently, if you were unable to satisfy your original obligations for any reason, you were released. This becomes understandable whether often for legitimate reasons or for the greater good of maintaining a streamlined Navy.

These stories turned out to be the least of my concerns. The letters of my own dismissal appeared to be materializing outside my control. Both the illness and my past were converging to make one sweeping determination. This same Thursday I was notified I would be receiving a psychiatric evaluation. Meanwhile, my OCD medical records from Dr. Warren and Dr. Meyer were summoned for the review; I would remain in H-Class until it was concluded.

SHOULD I QUIT?

I began to consider whether the better option would be to drop out in order to thwart what was feeling like a guaranteed pronouncement of NPQ if I showed up for that assessment. Despite the rapidly mounting evidence against my continuing in the Navy, I decided it was best to persevere trusting in the Lord to work out His plan rather than take things into my own hands. I did not want to forfeit any gain through being an impediment to the Lord's working out the impossible once more.

In the days that followed I had time to do some research based on the grounds that OCD is classified as an Axis I disorder. I found military medical documents that codified my formerly identified mental disorder. That condition required a stamp of disqualification for naval aviation pipelines even if it was treatable with a high likelihood of full recovery. It did not matter that I had been shown to have recovered. I would still have to face one of three ultimate dispositions. I would either have a permanent NPQ, have a NPQ with a waiver, or in the best case scenario, be found Physically Qualified if the Navy agreed with all my prior evaluations that I was fully relieved of OCD.[3] Considering I was also facing a possible diagnosis of IBS, combined with the Navy's release of so many in their aviation segments, it was becoming doubtful I would ever see *that* day. My parents saw the same outcome unfolding. Nevertheless, I sought to remain pliable for the Lord to do as He saw fit.

On Tuesday, November 16, I had another appointment at Branch Medical. From 7 until 10:30 that morning, I bounced between there and the Naval Aerospace Medical Institute (NAMI). The doctor who had given me warning was not in when I arrived, so I was seen by another skilled physician. Per Branch Medical's request, I reported my persisting symptoms, albeit milder in intensity. After he dug into my past as a pilot, I reiterated to him my wishes to carry out my time to the eventual goal of flying in the United States Navy. This doctor understood my predicament, and I was grateful he did. He closed his inquiry and referred me to an Internal Medicine specialist.

Before leaving the doctor's Branch Medical office, I pried for his personal opinion. The physician stated he couldn't make the final decision, but he then looked me square in the eye and said I was "symptomatic." Due to that, I would most likely be found NPQ. More crucially, he went on to explain that such a classification meant I would not be able to pursue having the NPQ waived.

My state of affairs was looking bleaker. I seemed inescapably locked in these proceedings. I was sent to talk to the Flight Surgeon who on my second day of Officer Candidate School had cleared me to continue. His signature was required before I could sit down with the Internal Medicine specialist.

Upon reviewing my file from the past weeks the Flight Surgeon said, "It looks like a lot has changed since we last met." I acknowledged in unenthused agreement. I then proceeded to underscore my longing to be a Naval Aviator as I had minutes ago with the other doctor. While looking up my history on his computer, he inquired the status of my symptoms. He gave no indication as to whether or not he agreed with the preliminary diagnosis of IBS, but he did follow through with signing the consent form.

All indications remained I would face a disposition of NPQ. The Flight Surgeon never said so directly, but he was the third doctor to at least imply as much. I wanted to fly in the Navy. Be that as it may, I *had* to concede there were consequences if it turned out to be true my body was incapable of dealing with the military. I reiterated my concerns over being able to overcome any illness for the sake of mitigating the unacceptable risk of putting others in danger. He understood and concurred. As I was walking out of the Flight Surgeon's office, he wished me the "best of luck." I turned and said, "Well, I just trust that whatever happens, the Lord is in control." In what I recall was a look of amazement, he replied, "Well, I can tell you're a very mature young man." His statement was the best encouragement I heard in days.

MORE PROBING

I had two appointments arranged. The first with Internal Medicine regarding my IBS diagnosis, and the second a psychiatric evaluation a week later. My future in the Navy was lying on two fronts—IBS and OCD. Either or both had the capability to end my service.

Was I invoking this progression of events by my honest but persistent inquiry? I originally wondered if I had, but the timeline said otherwise. I had been ordered by the Naval Hospital to go to Branch

Medical upon my return to NAS Pensacola. That Monday visit was inconclusive apart from the blood results. Two days later I was being summoned by a doctor wherein my past with OCD was resurrected. What followed was out of my hands.

Could I have pretended nothing had happened? Might the matter have died? Perhaps these *could* have occurred. This would have required I ignore the truth and lie to the doctors *and* to myself, something I was not willing to do. I *did* have extreme pain the night I was taken to the Naval Hospital. Neither had I fully recovered. Despite having been removed from the normal training environment after returning from the hospital, symptoms recurred. It was only reasonable they could return with a vengeance. I *knew* I had to find out what was ailing me, and afterward, to ensure it would not impede my progress. My only option was to be honest in my symptoms and allow the Lord to lead my steps.

The Lord had yet to fail in my life, much less allow any of my own words or actions of the past destroy His plans earmarked for me. His plan always came out on top. So, what would lead me to think any differently in this case? What human decision could I have made that would have propelled me into a position separated from His plan?

So, I found rest in His sovereign presence. The Father was overwhelming me with His peace in view of the potential loss of my Naval Aviator designator. Arguably the most important thing I did was truthfully relay to each doctor my symptoms and continued desire to fly in the Navy if it were at all possible.

I bathed my future in prayer. The health situation *did* need to be handled, but I continued pressing forward in the most recent direction the Lord had *led* me—to become a Naval Aviator. As long as I was truthful He would see to the end results. In a matter of days I would discover my resolve to rest *and* trust in Him a necessity.

On November 18 I experienced one of the worst bouts of pain. Through a mishandling of my prescribed medication the symptoms were instead becoming more severe. That evening, I had my normal duty to stand watch. My abdomen stiffened and the pain increased the longer I stood those three hours. How could this be? The prior day I had been feeling well, nearly forgetting my complaints. That is, until my abdominal pain relapsed as half-way incapacitating during the similar conduct of my duties. My symptoms had been lurking. Why, though, was I noticing *worsening* symptoms? These two days had delivered the greatest level of stress since I had been taken to the hospital. I admitted stress could be partly to blame. I had no choice but to be equally as forthright with the doctor the following Monday, and I knew what it would likely cost me.

November 22 came, the dreaded date for the Internal Medicine specialist to review my case and give a formal recommendation to the Flight Surgeon. Immediately the doctor asked about my symptoms. It appeared by his mannerisms he had not reviewed my personnel file. So, I candidly relayed to him all the symptoms I had experienced, my personal history, as well as my mother's medical history. I reiterated the moments of incapacitating pain I had over the past weeks, and even the fact most symptoms had subsided.

The specialist then asked about my history of OCD. I explained it was no longer an issue. He didn't dwell on the subject, but did ask if I thought the two were interconnected. I said I wouldn't know how to discern if they were. As with the others, I emphasized that I longed to fly in the United States Navy, but I had to be certain any pressures of Navy flight training, operational flying, combat, or military life in general would not be compromised by whatever was causing my symptoms.

THE NEWS I DREADED

After a quick physical examination, we returned to his office where he began to explain medical terminology. All of the tests pointed to a conclusive answer that there was nothing wrong physically. He went on to equate me to a two-month-old, colicky child and followed that with a diagnosis of Functional Bowel Disorder/Syndrome, which is the parent category for IBS. Aside from this condition, I was physically fit to serve in the military.

I began to get flustered. It sounded like the specialist was going to send me on my way. I had yet to be told how this was going to be resolved or why it had even happened. I had passed my official fitness and swim assessments. How was I not capable in every sense? Was there truly a stressor impeding my continuing in the Navy?

The immensity of the news I was hearing and its implications caused my patience to run thin, and so I began to butt into the conversation to seek clear answers. Amid my rudeness, the doctor calmly continued by saying there was medication to assist with the medical issue. There was not much else that could be done to alleviate it other than removing me from the settings that initiate the symptoms.

He went on to explain what I had been told by Branch Medical. The change in structure, controlling environment, and diet was the cause for the affair. Given the right set of circumstances, like surroundings I could not control, nerves commanded by the brain to govern my digestive system would respond negatively, creating at times severe and incapacitating pain.

I was not prepared to hear what came next. He said that because of my ailment, the head of Naval Medicine classifies it as *disqualifying*. It was strictly protocol. I asked if that meant I would be found NPQ. It did. Even more disappointing, the doctor added he was going to attach a statement of "waiver not recommended." His reasoning was that I might one day face a command outside my control, and the risk in such an event was simply too great. I had no choice but to agree. This meant I now had no recourse. For me, it also meant the Lord had just *visibly* closed the door to being a Naval Aviator, and quite possibly the Navy entirely. It was here, in the middle of my languishing, the Lord saw fit to offer a large piece of encouragement.

This specialist was a civilian Aviation Medical Examiner who could issue FAA medicals. I had drawn concern over how my Navy experiences might impact my aviation future, despite the FAA having already cleared my OCD while at LeTourneau. He reassured that I would not have a problem continuing to fly as a civilian, and if it had been needed, he would have had no qualm in granting me a medical.

The simple truth was I could not perform the duties of Naval Aviator on the required medication because it affected my central nervous system. Moving forward I initially perceived I had a choice. Either I could take the medication and be assigned a different designator; or, if I was convinced I was to fly aircraft then the only alternative available was to accept dismissal. The choice would become crystal clear.

On November 29, having retained my appointment per the request of the Internal Medicine specialist, I reported to NAMI to follow through with my psychiatric evaluation. Would it be permissible to waive my history of OCD? It didn't take me long to realize this determination would entail a lengthy process. Shortly into a 576-item questionnaire, I began to pray the evaluation would not negatively influence any future of civilian flying. In so doing I came to the awareness that the assessment was unnecessary if I had already been found NPQ for a *physical* condition. It made no sense to push forward to only then risk more than had already been dismantled. I immediately ceased filling out the forms and went down several halls to speak to my Flight Surgeon.

The Flight Surgeon never received the recommendation of the Internal Medicine specialist until this point. Had that not been the case, I presume the need to address my OCD would have been withdrawn. As I suspected, the Flight Surgeon concurred with my deductions, cancelled my psychiatric appointment, and documented my final, official disposition eliminating any ability for me to fly in the Navy. It stated, "Physical examination is complete. Member is

NPQ (Not Physically Qualified) for SNA (Student Naval Aviator). Waiver not recommended."

The possibility of *ever* navigating the skies in a Navy fighter jet had passed. It was now a matter of time and paperwork before I would be sent home.

I eventually made the last, required visit to Branch Medical where I would be issued the formal NPQ letter. The Flight Surgeon held the power to remove me from Duties Involving Flying, but the doctors at Branch Medical were the only ones who could remove me from the service entirely. This is why the Flight Surgeon was not authorized to say anything more than "NPQ for SNA."

Upon receiving his finding, the Branch Medical doctor filled out what served as my notice of comprehensive termination. It read, "Member diagnosed with Irritable Bowel Syndrome which is disqualifying all duty involving flying. Also, history of Obsessive-Compulsive Disorder is disqualifying. Disqualification from contracted designator is resulting in administrative separation from Naval service."

That was it. My time in the Navy was over. My discharge orders, DD-214, would assure me of this surreal truth. My designator of Naval Aviator, 13950, for which I had signed up, would never be a reality. I was not surprised after the events of the preceding weeks. But, to say I was not deeply disappointed would be a grave understatement. Though, somehow I remained unshaken. I knew the Lord had a plan. I just didn't see it yet.

The news quickly reached OCS Command. Without delay I was moved from H-Class to a holding area for those being discharged—Student Pool. The purpose was to isolate you from the active classes. I would remain there for nine days while I continued to serve the Navy conducting various daily facility services.

In the evenings we were released to do as we wished. For the first time in over a month I climbed into my car and aimlessly drove the streets of Pensacola. In the beginning it was a wonderful relief to have regained my freedom of movement. But, with each night away, the reality of what had transpired began to sink in as I had time to think it through. On one occasion I even snuck down to H-Class where Luke had made an undesired return. We talked and prayed over each other before concluding my time in Pensacola.

It was December 9, 2004. With my paid uniforms and gear packed in my car from the night before, I out-processed from the United States Navy, acquired my paperwork including my discharge orders, and was instructed to begin my drive home. It was a long and pensive drive.

In the midst of the rapid-fire events and in the weeks and months to follow, I firmly believed what I had been told—the military component had *triggered* the physical betrayal from my body. The stressful setting had been the instigator of my malady. Yet, I had been told I could mentally focus and exist in the military atmosphere as long as my body didn't tag along. So, which was it?

The more I mulled over my diagnosis, the more wonderings mounted. I was not so sure the Navy's conclusions fit my particular case. I agree the military entails an exponential level of stress. My body *was* reacting to some element. Perhaps not having control over my environment played some role. Was the stress, however, the primary causer they deemed it to be? How had I tolerated four years of stressful flying despite the nervousness? Any one of us could put a finger on ourselves or someone we know who now and then swallows a throng of butterflies. In the end, did my diagnosis make logical sense? Had I even correctly understood everything I had been told?

One truth held fast: I had no doubt the Lord had been entirely present in the process of being discharged. He had served many intangible purposes through the brief experience, but He was readying Himself to fulfill even grander purposes outside the Navy. He directed it. Yet, I was not going to be able to admire the entire painting for a couple more years.

Eighteen

Contentment and Redemption in His Purposes

Making Sense Out of It All

I had a lot of time to think on my way home from Pensacola. This was the first time in my life I did not possess God's clear blueprint. I was without a job, and that required a decision. Anxiousness set in.

So, what about flying? I did not yet know what future lay ahead. I did, however, remain convinced it was the Lord's will to fly somewhere. Repeatedly He had confirmed flying as my occupation in service to Him. This made it an easy decision not to reapply to the Navy with a different assignment. It was reasonable to conclude that the military option was closed. My body had been having a physiological reaction to something, whether it was stress outside my ability to control or a God-given temperament with its "quirky" nerves.

There was no room for regrets. If I couldn't fly in the military, I would pursue another venue.

In this directed pursuit the Lord had begun to move and lead. While on my bed in H-Class, I prayed about what step to take next. *Immediately*, the Lord brought to mind my commercial flight instructor. I remembered that he worked for a company called Dynamic Aviation. I sensed His Spirit instructing me to contact him once I left Pensacola.

As I was driving that Friday morning, I decided to stop and see everyone at the LeTourneau airport. It was then that I found encouragement and peace, evidenced by my broad smile.

The Lord's leading toward Dynamic Aviation had not seemed to embody the commissioning the Navy had. This time He was asking *me* to take a step of faith, but it was not because I feared my unknown future. I identified I was frightened by the thought of *ever* walking forward in life *without* the Lord. My relationship had grown into a singular dependence on Him. He had remained faithfully present. The step of faith was trusting He would never change. I *craved* His lordship *all* the time, and this comforted me. I rested knowing He would never let me make foolish choices as long as I was depending upon Him. I cannot describe the immense reassurance that knowledge brought.

TIME TO ASSESS

It was not until all the paperwork had stopped shuffling, the dust had settled, and I returned home that I was able to comprehend exactly what had transpired. It was as if someone had a camera capable of the brightest flash, held it one inch from my face, and then snapped a picture. It took a little while for my emotional "eyes" to readjust. Tears *did* streak down my face that first night home. I could no longer hold it in.

Those tender moments at the outset would nearly be my last expressions of grief. Why was my dismissal not more difficult? It was an unsettling thing for many to swallow. Why were there rarely more tears from me? It was because the Father had been *clearly* evident through it all. By His loving grace, my spiritual eyes had been granted the ability to observe the truth of His purposes. I would understand, at least in part, why He led me into the Navy and how He used me there. So much had become apparent that I found peace and contentment as I faced the conclusive nature of my discharge.

I had already come to terms with the detailed truth behind my compounded disposition. Looking back, my *visit* to the Naval Hospital had started a sequence of events that led to my being found Not Physically Qualified. The battle of my release from the Navy was waged on no less than three fronts. Two of them were capable of ending my service. Combined the result was irreversible.

The decision to be discharged was not driven by me, but by a set of circumstances. The only choice I had made was to be initially checked after that original, severe bout of pain. I could have done *nothing* to change the chain of events that ensued, and it was that *very* fact that made me realize that if I was not in control, someone else had to have been—and that was God.

My discharge was the Lord's will for me. God possesses all power and authority. He could have reversed my course *on His own* had he chosen to do so. He could have dissolved my symptoms or affected the doctor's determinations. He could have even intervened supernaturally. But, He didn't. What is more, I firmly maintain the belief that to have fought any denied waiver would have itself been an act *against* the Lord's sovereign will.

Had I been wrong about the Lord's leading to the Navy? Truth is, God called me to the Navy *and* removed me from it. I was *correct* in sensing Him on both fronts. If I had been led there, could I have then been wrong about flying? Maybe I could have similarly witnessed the Father's hand by staying in the Navy and doing something bigger than myself—to serve my country. I, too, may have misinterpreted my *expectations*, but I *never* misconstrued His leadings.

Step by Step He Leads Me

My time in the Navy was *not* wasted. My future character and life assignments would reveal my tenure was for a purposefully short time. The Lord had a plan. He was about to fulfill a greater, grander purpose. God's timetable would prove to be beyond my own. It was about perspective.

This drives me to my knees in gratitude to my Father. His guiding hand *never* left me. The Spirit's clearly distinct voice enabled me to consistently discern the correct path to take. The Father guarded me. I was convinced of it then, and even more now. He preserved me, and continues to do so.

What had the Navy served in my life? How had God used the time to affect me? The radically extreme pressures of entering and then serving provided one of the best scenarios for the Lord to teach me central life and spiritual lessons. He led me to the Navy for spiritually-based purposes, not as a career. It wasn't until I departed the Navy that I observed this.

By the time I reported to Pensacola, I already had been contemplating the next decade. I had signed the contract for as long. So, I went into the Navy thinking, "I know I am to fly. I also know I am being led to the Navy. Two plus two always equals four. So, it's just rudimentary math. I am going to the Navy to fly." My thinking had become flawed. It was "me" focused. I lost sight of God's singular, straight-forward command to follow Him out of obedience. I had begun to overlay my human intellect onto a direction that was largely unknown. I was the one making plans to fly the F-18. I was the one straining to look ten years down the road.

I never sensed the Lord placing *any* specific goals on my heart in Fall 2003. In a tender, non-condemning love, the Father began to orchestrate a melody of instruction out of the Navy experience. One of the first things was: He only asks us to take one day at a time.

I had jumped ahead of the Lord and proceeded to dream big. There is nothing inherently wrong with dreaming big. The problem arises when doing so leaves us susceptible to losing sight of God and His plan. My discharged status is living proof we do not know our future. Only God knows His full plan for us, and it remains up to His discretion how much of that plan He chooses to divulge at any time.

Isaiah 55:8-9 became a pivotal verse in my life: "For My thoughts are not your thoughts, neither are your ways My ways, declares the

Lord. As the heavens are higher than the earth, so are My ways higher than your ways and My thoughts than your thoughts." I learned I could not presume to know the Lord's plans, while at the same time I could rest knowing His purposes would come to fruition.

There was also no room for confusion about God's sovereignty. My removal did not depose God from His throne. Attempting to corroborate the fogginess related to my elimination and His plans for me did not grant latitude to question the validity of His past leadings. I was going to have problems if I attempted to superimpose my finite human reasoning upon an infinite God. Who was I to question His sovereignty? No, my inability to perceive the future would be the *most* probable cause for any confusion.

Scripture does not state we know the mind of God. It says the opposite. Satan promised Adam and Eve that they would be like God and understand Him. This brings me back to the verse in Isaiah. Who was I to know the thoughts and ways of God? It was as if He had said, "Peter, what you perceive is not what I have planned for you. Don't get ahead of Me." I was spared any confusion because I understood that.

This begs a clarifying question. How, then, could I have known His commands at any point? Time. Time equals relationship. Relationship equals His Spirit to sense the things of God. The Lord repeatedly had confirmed His leading me to fly at LeTourneau. Similarly, the command to join the military came first and the affirmations came later.

Consider if we were to always know what He was thinking. What depth could there be to such a relationship with Christ? Truth is there would not be. It's the uncertain times He often draws us close. For Him to have displaced me from a career in Naval Aviation, He must have had better things in store. Flowing from this maturing relationship, I realized those times will be fulfilling, although probably not easy.

In that relationship I find joy in the past, peace for the present, and hope for the future. In that indwelling bond I comprehend His purposes.

A Lesson in Humility

Maybe it would be possible to abide in the disappointment if there were not another human trait getting in the way—pride. The Lord humbled me. I had pride welling inside of me before I ever reported to Pensacola. Who wouldn't like to sport that dress white Navy uniform? Who wouldn't want to have fun flying sophisticated, multi-million dollar supersonic aircraft off the pitching deck of an aircraft carrier?

The truth of pride in me came to light when I read 1 John 2:15-17,

> Do not love the world or anything in the world. If anyone loves the world, the love of the Father is not in him. For everything in the world—the cravings of sinful man, the lust of his eyes and the boasting of what he has and does [some translations say: the pride of life]—comes not from the Father but from the world. The world and its desires pass away, but the man who does the will of God lives forever.

I did not want any pride in the things of this world to distract me from what I *really* desired—undying relationship with Him.

That craving had existed for a long time and had been a driving force in my seeking and following His will as He revealed it to me.

Does that Scripture mean my Father does not bestow good things upon me? Am I supposed to shun any enjoyment of life or fulfillment in my career? No. He *longs* for my best. The inherently unwelcome misery or danger of losing out on that kind of gift reinforced for me the importance of following His lead, rather than seeking my own fulfillment apart from Him.

Following God was never about doing what I wanted. If it had been, I would probably have not obeyed the Lord's command to enter the military in the first place. I already knew that being outside His will is unpleasant. Mark 1:16-18 describes Christ's summon for Simon Peter and Andrew to follow Him. Without hesitation they put aside their lives to follow Him. My life was no different than theirs. My free will was expressed by following Jesus Christ. It was because I had been in sync with His desires that my life had truly taken on an air of fulfilling satisfaction. It is a *privilege* to join my career to His plan.

A New Direction

The formula is simple: one day at a time, without confusion, without pride, *follow* Jesus. I may not have done so perfectly, but I *had* followed Him. It becomes unmistakable therefore that obedience and trust *had* been intertwined in my life.

The more I think about it, a life that follows His will *should* be one of radical obedience that does not ask questions. Obeying means having a life of peace because it trusts God has a better plan. More in my time at NAS Pensacola than in any other I came to concede my life and career served only one solitary purpose—to be used by God to reveal His salvation and relationship to those searching for more. This being true, the more flexible I was to being obedient to His leading the more people my life might touch.

Who was I to say that among many purposes the Father had not been testing to see how far I would go in following Him? If I followed Him to the Navy, then perhaps I would trust His lead to something more radical. I *had* been learning to lovingly trust Him every step of the way, and it was becoming easier to apply after every instance of obedience to Him.

The Father *had* accomplished exactly what He had intended: to encourage me to trust Him. Nevertheless, my trust was only in its infantile stages. Frankly, it would become a resounding theme as the years progressed.

BACK TO THE BASICS

To *fully* understand what had happened to me and make sense of God's actions of appointment and dismissal from the Navy, it is a necessity to step back. Long before the Navy and even college my walk with Christ had brought me to accept the truth that my salvation had nothing to do with any good I might do. Perfection is the criteria for my presence in His Kingdom. I had no hesitation believing my life had fallen short and far beyond any remote chance of being perfect enough. I had been stained by Adam's blood when it began coursing my cells at the moment of conception. Still, I grew up in a family whose members tried to live biblically, good, and obedient lives.

Doing good is admirable as long as its goal is to be a life pleasing to God. Consider Christ's words in Matthew 5:48, "Be perfect, therefore, as your heavenly Father is perfect."

Likewise, Peter and Paul echo this principle. In Ephesians 2:10 Paul writes, "For we are God's workmanship, created in Christ Jesus to do good works, which God prepared in advance for us to do." I loved the Lord and I wanted to please Him.

My good deeds had begun to indiscriminately cloud the *whole* truth. I had not yet grasped the Father's love for me. I wasn't trying to be good enough to be saved, but I was retaining a lack of understanding of how He could continue to love me when I failed to please Him. Indisputably, I was saved through faith in Jesus. Sadly, I had missed the importance of seizing how it was possible His *enormous* measure of love could meet me in my imperfections.

This opened the floodgates to an ever-increasing susceptibility of being tempted to doubt my salvation. When I would talk to someone about Christ, reminders of how imperfect I was lurked in the shadows. So, I would become timid and distracted, restrained from being an effective tool. The Adversary had undoubtedly taken advantage of my immature faith. His incessant nagging was wreaking havoc in my mind and driving me toward burdensome doubt.

The Father sought to clear my spiritual cobwebs and bring me to a mature and conclusive answer. I had fought long enough. Through the powerful event of the 2003 summer and the initiating proceedings toward the Navy in the months that followed, the Lord brought an end to the misery.

His vivid interactions and confirmations during the application to the Navy affirmed a connection existed between us. Then, as I testified to others about this working of God in my life during OCS, I knew I could not profess Christ if I did not possess His Spirit. I recall still how near He was to me when He beckoned and then commanded me to the military. It was a face-to-face interaction with an Almighty God. I identified with the record of Moses in Exodus 3:5-6. He had hidden his face because he had entered into the presence of the King's lordship. I *knew* I had encountered the same.

The red tape of the application process showed His clear orchestrations. There had been no financial help, my OCD might not have been waived, and the window for a slot had been narrow in a Navy that didn't need pilots. For the guiding hand of the Father to have overcome these challenging hurdles and divinely orchestrate my entry into the Naval Aviator pipeline showed me that absolutely *nothing* was impossible with God.

My attaining the coveted Naval Aviator's slot was not the Lord's end goal. It was His real, personal interaction coursing my life through this adversity laden, improbable achievement that showed me—*He was* alive *in my life*. Unless I had already been His child, how could I have recognized my Father's voice when He gave His command to me? There is no other conceivable way how I experienced the intimacy of His presence through it all.

This one thing I did know: *I was* assured *I was saved*. The Lord had staked a claim on my life. Almighty God had pronounced His declaration of possession! The life-long temptation to doubt had been stifled.

My youthful fears of physical death were quickly ebbing away because I knew whose child I was and where I would be if I died. I now became a viable threat to the Adversary's attempts to thwart God's plans.

Why elaborate on my assurance of salvation? Knowing I was His child in a real and vibrant relationship made my Navy challenge worthwhile. Nothing comes before salvation, and everything, including a career in the United States Navy, pales in comparison. Since God had been the one to use the Navy to assure me of my position, *all glory is* His. I had nothing to do with it—and it feels *great* having it that way.

ASSURANCE IN PRAYER

The most significant factor convincing me of the reality of my status as the Father's child was His hearing and answering all my prayers in accordance with His Word. It became a lesson in how to pray *with power.* Christ says in Matthew 21:22, "If you believe, you will receive whatever you ask for in prayer." Mark 11:24 resounds this word, as does James 4:3, which underscores the need to pray according to His will. My prayers in regard to acquiring the Naval Aviator slot afforded me the ability to say, "God, this is what Your Word says. So, I pray this in belief You are true to Your Word and will fulfill Your promises as You answer my prayer." Through this application of His Word in prayer I caught a glimpse of the power behind prayer.

I have come to prize what Psalm 145:18-19 promises: "The Lord is near to all who call on Him, to all who call on Him in truth. He fulfills the desires of those who fear Him; He hears their cry and saves them."

Peter affirms this: "For the eyes of the Lord are on the righteous and His ears are attentive to their prayer, but the face of the Lord is against those who do evil" (1 Pet. 3:12). For the Father to have heard my prayers *and* answered as He did asserted I had accepted Christ's robe of righteousness for my life. I *had* to truly be His!

God Alone

One of the most deeply meaningful reflections I carried from the Navy was being able to *see* how much I loved the Lord and was content in Him alone. In Officer Candidate School, I learned what it was like to be stripped of everything. I was rarely allowed to talk to family or friends. For a time I became a member of a new family—those who shared in the training experience. Being somehow worse, I was not permitted to look at the moon at night. I was not allowed to look at the Blue Angel F-18 flying overhead. I was deprived of enjoying *every* visual stimulus.

Outside physical training or drilling, time in OCS was often inside one of two buildings. For the first week of training, you were not allowed to drink anything other than water. You initially could not have a salad or even a peanut butter and jelly sandwich. As I recall, at *no* time were desserts permitted during the first eight to nine weeks. It was training. What I *am* trying to express is how everything I had *ever come to know* had been stripped from me. Whether it was people, food, the simplicity of savoring a sunny day, or listening to the falling rain while standing out on my room's veranda—it was *all* taken away.

Then, during the forty hours spent in the Naval Hospital, I encountered the loneliest times. There were few patients and a handful of nurses and doctors on my floor. Half of the floor was unlit and, at least by appearances, unoccupied. As I walked the lonely halls of the desolate hospital floor, my IV apparatus in tow, I was heartbroken.

In these piercingly quiet moments I shed excruciating tears of loneliness. I had lost grip of *everything* I had come to know in my life, even food and water. On the walls there were paintings of sandy beaches and enticing tropical paradises. Perpetuating my now anguishing and streaming tears, I found myself stopping at each one, gazing at them as if I had *never* seen what a human hand could do with something called a paintbrush. I wished I could have been transported to the places that inspired them. It was as though OCS had taken everything possible from me. More painful to my soul was that the family I had most recently come to know—my fellow midshipmen—had in a flash been ripped from my sight. I never felt more alone. I knew absolutely *no one*.

I was near perishing. Then, in the darkest reaches of my unspoken agony, I was inescapably blanketed in the nearness of my loving Father. He hadn't left. I *cried* to Him not to leave me. I needed Him now more than ever. I appealed in desperation for Him to walk with me through this uncertainty. I believe He had intended for me to be left with nothing but Him. In a heart filled with comforting peace, I learned what it felt like to be completely alone with God—and, yet, to be perfectly satisfied in His love and rest assured of His presence.

PEOPLE ENCOUNTERS IN PENSACOLA

My ability to face and cope with being found Not Physically Qualified proved to have significant impacts on those with whom I came in contact while at NAS Pensacola.

Fellow candidates, including a classmate also found NPQ, were curious about my positive outlook. They could not understand how I could be so calm. One of my peers was shocked after witnessing how my unashamed proclamation of the Father's consistent hand in my life affected the others in H-Class. Some even stopped using foul language in my presence. I never told them I thought it was wrong. I did not *have* to give a word of reproach.

How *could* I have had such a gleaming attitude knowing the dream had been extinguished? It was the same thing everyone noticed without a single word from me. It was the loving Father shining like a beacon.

Luke and I were witnesses to the effect the Father's touch had on the lives of our peers at the naval base. It may never be fully appreciated until eternity the imprint the Lord left on them. I firmly grasped the way God can use my life to impact others for His kingdom.

I rejoice to see how naturally Jesus influences every aspect of my existence. His testimony was breathed from my lips day in and day out for people to see. These observations along with God's ability to work through my imperfections gave me less despondency over my loss.

Look at all the praiseworthy triumphs the Father fielded. I made it into one of the most coveted and extremely impossible military and flight avenues—Naval Aviator. I made it farther than most people even *dream*. That is a blessing of accomplishment in itself. I made it through Indoctrination week, the week the Navy weeds out those they know do not belong or won't make it in the military. I passed the physical requirements and swim tests. I became an Officer Candidate. Shoving all this aside, both Luke and I agreed that had the Lord done nothing else but plant one lone seed of the gospel of Christ, the briefness of my Navy tenure still served a purpose. What is there to be disappointed about when God had done all this? I will always savor and reminisce on my time in the Navy, not to remember what "could have been," but to be reminded of what God did.

I departed with a notably deeper respect for authority, respect for the military and their sacrifice, and love of my country. Nevertheless, I confess it would have been amazing to have been able to fly an F-18 off the USS Ronald Reagan. I was saddened that Luke and I were not able to live out the dream of being bulwarks for each other through OCS and the Navy leading to a shared graduation. However, the military was not His plan, and my personal yearnings could not take precedence over God's will.

As had my family, Luke and I had bathed my potential discharge in prayer. We were specific: if the Lord did not want me to continue He would deny the waiver. As Christians, we knew it was not our place to coerce the hand of God, but only to trustingly follow Him and do those things within our realm of control. Neither of us had been stirred by the outcome because we had already resolved the Father was in control. We knew He had taken the lead. I never shed many tears because His consuming presence and grace had washed over me. Instead of being overwhelmed in sadness and disbelief, I was ecstatic and rejoiced in the truth that every minute facet of my Navy experience resided in His grand purpose.

Jeremiah 9:23-24 says,

> This is what the Lord says: "Let not the wise man boast of his wisdom or the strong man boast of his strength or the rich man boast of his riches, but let him who boasts boast about this: that he understands and knows Me, that I am the Lord, who exercises kindness, justice and righteousness on earth, for in these I delight," declares the Lord.

So any boasting I do related to that time boasts that I understood and knew the Father.

It bears repeating: *Boast that I understand and know the Lord Jesus.* God had been gracious in letting me perceive more than a *glimpse* of His purposes, therein assuring me of my standing in Him. Why *shouldn't* I boast over what He had and was doing in my life? I bear witness to the most grandiose purposes ever to be attained in this life, the capstone of all His intentions in leading me through the events of the Navy—to soundly know my life was intertwined with His. Praise the Lord I learned my life can be overwhelmed with hope because I know Christ.

I may never know all the reasons God chose to take me from the United States Navy. He did, however, give me more than enough convincing and redeeming reasons.

Many loved ones were perplexed by my calmness through it all. Why was there no need to be anxious? There is only one answer, and His name is—Jesus Christ.

Nineteen

CLOSURE TO MY TIME IN THE UNITED STATES NAVY

I was disappointed that I would not graduate with Luke as his classmate, but I was not disconcerted. My dismissal from the United States Navy would not prevent me from graduating with Luke as his friend. Upon my departure from Naval Air Station Pensacola, I had promised Luke that what we had started together in Officer Candidate School, we would finish together. We both knew this would come to pass if it were the Lord's will. In that light, I prayed that the Father would permit me to keep this promise to Luke, holding off any future job until after his graduation the following spring.

I was getting choked up as Luke's Commissioning neared. I found myself back to times I had in the Navy. I was struggling with pressing forward despite my peace it was the correct direction. I was, however, comforted knowing the Father understood it was one of the biggest transitional periods of my life. Spending even one day much less forty-nine in the military *will* leave a lasting life imprint.

Since the Lord had moved so purposefully through the Navy experience, heartfelt reflection and mental refreshing would need to continue in a balanced approach. The testimony of His dealings during my short stint would remain as long as I had markers of remembrance.

My request *did* fit the Lord's purposes. He honored my appeal.

His design in enabling me to attend Luke's Commissioning would facilitate needed closure to my Navy service. What follows are the deeply moving and indelible impressions God left upon my life during this ceremonial weekend—used by Him to bring firm closure for me.

Both Luke and I had encouraged my parents to attend. They enthusiastically obliged. A few days before, the three of us departed Texas for Pensacola where we would celebrate with Luke, his family, and friends. His Commissioning as an Ensign in the United States Navy would take place on March 11, 2005. This was Luke's shining moment. Any of my pain of being released from the Navy paled in comparison, and I wanted to make certain my feelings did not detract from his celebration. I was soon to find my wishes dashed, but not by my hand.

As Navy OCS tradition would have it, a ceremonial run would be performed early graduation morning. Family and friends were invited to participate with the soon-to-be officers. I was moved and honored when Luke invited his college roommate David and me to run with him.

It would be an early rise that Friday. Luke's victory run started at 0500. On the way to the base that crisp morning, I drove the coastal highway that ran from Interstate 10 to Downtown Pensacola. With most still sound asleep, I enjoyed the quiet and beautiful drive to the Naval Air Station. With enthusiastic spirits, David and I joined the class for the run.

I cherished this bittersweet run with Luke. It reminded me of times I reported at the crack of dawn to train with my Navy comrades. I still felt like one of them, though I no longer was. All the same, God's grace persisted enabling me to focus instead on the prize of these shared minutes. After the run I returned to the hotel, changed into my dress attire, and drove back to NAS Pensacola with my parents for Luke's class ceremony.

It turned out to be a pristine morning. The sky was a soothing shade of blue offset by the green expanse of the parade field. Seated with David and the Brown family, I roared in riotous cheer as Luke jointly led his class of candidate officers. It was a fabulous, eye-catching experience.

After the ceremonial parade, with hesitation I walked over to meet Luke. I was swept away in a sea of emotions as he thanked me for coming to his commissioning. I fought back tears.

Everyone else joined us on the parade field for pictures. David walked over to be in one with Luke. I stood in the background. I did not want to diminish his light or their moment. Luke was not going to have *any* of it. In a genuinely compassionate tone of a close friend, he demanded I get in the picture with them. Again, I was speechless.

After the Navy's post-parade reception had ended, we made our way to the Naval Aviation Memorial Chapel across from the parade green. It was time for the class to officially swear in as Navy Ensigns. Luke Brown was now a Naval Officer.

The official proceedings concluded. Everyone moved outside the heavy white doors of the Naval Chapel to the area surrounding Old Glory majestically perched in the open air. There Luke's Drill Instructor and Class Officer were already staged. It was time for another Navy tradition. In commemoration of their new standing as Naval Officers, one and then the other would give each new officer their first salute at which time each officer would return salute, firmly shake their hand, and present them with a ceremonial silver dollar. Standing off to one side I watched as each new Ensign approached their class leadership.

Dealing with the aftermath of my unexpected dismissal from the Navy entailed an ebb and flow of emotion. Some days I was fine. Other moments, like this one, were difficult to hold back tears. Even during these solemn minutes, Luke's family came alongside with affirmation of what my presence meant to Luke. Hearing these words as I watched each salute, my throat finally constricted. I instantly appreciated everyone knew how truly stinging it was for me to be pondering all the "could-have-been" moments, watching Luke continue alone. Here I wanted to be respectful and hide in the shadows. The Lord, however, had another plan.

Luke saw me standing alone in the open lawn. Unaccompanied, he walked over. He told me I was strong. His voice had a tone that echoed our unique bond. Then he said, "You still served!" He pronounced in clarity that regardless of what had happened, I had been in the Navy—I had served in the United States Navy. I could discern he meant every word. To this day I fail in my ability to describe how moving and emboldening each one was to me.

Luke's remarks resounded even stronger as I considered they had come not just from a friend, but from a Naval Officer. Luke understood what being in the military required. He knew what I went through and the disappointments we *both* had. He valued the effort I had given while I was in the Navy along with the desire and commitment I had to finish what I had come to do. I *had* served.

All day I had been awaiting a moment to give Luke one of his first non-military salutes. In this shared moment the opportunity presented itself. I put down my camera bag and phrased closely to these words, I said, "Luke, I have wanted to do this," as I raised my right hand in salute. He initially hesitated to return the salute as he told me I did not have to salute him. In urgent insistence and growing awkwardness I told him, "It would mean a lot to me. So, please just do it."

Time stood still as we saluted each other. Luke and I had finished what we had both begun just over four months ago. It meant *so* much for me to be able to be present to do that out of honor for Luke. It was also one of the many times over that weekend that helped me find closure.

Later that afternoon, Luke and his new roommate along with their other friends hosted a banquet in Downtown Pensacola. Afterward, while our families and David were chatting, I pulled Luke aside and asked him to follow me to my car.

I gave him a piece of paper on which I had written questions. I wanted to know if *he* thought I had given up, perhaps given up on myself, or, worse, given up on God. I told him to take it and look it over. Luke looked square into my eyes and said in the most sincere yet stern voice I had ever heard come from his mouth, "It meant a lot to me that you came." I again fought back the choking tears. He then left an open invitation to get together any time I was in Pensacola.

After the banquet my parents and I drove to Destin, Fla., for the night. I had chosen to stay at the same hotel I had been in the night before I reported to Officer Candidate School. My dad and I had the opportunity to share sweet time together. No words were said as I recall. They didn't need to be.

The following morning we were due to meet Luke and the rest at the National Museum of Naval Aviation on NAS Pensacola. Before we departed Destin, I wanted to visit one quiet place. Alone, I traveled the distance to the beach. The sun's early light had just broken the horizon. It was refreshing to feel the unusual silkiness of the sand between my toes, the thrust of the waves, the chill of the deep blue water, and all the natural sounds of a beach. I needed this serenity.

I could not keep these wonders to myself. After returning to the hotel to pick up my parents, I took them to the same place. I knew they would appreciate the pristine water and pure, undefiled sandy beach. My mom was giddy. She had never seen such white sand. My dad snapped a picture of her holding a handful in her cupped hand. She looked like a kid discovering something new for the first time. It was a precious moment.

We rendezvoused with everyone at the museum. We spent several hours looking at the impressive and meticulously preserved historic artifacts. My parents along with Luke's parents, Max and Nancy, and grandmother, Betty, decided to see a couple of the museum's IMAX movies. Luke's sisters as well as David had other goals in mind while Luke needed to wrap up a few administrative matters. I chose to spend my remaining time with Luke. I expected little future social interaction with him considering his packed flight training regimen.

I tagged along as Luke attempted to arrange for housing in Pensacola. He was instead redirected to NAS Corry Field a few miles away. He and I drove to Corry Station where he was *finally* able to make formal arrangements. Having a few laughs over the runaround, we departed the base.

Leaving the Corry gate, Luke said he had read the questions I had given him the previous evening. He emphatically stated I had *not* given up. He said if I had, I would have dropped out. He emphasized if my body did not want to cooperate, then it simply would not. There was nothing I could have done about that. He continued in so many words, "I know it must have been hard to see me get commissioned, but I am glad you came."

I sat speechless amid the quiet. Luke went on to remind me of the facts. "I mean, you still got a slot, something most people don't ever get. You got something most people only dream of." Whether he verbalized it in *precisely* those words or not, it was true. Not everyone is offered such a premier avenue in which to fly. Many people desire it but never get it.

Honored, encouraged, and emboldened by Luke's comments, I shared with him my conclusion. It really all boiled down to just trusting God in what He was doing. There had been some struggles in those early stages as I faced and then realized my dismissal. Ultimately, however, in the knowledge that the Father possessed the grander plan and in the strength of His Spirit, any doubts or regrets were quickly washed away.

When Luke told me I had *not* given up, it meant worlds to me hearing through his honest frankness about not only what I *had* attained, but what I *had still* performed in duties while in the Navy. The time during these administrative errands topped the string of encouraging moments throughout that Commissioning weekend.

The two of us returned to the base. My parents and I would soon begin our drive home. But, before the three of us could pile in my car, Luke and his family invited us to accompany them for dinner in Forney, Alabama. We caravanned westward in the setting sun.

After savoring laughs and the home-cooked food at Lambert's Café, we congregated outdoors. Luke emphasized one more time how much it meant to him that I came. I assured him I had prayed for him every day he was in OCS, and I would continue to pray as he embarked on his training. He replied it was God and prayers that had gotten him through thus far. We *both* knew the solid truth behind such a candid statement. He and I embraced one final time before I began heading home.

There were many times that weekend that I had to fight back emotions. Luke and I had begun the Navy endeavor together. Our shared experiences formed a camaraderie that drew our friendship closer than ever. I would be lying if I said it was an easy affair. Nonetheless, it was a momentous day for Luke, and I sensed God's presence, peace, and grace through it all. I was content in knowing we were individually competent in serving Him because our bond of brotherhood in Christ unified us. I am grateful to the loving Father for having encircled me with so many close family and friends throughout the event of my dismissal from the Navy. They enabled me to receive the Father's healing rather than wallow in bitterness. God's idea of love gave me cause to celebrate.

I enjoyed every moment of the Navy. I walked away with my head held high. I have no room for regret. I have peace knowing God had much weightier goals when He took me to the Navy. I concede God is often beyond my understanding, and I am perfectly fine with that truth. *This* is precisely where He wants me—a relationship cemented in faith and believing in trust. It is a learning process, and even I had much farther yet to grow.

Two strong passions were already coming to the forefront. My heart was yearning for all of Christ's followers to unite with me in living a life reflective of Christ and His love. Simultaneously, I retained a growing craving to fight for the United States and for human freedom around the world. This grew stronger on the way home from Luke's commissioning when my parents and I stopped at the D-day Museum in New Orleans, La. Absorbing all the stories and pictures of the young men that gave their lives made me wish I had been with them. I sought to fight for something bigger than myself and share that camaraderie. I wanted to battle for those causes still noble, good, and true.

I did not recognize it at the time, but these were God's desires. He was preparing me for both of them. I could *not* have conceived how my loving and gracious Father would begin to fulfill both of these in the next two years. What is more, He had already lined up a multitude of events to accomplish what human minds would reason as utterly amazing, if not impossible. He would intricately weave them into my spirit and character for the purpose of nurturing and perfecting my understandings so I could be His effective tool. It would all bring indisputable glory to His name. I had not seen *anything* yet.

Twenty

DYNAMIC LESSONS

The United States Navy had been pivotal and paramount to my future. The Lord Jesus had solidly placed my feet within His decree of identity. This was to create in me an unshakeable component of implicit trust to face the coming events and spiritual trials. Still, the sense of spiritual love and urgency that had grown out of God's obvious and reaffirmed presence in my life had no solid bearing or direction. Even missionary aviation did not seem to match the intense yearnings in my heart. What I needed was definition. The Lord would refine, shape, and mold this craving. Remarkably, it would begin to take form within the year. Then, when I would think I had locked on to His plan, I would discover I was again leaning forward beyond His steps. Eventually, He would materialize around me a work of ministry when I was not even looking.

The Lord knew my military discharge was going to require a healing process. I thought I had been able to put it all behind me. The Father knew. What is more, He understood the longings toward serving my country that materialized in that time. Not only would He quickly fulfill those desires, but He would use them to mend the disappointment.

The Lord had given me another promise He had yet to fulfill. He had assured my indebtedness would be taken care of in His time. With my college loans combined with the used car I had purchased before entering the Navy, I was staring down close to $150,000. I had no concept of when, much less *how*, this would be resolved. I had only a small window of time remaining to postpone repayment. My parents had been paying on their portion. In both cases, the interest was continuing to accrue. It became intensely more challenging to trust His timing. Nonetheless, I knew it was my sole task.

I had much to learn and a lot of spiritual growth was required to arrive at that depth of relationship. But, God had jumpstarted it, and I'd become enamored in love and satisfaction as the Father further crafted our bond at an exponential rate. As these encounters increased I'd reciprocate by placing more of my life in His capable hands. One item of particular note that had become apparent was that I had come to identify His distinct voice. To kick off what would be a long series of tests of my trust I had understood His Spirit to direct me to inquire about a position with Dynamic Aviation.

After gathering myself during the remainder of December 2004, I entered January with this new assignment. I called my former flight instructor and applied to the company. There was zero delay in trusting God through *this* instance of obedience. Weeks, then months passed with no word. I was finding this period of waiting was not without purpose and benefit.

I was relinquishing to Him all the desires I had built up toward flying. The Lord pricked my heart to search whether I was willing to altogether give up flight. He led me back to a simple understanding of my priorities as seen through His eyes. My hand needed to stay open, but I *knew* God would honor His direction.

I was fascinated when I learned the Lord had chosen to *doubly* bless me through one delay. Less than one month after returning home from Luke's commissioning, the company where my dad worked had given me provisional work. Filling in over lunch at the receptionist's desk I received a phone call from a not-so-familiar area code. It was Human Resources at Dynamic Aviation. In a tone of deepest apology I was quickly informed a personnel transition within the department was cause for the delay.

After a short conversation, mostly surrounding opportunities and pay, I was asked if I would like to come onboard with Dynamic. God's peace having been established in my heart toward this direction, I accepted. Because I had not been expecting this call I stated that I could not meet their suggested start date of the following Monday. Not only did I need to pack up, but I had to drive the over 1,200 miles to the company's base of operations and locate living accommodations.

They offered one extra week to handle these details. *Great news.*

My oldest brother, Mark, booked a ticket on Southwest Airlines for my brother, Matt, who eagerly agreed to assist in my drive out to Virginia. The Father even graciously provided housing while I searched for a permanent dwelling. This life transition couldn't have gone easier.

My attentions delved deep into applying myself in my new assignment. Though I retained the strong passion to fly, the initial position was as a pilot and mechanic. There were not many opportunities to fly as part of the team of First Officers on their fleet of Beechcraft King Airs. In the meantime I continued to function as a mechanic. It was a welcome change of pace at first. If the Lord still intended for me to become a missionary pilot and mechanic, hands-on aircraft maintenance skills would prove necessary.

My Obvious Aptitudes

Dynamic Aviation is like a family. The company is family owned, and was founded with a strong Christian heritage that has been maintained as their guide for business. So, it did not take me long to appreciate the blessing it was to be viewed, treated, and spoken to like a member of a family. When I came aboard in April 2005 I was one of no more than 200 employees worldwide. We knew each other personally then. We still do, today.

Dynamic Aviation has made its mark in the aviation industry for decades. They are known for their ingenuity and ability to meet customer demands through the tireless efforts of all their employees. They have obtained and fulfilled contracts for local, state, federal, and even international governments. Much of their success came through the company's specialized modifications to small and medium-sized turboprop aircraft, mostly the King Air.

The company has provided aircraft, pilots, and mechanics to support efforts ranging from aerial mapping, to environmental disease protection, to defense and law enforcement support, and beyond. One of my first memories in the hangar was working as a team to provide rapid aid to mitigate the health risks of those who had survived Hurricane Katrina.

During my first few months in the maintenance shop I grappled with the many new trades required to repair and improve each King Air in our particular hangar. My immediate management team and peers shepherded me through my tasks and taught me the necessary skills. They accepted me with care, even though I was a rookie.

My manager, Brian Miklos, and I got to know one another early on. He possessed an uncanny ability of connecting interpersonally. He came to know of my itching desires to fly, my strivings toward the mission field, and the difficulties in achieving either. In particular, the pay of an aviation novice would at best nibble at my debt. The mission field would remain a distant dream even if I had decided to cease financial giving to my Lord. The Father had done too much for me to do that. I sensed His Spirit reassuring me that if I honored Him He would take care of the rest.

Grateful alone for the peace knowing my manager appreciated my predicament, a spirit of eagerness formed when he began affording me nearly every opportunity to obtain flight time. Less than a quarter of a year with the company and I had been assigned as First Officer on several projects, including back in Texas and as far away as Toronto. Not only were these lucrative, but they opened a new and exciting world. What I did not expect were the fresh uncertainties interwoven with this flying.

Caring for People

Three months with Dynamic and I was beginning to have doubts of my aptitudes as well as pursuits. The assignment to Canada evidenced an undiscovered attribute of my character. I was finding I enjoyed the interaction with people who approached life in different ways. It was an interest aligned with my passion of giving witness to the Lord's reality. I deduced this characteristic in Dynamic's global travels would be beneficial and productive toward serving on the mission field, but difficult to reproduce while working in a hangar.

Prior to my project in Canada I began to observe a visible lack of propensity toward mechanical skills. I had the distinct impression my abilities to solve the most mundane *and* expected snags of aircraft repair found me wanting. My capabilities to apply common sense knowledge and practical conflict resolution in flight dilemmas were higher.

I had to be careful not to allow personal feelings to cloud reality. I had been turning wrenches for less than four months. How could I expect to possess a wealth of mechanical knowledge? Yet even at LeTourneau I regularly lagged behind my peers because I wanted to do a task neatly. In college this was acceptable, but in the real world, it was a necessity to be on one's game. I was taking an exorbitant amount of time to accomplish tasks.

Though time and experience might have afforded a more proficient skill set, it did not negate calling the pursuit into question. Was I using what the Father had shown to be my greatest skills, talents, and abilities to the broadest range possible? Was I following God's leading accurately? Sitting outside my apartment one sunny Tuesday afternoon in early August I sought clarification. Reengaging the memories of what the Lord had accomplished in my past helped me rediscover the many occasions in which I had been blessed with affirmations toward flying.

It seemed I had a natural capacity to *maneuver* aircraft more than fix them. No evidence of equal skill level had ever to my memory been referenced regarding my mechanical aptitudes. Whether it was compliments on my comfortable flying, my precise control, or my conscientious attitude, all of the admirable comments from the LeTourneau staff revolved around my being a pilot. Then, after my Navy dismissal, one of the assistant chief pilots who had been the most outspoken of my abilities suggested I return to flight instructing. During my six months of teaching he had observed how deeply I had enjoyed caring about my students. According to him, I owned an attribute that was hard to find. God had endowed me with everything I needed to fly, the most important of which was a care for people.

This was a relatively recent and stunning character development considering my earlier propensities toward introversion. I was thankful I had not initially seen my care for people because I otherwise might have deduced it was self-intentioned. In reality, it was an improbable trait to have attained in the flesh. What joy it was to know I was being conformed to the likeness of Jesus deep within my heart's core.

According to others I also had a propensity toward leadership. I believed *spiritual* leadership through edification offered the depth of interpersonal interaction I was seeking, and flying would broaden that realm.

On the surface it might appear I should have resumed flight instructing. Doing so was not part of the Father's perfect plan. Had it been my own presupposition that in-depth mechanical skill would be a necessity in missionary aviation? I admit I did not relish the idea I might not make a good mechanic.

I had no doubt that God had orchestrated my placement at Dynamic. I was getting a crisper image of who He had made me to be along with His specifically bequeathed skills. It only made sense that flying would be the primary outlet. Remaining in the shop, as great as it was to work with everyone, could not provide the breadth these aspects required.

What I was longing to know was what role, if any, a maintenance background was going to play in the immediate and the future. Having given due introspection, I again found myself before His throne of grace asking Him what His desires were for my life. I needed Him to be precise, and that would require I check my emotions at the door.

The Lord used this submissiveness as well as a series of discussions with my manager and human resources. The more I evaluated all the indicators and tested their genuineness against His Spirit of truth, the clearer everything became. God likely had navigated me to Dynamic Aviation for two purposes. The mission field continued to make sense, particularly in the function as a pilot. Pursuing it necessitated my college loans be paid. The Father's other intent had been to reveal and nurture my strength of helping others see Christ.

I *Have* to Fly

For either of these to occur I would have to step outside the hangar doors. I was not intended to do everything. I had applied Ephesians 2:10 after my discharge from the Navy; it was no less fitting here. "For we are God's workmanship, created in Christ Jesus to do good works, which God prepared in advance for us to do." In that individuality and empowerment God *is* most glorified.

It became affirmed in my heart—I *needed* to fly. My natural, vocal proclamations of God's reality could best be shared there interpersonally. This honing of my focus away from maintenance appeared to be His will. The Father persisted in pruning my life. He was making me into a single-minded and increasingly unashamed follower of Jesus Christ. This was a joyous realization.

I would soon find out I sensed the Spirit correctly, but not before taking another step of faith. In August I again met with my maintenance manager, Brian Miklos. It was an emotional conversation as I shared my heart with him. We agreed there was no more important task than following the Lord. It was time to approach human resources. Either I could be placed in a different position within Dynamic or face the possibility I did not have a fit in the company. I knew I had to trust God with the outcome.

Twenty-one

HEART OF MINISTRY
AT LAST DEFINED

I was willing to follow the Lord and at all costs, even at the expense of my new job. Was this radical? No, radical would have been to think otherwise. I had come to Dynamic Aviation with no guarantees of a future as a pilot. That was in the face of flying being my passion. What more of a blessing it then was to have engaged an ever-expanding world of people through sporadic duties as First Officer.

Early on I heard passing mention our company had a small-scale operation overseas, but I never learned or chased any details. I had no expectations, no pursuits. My Lord had been *more* than gracious already. I was content to keep following.

Then, shortly after I began work in the shop, Brian Miklos discussed with me just such an opportunity. He suggested I look into this niche of Dynamic. It might turn out to be a perfect fit to my promptings as well as my financial needs. My ears perked as he recommended I inquire about going to Iraq. Could this be? Had God taken me out of the Navy to serve in a similar capacity in the civilian sector? Was God's divine hand of orchestration in this?

There were not many company projects in that part of the world at the time. There was, however, one contract set to be extended. The company needed a crew immediately. Already sensing the Spirit's peace and affirmation, I pursued this small, hand-selected operation. I recognized the odds would be slim. I also remembered the Lord had done the *same* thing through the Navy.

I approached Shirley Trobaugh, the manager of these overseas operations, and shared with her my yearnings and the need to pay off my indebtedness prior to a future in ministry. She understood and looked into the possibilities. We all agreed that I would continue in my current position until I heard further. I did so with considerably more enabling peace combined with a renewed vigor.

In Autumn 2005, this manager approached me on the shop floor with disappointing news: the contract renewal that had been anticipated fell through. Iraq was off the table, at least for now.

Yet God again had a purpose in delay. She told me there was a need for a brief assignment in Afghanistan. It was a single, pressurized Beechcraft King Air 200 project tasked with assisting the reconstruction and infrastructure. One of the two pilots on location was taking a one-month vacation. Dynamic needed a fill-in pilot to support the lead pilot with mechanical duties.

Although this was more of a humanitarian effort than mission work, I eagerly agreed to it. Even so, I still sensed the Lord's leading toward the mission field. Since this would involve working among local people of a different part of the world, it might prove to be an opening test of missionary aviation.

So, I began to bathe the prospect in prayer. I asked that the Lord would use the time abroad as confirmation or denial of His direction to the mission field. I conceded that I wanted His will above mine. After all, I knew I had a nasty habit of presuming His thoughts and ways.

Certainly, I needed to continue pursuing missionary aviation as the Lord had been impressing upon my heart to do since college. That was the most recent direction I knew. I would be lying, however, to deny my heart was being driven to something even deeper. It was as if His Spirit had been filling me with a strong sense of urgency. The only way my life had amounted to anything was through my connection to Jesus Christ. What I could *not* identify was how to carry out His will for me. I had no place to turn except to the amazing and yet sobering notion that God was indeed staging to clearly define my path.

I awaited to hear the details of my sendoff. Mere days passed when I learned I would be leaving the last week of October. I would be stepping off the terra firma of North America for only the second time in my life. I would also be flying the largest and heaviest airplane to date. Excitedly I packed my bags for the journey.

WHAT IS A MISSIONARY?

I briefly met the counterpart I was relieving as I arrived in Afghanistan. Then, within my first few hours on site God began to answer my prayer. My captain had concluded there was more to life than flying. He was similarly prepared to sacrifice his flying career for the sake of Christ.

Two days after my arrival, I joined my captain in worshipping with fellow Christians in the area. I was overwhelmed as I shared in a unified voice of praise. This time with thirty others of varying ethnicities rendered me speechless. To me, the implications were evident. I was awed by the depth of faith and relationship these fellow Christians had in Christ. In the United States, it was rare I met a fellow believer possessing such a sacrificial relationship with Christ. More horrifying was my belief this was lacking in my own heart. I recognized I had not been seeking the Lord with the same passion these Christians demonstrated.

The Lord was awakening my heart to discern the truth. In my younger years I had come to the spiritually immature premise that being a missionary meant going to a country not labeled as Christian. The Father had been chipping away at this presupposition. God was showing me equally critical needs back home. Spiritual revitalization may be more needed in a land of ease, where there is less impetus to rely on Him.

It was not that the Father was unable to give me the bold strength to handle mission work in foreign territories. Rather, He had begun to turn my heart toward my Christian brothers and sisters at home. I observed a welling eagerness to share with them Christ's power to do for them the same as He had done for me. The gracious Father had revealed to me His capability to handle my temporal affairs all the while supplying me with surpassing fulfillment in the indescribable peace of relationship with Christ. This was not a personally derived passion. It was God's heart expression for me.

Nearing the end of my stay in Afghanistan I could see the Lord was changing me. As He had made me willing to serve as a missionary pilot in college and reversed my oppositions to entering the military, so, too, He was bringing me to new understandings of the scope of ministry. He was rekindling my earliest childhood drives toward pouring into the hearts of others.

The Lord cemented these revived cravings as I considered the ramifications of sending missionaries outside the borders of any country. The greater risk would be to send a diluted or untrue message. I was discovering the critical job was not necessarily working in the manufacturing plant. Instead, the paramount task was to ensure the parts being sent were of high quality.

Although it may sound like I had reached a firm decision on the matter, it wasn't until several days later that the Lord placed His seal on my orders.

Fatigued and wearied again from relating with the Lord, I found my interest and enthusiasm for flying mellowing while my loving concern for His children's spiritual health increased. I found the thought of being a missionary pilot as insufficient to meet such a need. After nearly a month in Afghanistan, even *this* flying had proven incapable of satiating this burning passion. He patiently waited for one moment.

A Closed Door

I had fallen behind in my reading of the *One Year Bible*. I was just getting into November although it was almost Thanksgiving. On the night before I left Kabul the assigned reading was from the Old Testament prophet Ezekiel. My pupils froze. I had to reread it and the surrounding verses several times.

> He then said to me, "Son of man, go now to the house of Israel and speak my words to them. You are not being sent to a people of obscure speech and difficult language, but to the house of Israel—not to many peoples of obscure speech and difficult language, whose words you cannot understand. Surely if I had sent you to them, they would have listened to you." (Ezek. 3:4-6).

God had met me in His Word and spoke to me words of peace and affirmation within the eerily similar command He once gave to Ezekiel.

The repercussions of this Scripture were powerful. Before I departed the States I requested the Lord use my assignment abroad to either confirm or deny His intention to have me become a missionary pilot. I had become unsettled by the language barriers I had encountered while in Afghanistan. I asked He likewise undertake to answer this troubling insight into my competency to handle serving in foreign lands.

In this Scripture I found my eureka moment. He affirmed through His Spirit that my purpose, whatever it was, would not unfold among another people, but with those to whom I was most equipped to share Christ. After months of feeling my heart boil with spiritual urgency, I grasped the passion that had been driving me. I yearned to express my heart to those in the Church in America. I wanted them to obtain the blessed reward of having a personal relationship with

Christ. The purity of this moment is what made these conclusions all the more inescapable. I did not sense my thoughts had been prejudiced because I was not even searching for answers when I began reading.

The Lord had met *me* through His Word. I realized a career of flying would never assuage what God had powerfully placed upon my heart with its culmination in Afghanistan. By November 26, I was convinced *the Lord had* closed *the door to being a missionary pilot*. He drew my heart home. My mission: to share Jesus Christ.

God had placed the desire of being a missionary pilot upon my heart for the purpose of getting me to Afghanistan. Only He knew how to work around my analytical brain. He needed to foster that proposal so I would be amiable to venturing half way around the world. His superior purpose was to get me, with the spiritually attuned heart He had put in place, to look back to the United States and gain an outsider's perspective—His perspective. What He had intended all along was to assign me to serve my own people. It had simply taken me six years to see it.

Only time would reveal the when, how, and what. Anything more and I have no doubt I would become overwhelmed. A month later God would usher me to the opening ceremonies of fulfilling His strong promises through this newly clear vision.

Twenty-two

A Second Chance to Serve My Country

My return to Virginia was bittersweet. I was glad to be home, but the intimacy I had encountered with the loving Father while I was overseas remained fresh. I persisted in mulling over, praying, and seeking the counsel of others as to what God's intent was for drawing my focus away from aircraft maintenance and missionary aviation. The Lord was, after all, leading me into *some* ministry.

The more pressing matter to consider was the lingering school and car loans. This had to be resolved before any ministry—or did it?

With this newfound passion and focus of direction, I began to target my prayers with the same measure of forcefulness I invoked when seeking further confirmations during the process of applying for the United States Navy. On the Monday before Christmas 2005, I humbly asked the Father that if He was leading me toward a full-time ministry, whether it were to mean leaving aviation or going to Iraq, that He would confirm the direction I was sensing. I didn't know the form of answer I'd receive, but I asked that He'd grant it *by the end of the week.* I was specific for a reason. I believed His plan was to fulfill His promise from LeTourneau. I told Him I believed He had always been leading down the road to Iraq, so I believed as strongly that He would provide further affirmation.

While I had been overseas, newly proposed contracts were expected to come online in Iraq in 2006. Our purpose would be to gather intelligence to provide the military with much needed life-saving information. It would be part of a company division that had yet to be formally established. It appeared that the Lord was going to take me to Iraq after all. I did not see how it would fit into ministry, but it fit the bill of paying my educational loans more quickly.

In the weeks that followed Afghanistan I had conversations with several divisional managers. I laid before them my energized aspirations toward ministry. They suggested I talk with Dynamic Aviation's Director of Flight Operations, Aaron Lorson. I had been slated to chat with him on Wednesday or Thursday. Those days came and went. It was now Friday, the last work day before the extended Christmas weekend when I'd fly home. I began to believe the meeting wouldn't happen before that break. But, God desired to powerfully reveal Himself.

BOLD REQUESTS

In the middle of that Friday morning I was working in the hangar when I received a page to the Director's office. I scurried through the hangars to his corner office near the airfield's beacon. I poured out my heart. I described the events in Afghanistan and explained that ministry was becoming my focus. I imagined the Lord would provide further direction toward ministry, perhaps to the extent of resigning from the company. I expressed my firm belief God's foremost objective in the interim was to resolve the indebtedness. I told him that was why I was prepared to commit to the two-year contract in Iraq.

To make the tentative deployment of August 2006, I foresaw several things that would need to transpire. There were flight time requirements for the contract. I would need to accumulate several hundred more hours of flying experience to meet the qualifications. That would necessitate being transferred out of aircraft maintenance to the supervision of flight operations.

I remember not being sure how he would receive such boldness from someone who had only worked eight months for the company. He said he agreed with the notion of gaining flight experience. A move into mainline flight operations was a reasonable deduction.

Unfortunately, the Dynamic Aviation business load during the winter did not afford many opportunities to fly. Though, there was another option immediately available. The pilot of whose duty slot I had temporarily filled in Afghanistan was leaving the company. A two-month position needed to be filled again until they could find a permanent replacement. Upon the conclusion of that commitment, Aaron Lorson would bring me back state-side and place me in other flight duties to build time. There would be ample prospects to be prepared in time for the anticipated deployment. He was certain the Iraq contracts would transpire this time.

I had another concern to share with him. Having prayed and discussed a potential move with my parents, we believed the wise thing to do to expedite the repayment of the loans would be to leave Virginia. I told the director that if I was going to aim toward an assignment in Iraq, I desired to move back home. He said I could anticipate a move back to Dallas by the end of 2006 at the latest, earlier if the deployment date remained firm.

He told me how excited he was to see what God would reveal to me as His ministerial goals. He said he was happy to play a part in assisting in any way he could to help me move in that direction.

I was uncertain how he would receive my suggestion of leaving the company at some point. Even in this, he offered reassuring peace. Any time they were able to retain a pilot for three years they would be doing great.

Excitement and Trepidation

I left his office beaming in excitement and yet harboring some trepidation. I was amazed that the Lord had seen fit to fulfill for the *second* time in my life the desire to serve my country. I was astounded that the Father had provided *so* much direction, confirmation, *and* thorough answers to the prayer that had opened the week. Not only this, but God used this key company figure who carried substantial clout to be the vessel of affirming *His* plan of Iraq. I could not have fathomed the Lord having orchestrated a clearer, more precise answer.

The paved road to ministry lay before me. All the tasks that had to take place were in motion. Was I correct to presume the Father would require that I cease flying? It was more of an assumption on my part as an outflow from my core desire to place God's will at the forefront.

I did not see it at the time, but His plan to allow me to serve my country would be part of a triple purpose. In ways I was not expecting, this prospect would be conjoined with fulfilling the burden of ministry He had placed upon my heart. Beyond those two foremost goals, He'd fulfill hidden and unspoken longings only He knew I held.

Fears and Faith

Now more than ever, the Lord's courage that had propelled me to commit to Iraq bolstered me. Yet, there would also be grave risks to my life. I was not going to be serving in the security of a state-side installation like when I was stationed in Pensacola, but I would be flying over a part of the world that for the previous three years had proven deadly. His Spirit reminded me it was again time to trust Him. As He had shown me His ability to spiritually protect me through OCS and the Navy, He could safeguard me here as well. I did not know every detail of what would result from going to Iraq, but the Lord was making clear that the preparations to that indefinite end needed to begin.

The Lord already *had* given me spiritual armor for the experience. Being witness and recipient of His power during the events surrounding the Navy and Afghanistan gave me the courage and boldness to step into the unknown. The wonders and benefits of relationship with Jesus Christ and the *power* of the Holy Spirit gave me the helmet of assurance that I was His child. I also had the sword to fight through to the final battle of trust in His promise to reconcile the loans. I heard David Jeremiah recall a powerful truth, "God's man in the center of God's will is immortal until God is finished with him." I knew He wanted me to *own* that truth.

Taking Flight Again

When I returned from Afghanistan the first week of March, I learned I was transferred into flight operations. My time became occupied in the preparations necessary for deployment to Iraq.

First, I spent a week going through King Air ground school. During a lunch break one of those afternoons, my proactive flight manager, Shirley Trobaugh, came up to me with spectacular news that "a new division in the company, ISR, or Intelligence, Surveillance, and Reconnaissance, has been officially formed. Welcome aboard. You are on the ground floor. It will become the biggest segment of Dynamic Aviation." She was also going to be my ISR manager. I felt as though I could have run a marathon. It was far more than having some minor confirmation that Iraq was an eventuality. Rather, it was a paramount understanding that my placement was in God's divine plan.

Summer raced into view. The packed preceding months had satisfied my urgent need of flight time. The next rapid-fire task was to schedule my move to Texas the last week of July. I asked my parents to help by driving my car. They happily agreed. So, to make it worth their while, my oldest brother, Mark, and I lined up a week of vacation. We could not have asked for a more blessed reunion as we traced history from Williamsburg to Washington, D.C.

While in Washington, D.C., I received a call from my ISR manager saying they needed me to get to San Diego, California as soon as possible. The full test of the first official ISR project was taking place, and I needed to be there.

My parents and I returned to my Virginia residence nestled between the peaceful, green mountains of the Shenandoah Valley. We spent two days packing, cleaning, and closing my affairs in Virginia, and then started the nearly 1,300-mile trip to Texas.

Hurriedly finding a storage unit in town, I unloaded my belongings into a five by ten space. Within days I was on an airliner to California. Off and on over the next three months we would qualify the aircraft platform and establish team cohesion that would be necessary once we crossed the Ocean.

Some of my preparations would serve as welcome relief. Each deploying aircrew member was required to be trained and qualified to military standards on a handgun and rifle. We would be issued and carry them for our safety when flying in Iraq. My brother, Matthew, was in the United States Army and was a certified weapons instructor, so he agreed to train me. The last week of August I was released from duties in San Diego to accomplish this task.

I went back to Dallas and drove to my brother's home in Missouri. We tackled my first formal exposure to weapons. I had fired a few handguns and shotguns for recreation during college, but this was the first occasion that mandated serious and objective standards. My brother's expertise prepared me to remain steady and precise.

Feeling equipped to head overseas, I had a few days left with him and his family. It proved to be another rewarding time of fun and memories, but the reality of what I was about to undertake was deepening. This was not going to be preparation or a military exercise. There was more at stake.

The gravity of the stress and consequences of what I would face was becoming my sobering cross. Still, I knew God had His purposes and would protect me.

After everyone had gone to bed the night of August 31, I decided to watch *We Were Soldiers*. It was a moving experience. In the wee hours of Labor Day morning, I cried out to the Lord in tearful prayer:

> Lord, if I must go to witness where life and death meet . . . if only for the sake of sharing with Americans, Christians—the Church, Lord . . . if only for showing them the things I have seen with my eyes and heard with my ears . . . telling them the reality of this life . . . telling them how we are to be *so* grateful for every day we live . . . not to take our lives for granted, and with that realization, to motivate us to become serious about our devotion to You . . . if my going will serve this purpose—Your glory, Lord . . . then *I **WILL** go.* I will go in Your *power* . . . in Your *strength* . . . in Your *might* . . . and I will serve bravely among, not my military counterpart, but next to my brothers and sisters . . . among my fellow Americans. Grant me the eyes to see what You would have me to see. Let me ne'er forget what I see and what I learn. Nor, let me never forget Your life and love for *all humanity*. Let the people of this land, which You and *You alone* have blessed, Lord Jesus, be reminded of this very thing; and, that it will, is, and always has been Your plan and desire for all men to know Your love . . . Your peace . . . Your grace—the *only* thing that will *ever* give promise, hope, and an explanation of our mortal lives to a world that seems so messed up. . . . And, so it begins.

I was commissioned and was being sent from the presence of the King with a purpose. I can remember wiping the tears from my eyes as I typed those words after the movie. Reality had hit home. Emotionally drained, I slept through that night.

I headed back to California. Training and testing moved forward as did my persistent introspections. I began to question whether my physical capabilities would be up to par. Memories of my discharge from the Navy replayed as September drew to a close. The jitters I normally felt prior to any dramatic life event were present as my moment to depart for Iraq drew near. This, however, enabled the Lord to grant me renewed and revived insights.

Due to God's leadings during Afghanistan and His wisdom and direction in placing me on the new Iraq contract, I could not ignore the truth that He had both sent me to the Navy and removed me from that responsibility. I wondered, though, whether my physical problems could have been explained entirely by my apprehension over my future in the Navy combined with the physical strains, reduced sleep schedule, and rapid diet change of that first week.

In Iraq I would be encircled by stresses. I would discover if the military facet had any connection whatsoever to my medical condition, or if it even existed at all. I still had lingering doubts. Never far from my remembrance were the comments from the doctors on NAS Pensacola declaring me mentally fit to handle the military. Perhaps I had been physically fit as well. In either case, the Lord God Almighty had remained sovereign acting through my circumstances to perfect my spiritual fortitude.

I realized in these moments that my NPQ *might* have no bearing on my capabilities. I was soon to be functioning as part of a military task force in Iraq, and I had yet to notice physical snags. I was enveloped in the Father's love, peace, and contentment. The Lord was showing me it had all along been in His grand design. In this joy and strength I calmly pressed on.

Before I embarked to Iraq, aircraft testing continued and I underwent readiness training, to include pre-deployment preparations at Fort Benning. The United States Army eventually approved the contract, the location, and deployment date. The aircraft with its single crew would depart the United States in November 2006. The remaining crew and other personnel would follow behind. I would be a part of this second group. We would rendezvous at our destination—Camp Speicher in Tikrit, Iraq. The Lord had blessed me. I was part of something bigger than myself—*His* plan and purpose.

Twenty-three

SALVATION REAFFIRMED

I was commencing something that could cost me my earthly life. I was keenly aware of that possibility. The Father knew this uncertainty uniquely positioned me with the greatest measure of receptiveness to hear His reinforcing voice. I *needed* to hear His reaffirming proclamation of loving possession, despite my notably more profound faith and quiet trust.

It was November 5, 2006. After tearful good-byes, tightly embracing hugs, and piercing words of love between my parents and me, I checked through security and boarded the first flight. This initial leg required a layover in Houston Hobby airport. The break in travel was substantial enough to offer time to mull over the gravity of the movement. The Lord had encouragement waiting at this terminal.

I wanted reassurance, again, of where I stood with Christ. Facing the brevity of life brought back the single, most crucial question—was I positive I would spend eternity with the Father? I recalled what He had supernaturally told me through the Navy, but I needed another self-check.

Sitting on the terminal bench staring through the glass into a world that seemed to be moving in slow motion, I begged the Lord to help me through the questions. He was eager to answer.

Did I truly believe Jesus Christ was real? Yes.

Did I believe that He had come to the earth? Yes. I reasoned it was true not only due to His past, real interactions with me, but also because I knew history attested to His having lived in human form on the earth.

Did I believe Jesus was God? Yes. For much the same reasons. Years of inexplicable and truly spiritual exchanges with the Lord through His Spirit confirmed it. My response to these questions resided heavily in the fact I believed the Bible to be true. A man named Jesus declared Himself one with the Father.

Did I then believe Jesus had died on the cross for me? Yes, by faith. Recorded history corroborates a man doing just that—dying on a Roman cross. That was Jesus.

I was driven further to refine and narrow that query into a series of introspectively crucial questions.

Did Christ really have to die? Was it the *only* way?

Is belief in Christ the only option and consequently the only true religion? I knew it had often been said that knowledge of God is never enough. Was that all I had? Frankly, this had often muddied my thoughts in the past. Had I truly grasped why He had to die?

I knew I needed to voice, clarify, and confirm what I had come to believe.

I believe that a creator is responsible for my existence. Since the created is not greater than the creator like a servant is not greater than the master, this points to one who is in every way superior. This would make the creator perfect in thought and purity, knowledge-able of my inmost thoughts. It sounds a lot like the God of the Bible.

It then makes sense He has designed me to follow His best pattern for my life. For me to oppose that would be effectively the same as slapping my earthly father. The disobedience would be a sign of disre-spect and would certainly negatively impact our relationship. One evil thought or outward act next to such holiness affirms I do not possess the ability to be pure like Him, and there will never be enough good I can do in my error-prone state to be in the presence of His holiness.

God swiftly ushered me to the knowledge of which I already believed. Faith in Christ and His gift of eternal, perfect unity with Him was based on grace. In every system of faith there is some standard of acceptance to attain a life beyond this world. God Almighty had only one standard to be met, and it came at the price of shedding innocent, unblemished blood. He had *met* that requirement through His Son, Jesus Christ. This meant I did not have to tow my own, mortal line of good deeds to gain eternal life.

It was impossible for me to believe any other solution. If I believed that my salvation was dependent upon how good I was, how good would I have to be? There was no clear answer. In theory, I could hold to one criteria of goodness in *hopes* of satisfying the scales of everlasting life. Someone could approach me and suggest a higher standard rendering mine insufficient. Who would be right? A standard based on human performance would only lend to countless interpretations. My heart was filling with peace in the reconstituted knowledge God's standard had been clearly defined in one simple word—*grace*. It was not complicated, nor did it need to be.

Two biblical truths said it all. Romans 6:23: "For the wages of sin is death, but the gift of God is eternal life in Christ Jesus our Lord." Romans 3:21-24 offers the solution: "But now a righteousness from God, apart from law, has been made known, to which the Law and the Prophets testify. This righteousness from God comes through faith in Jesus Christ to all who believe. There is no difference, for all have sinned and fall short of the glory of God, and are justified freely by His grace through the redemption that came by Christ Jesus."

I concluded it made sense there be only one standard. Indeed, there *was* only one worthy—Christ's perfect sacrifice on the cross. The caveat was I had to choose to grab hold of His free offering of unquenchable love.

I identified with these scriptural truths. For me to attain God's standard I had to receive His gift of righteousness from His Son. My history of communication with the Father through His Spirit meant Jesus bestowed His righteousness on me because I believed in Him. I had long ago received such grace. I needed to coherently develop my understanding one detailed step at a time to see my heart. The miracle was the Lord Jesus had given me His Spirit to concisely understand the truth of who He *is*. I was overjoyed to again witness Him proclaiming my adoption as His son through immediate answer to my heart's prayer.

With this refreshing peace soaking my soul and emotions, I grabbed my things and found something to eat before my flight. I *knew* I had the answer. I knew I held to the truth. No one could believe it for me, and no one could deny me the ability to believe it. This hope *empowered* me. I felt a tender love for *all* living people. I longed for them to encounter the freedom I had.

A SIMILAR ANSWER TO PRAYER

For most of that Sunday I didn't have time to read the devotional entry for the day in *Our Daily Bread*. Later, though, I read the entry, titled *A Surprise Answer* and written by Josh McDowell. It referenced 1 John 3:16-23. Josh told how after his mother's death his uncertainty about her salvation drove him into depression. So, he asked God to give him an answer, although it seemed impossible. Two days passed. Having driven out to the beach, he walked alone on a pier. There an elderly woman had been sitting in a lawn chair fishing. They began to talk and she asked about Josh's roots. He replied that he was from Union City, Mich. He was surprised that she knew the city. She then asked whether he knew the McDowell family. A stunned Josh told her who he was. She turned out to be his mother's cousin.

He asked the newfound relative, "Do you remember anything at all about my mother's spiritual life?"

"Why sure. Your mom and I were just girls—teenagers—when a

tent revival came to town. We both went forward to accept Christ." Josh startled the other fisherman as he yelled, "*Praise God!*"

The Father used Josh McDowell's testimony to meet me. Josh heard the Lord's intimate and personal answer to his prayer, as I heard His tender answer to mine the *instant* I sought Him that Sunday. I recognized that both Josh and I had been concerned with the things that concerned God. They had *everything* to do with His will. The Father cared so much for us to have taken the time to speak His response to our requests.

At the close of the devotional the Lord spoke one more word of encouragement. The words read, "God delights to give us what we ask when it is in His will. Never underestimate His desire to respond to our prayers. A surprise may be just around the corner. If you get definite with God, He'll get definite with you." Through all the days that followed my Navy experience, this statement became true: *I had learned to get appropriately definite with Him.*

I *knew* I was the Father's, and I knew He was more than delighted to have answered every question. I was blessed. If God was not real, then *I was not alive.* In tearful joy and exaltation I exclaimed, "I love You, Lord!" What strength and boldness He infused in me to step into the uncertain days and months ahead in Iraq.

Twenty-four

FIRST ROTATION TO IRAQ: VALIDATION

Being so far away from home, I spent the first seven weeks in Iraq feeling desolate and lonely. Despite having had plenty of work to accomplish in establishing our operation in the country, there was enough time left over to feel isolated. Christmas was approaching—my first away from family. I knew I was going to miss all the smells, sounds, lights, and traditions. Nevertheless, I knew I sacrificed it all for a noble cause.

In the demanding tasks of those initial days, the Father didn't allow me to wander aimlessly into disappointment. He always sought my best. For the moment, this meant healing in regard to my dismissal from the Navy. He used this new, intense life to usher me into a series of powerful words of emboldening purpose and confirmation.

These encounters kicked off early in my first rotation while I accompanied our customer's project manager on a drive across base. I briefly shared with him my reasons for choosing to serve in this capacity. He appreciated my focused motivation derived from the Navy was not without cause. He declared my motives noble and noted my dedication in my duties.

God's words through this retired-Marine had a profound impact on me.

I had begun to feel glib toward how well I was grabbing hold of the way everything flowed on a defense contract. I was not in the management chain or a position of authority on our mission flights. So, I was not always privy to the functions taking place behind the scenes that could have otherwise offered me insight.

The Lord continued to humble and encourage me through the words of our Task Force commander and Army Lieutenant Colonel. He reminded us we were embarking upon something never before attempted. It was important enough that an entire unit of military and contractors had been established. We were all learning something new. We shared a common obligation, a goal to save lives. We were all here to support one another—soldier and contractor alike. What I gleaned from his comments was that the contracting element was a facet contributing as much value to the broader goal as the soldier.

It was a privilege to be a part of an assignment of this caliber. Why had I been so blessed by God? Humility had the upper hand as I considered the grace and love the Father had showered upon me.

FLASHBACKS

Participating in such a larger military agenda as a civilian brought my Navy memories, passions, and motivations rushing back. The Lord knew He needed to address the hidden pain. He was able to see the sorrow.

A couple weeks after that outdoor mustering, two of my coworkers shared with me something they had concluded in their observation of me in theater. Earlier in the day they had remarked to one another that I would have made *good officer material* had I been able to remain in the Navy. One of them, a former military pilot, said he had no doubt of that in his mind. What had motivated him to say that about me?

This was the message of encouragement the loving Father knew I needed. He used it to carry on His process of mending my underlying, residual anguish and hidden disappointment. It did not lock me in the yesterdays, but catapulted me into my future.

The Lord also used these statements to refresh my memory. I had already forgotten the declarations made by many surrounding my time in the Navy. "The Navy needs a good leader such as you." This was not flattery. Knowing of my current assignment, the Navy recruiter requested I reenlist as a reservist on the intelligence side upon satisfying my school loans.

Clearly the Lord's purpose had not been to inflate my ego. It was to create within me a humble confidence and an ability to see a larger plan He was setting in motion.

By Thursday, December 21, I was pleasantly surprised to hear I would be traveling with two others to Balad Air Force Base in central Iraq. We needed training to aid us in surviving isolation or capture should we ever be forced to put our aircraft down somewhere other than planned. This military requirement afforded me the opportunity to venture beyond the earthen fence line of our base. We were scheduled to depart on a fixed wing military transport flight that night. Due to what I believe was the Lord's planned kindness to me through a strange set of circumstances, we missed the flight.

While the three of us now waited for what we hoped was going to be a helicopter flight, I had a chance to chat with another one of my colleagues, Victor Matakas. He had been in the Navy on the F-14. Having spent time together in the states in preparation for deployment, we were on cordially honest terms. Before long, the discussion started to turn toward our mutual interest of flying and how unique it was to fly in Iraq.

Victor described missions he flew. He would circle at a high altitude for a couple of hours and return to the carrier. That would be tagged a combat mission. Here I was flying notably longer at a much lower altitude over a hostile region. He exclaimed *that* was combat flying. Although as a rookie I didn't grasp all his terminology, I grasped his point.

He said how fortunate I was to pilot the aircraft and to be accumulating flight hours so quickly.

"Well, actually, I don't care about the hours because I believe the Lord is intending to move me into ministry at some point. So, the flight hours are really just cursory to me," I told him.

He explained it was not about needing the hours, but that I had the *opportunity* to build so much flight experience. As we talked I learned the frequency of flying in the Navy was lower than most people think. What is more, a number of pilots in the Navy never got actively deployed with a carrier or in a foreign land. His comments made it clear to me that flying a long duration mission on a fixed-wing aircraft, like I was, could be a rare event for many Naval Aviators and aircrew. I was a part of a task envied by military aviators.

Through Victor's words I realized the blessing behind doing what I was. I saw a new perspective on God's hand moving me to this unimaginable point. My peer acknowledged that I was serving my country as I would have in the Navy. Indisputably, there was no one else who deserved the honor for that other than God, and my smile showed my thanks.

God had known what I could not have. Had I become a Naval Aviator I might not have had the ability to fly often. I might never have deployed. I might never have flown fighter jets. This was my time and place to be, and it was all *His* design. Only He saw my future to know what avenue would best accomplish His goals. I had yet to witness all the reasons to believe that truth as it related to this undertaking. For the moment, His grace and blessing were enough.

On the Chinook

Renewed and refreshed, it finally came time to board our flight to Balad. Not only that, but it *was* a helicopter. For the first time in my life I would ride on a CH-47 Chinook. Unbeknownst to anyone but the Lord and me, I had always wished to ride on a helicopter.

It was eight o'clock in the evening and extremely dark. The noise and the thrust from the counter-rotating blades battered the air and sent its percussions piercing through our bodies. Body armor and helmet on and sidearm in its holster, I walked up the ramp at the rear of the helicopter. My face and body were blasted by heat as the engine exhaust rushed toward me from the rotor downwash.

With the flight crew in their tactical positions, they extinguished cabin lights. Darkness would be our cloak on the potentially dangerous journey. All of the aircrew used night vision goggles. One was situated on his hind end on the half-drawn cargo door, machine gun in his grasp. Stealth and preparation on this flight would be key to its success. Once underway it became so dark that I could not even see my hand inches away. Only the occasional, narrow beam of green light from the cockpit enabled me to observe my surroundings.

This was an adventure above comparison. Every one of my senses had been tapped. There was the smell of the fresh night air as it mixed with the causticness of the engine exhaust. There were the relentless, pounding vibrations thrashing the deepest, innermost core of my physical frame. The sound of the rotors lashing air against the fuselage was of particular note because my ear protection was inadequate. There was the blinding darkness. There was the taste of dust in the air, and, the inevitable touch of those around me as we all were tightly packed between cargo.

Finally I saw the lights of our destination. After the sensory stimulation of the flight, landing seemed an unfortunate necessity. The three of us disembarked as another group of soldiers and passengers awaited this crew's next exciting mission. I shared my enthusiasm with my two, military-skilled comrades. I confessed the only other wish I could claim would be to one day ride on a UH-60 Blackhawk. Who could finagle such a thing?

Even Farther from Home

Isolation training completed, it was time to head back to our "new home." Christmas was a couple of days away, and we all wanted to spend it with the people we had come to know. Weather would work against that desire. Days dragged as one return flight after another was cancelled or jammed with backlogged travelers.

Our base of operations considered picking us up with our own aircraft. Unfortunately, this would not bear out as a possibility, and it agitated me. It started to cloud and disrupt my Christmas joy.

Christmas Eve came, and even though the three of us had the unique opportunity to worship in a candlelight service, it did not change one fact. It was inevitable: my first Christmas away from home would be spent away from my home abroad. To my dismay, I was letting sin enter my life. As Christmas arrived, my patience ran paper thin. In continued email correspondence with our team seventy miles away, I began writing in frustrated jest. Sadly, I was not exhibiting the character Christ desired for me.

Realizing my waywardness, I returned to my tent to seek His face in repentance. I was searching for an attitude adjustment. It didn't take long before this simple child-to-father discussion made me ashamed of my behavior. I scorned my lack of spiritual maturity. I became even more disappointed in myself later that evening as we rode the shuttle across the base to attempt to get on another return helicopter flight. Why had I not been obedient? I was supposed to remain grateful in all circumstances, not only the good. How could I have been missing the fact the Lord had been blessing me? After all, He *had* allowed me to spend Christmas in the more festive of the two bases. How could I be grumbling over the delay He might be intending for my good?

That night we were on the list for a military flight out of Balad. We stood on the helicopter ramp waiting for our entourage of one

Chinook and one Blackhawk. Waves of anticipation swelled as we watched the incoming passengers walk off, but our hopes of getting home began to wane as rapidly. A cargo crate was being loaded onboard the Chinook. The few of us hoping to get onboard were sternly motioned to assist with lifting it into the helicopter's cargo bay. That's when we saw how fully loaded it already was with gear and personnel. We loaded the crate and assumed our previous posts on the ramp. One of my cohorts glanced, yelling above the rotor and engine noise, "There goes our flight home." I nodded.

Then, to all of our amazement, we were directed to proceed to the Blackhawk. Could it be? We boarded, strapped ourselves in, and lifted off at about 2:15 in the morning. Surprisingly, the noise and vibrations seemed more noticeable than onboard the Chinook. During the flight, I found myself watching out the side Plexiglas windows for tracer rounds from the ground below. From time to time my curiosity would gain the better of me as I strained to see over the passenger's heads and catch a glimpse of the terrain. This was something I had not been in a position to do on the flight down, and it was a fun, new experience. I probably would have preferred to have remained in blissful ignorance. The low flight was uneventful as the Lord had assured me it would be. We reached our home base, and in exhausted relief we departed the Blackhawk.

I then learned that my happiness in getting to fly on a Blackhawk had been evidenced by a huge grin. I alone knew there had been more involved than having my long-lived dreams of riding *both* heli-copters materialize. It was that the circumstances surrounding both flights pointed to Divine intervention and blessing from the Lord. God's graciousness had been imparted despite my failures.

The intense schedule and spiritually challenging environment of this first rotation left me fatigued and spiritually drained. This gave me a personal, spiritual hunger for His words of truth and prom-ise. It forced me to pursue Him through daily reading of the Bible.

Something once intermittent had become a yearning. I witnessed its value, and I have not been the same since.

Throughout these opening weeks in the sand, some of the most searching cries of my spirit had been met. The Father in His sovereignty understood an effective way to clarify and heal the past was to affirm the present. There remained one fundamental question, and its answer would come in a matter of weeks.

Twenty-five

THE FATHER'S GRANTING LIGHT TO THE NAVY DISMISSAL

The Lord was determined to rectify another piece of my personal history while I was in Iraq. Though content in resting in the knowledge the Father had been ultimately responsible for my dismissal from the United States Navy, a nagging confusion was persisting. What had been the *true* culprit of my physical symptoms? I was elated seeing the Lord work such magnificent purposes. Because of that I really had not cared about the reason. All the same, I had *grown* curious.

After nearly three months working in the rigorous setting of Iraq there was *no* indication of relapse. The Navy's disqualifying determination did not make logical sense. The Lord knew it was the ideal moment to clarify this matter forever, but His reply would be physically excruciating.

On January 31, 2007, ninety days since I had left home in the States, I went to the Combat Support Hospital on orders from our task force's flight surgeon. I had gone to him complaining of an onset of severe pain in my groin combined with intestinal incontinence. I had been dealing with it for several weeks. He decided it was essential we get to the base hospital without delay.

When the surgeon and I arrived at the emergency room, we were informed that there was a mass casualty, or "Mass-Cal," coming and they were about to have their hands full. An ER surgeon did manage to see me and he had determined I had epididymitis and CDIF—an infection that disrupted my digestive tract and came to rest in my groin. He prescribed two oral antibiotics and a narcotic pain reliever and sent me back to my room.

I hoped this was going to be the end of it. Unfortunately, my pain was worse the following morning. I began to hallucinate and become nauseous as a result of the drugs. The pain I had was localized. Any slight touch or movement rendered me helpless. I wanted it to stop.

I needed help. Everyone was at work and there was no way to contact them. It was a fifteen minute drive across base. I was torn between waiting to send a note to the flight surgeon in the care of one of my coworkers later in the day or attempt to return to the hospital on my own recognizance. Unable to stand the increasing pain and hallucinations, I decided to do the latter. Standing outside I waited to hail someone who could take me to emergency. An acquaintance from a sister contract walked by and rushed me there.

The ER doctor performed another painful physical exam in addition to an ultrasound and blood workup. He determined his initial diagnosis was accurate. For whatever reason, however, the oral antibiotics were not working fast enough or not correcting the epididymitis at all. The doctor decided it was time to check me into the hospital and begin IV antibiotic with the oral one he had prescribed.

Glimpses of War

The first night I didn't get much sleep as I was quartered with three others in the Intensive Care Ward (ICW). Two were local citizens who were victims of the Mass-Cal that Wednesday. One, age 33 and with two children, had burns to his buttocks, hands, and shins. The other man, age 20, had burns to his hands and right face.

It was nearing midnight as the nurse cleaned and redressed their wounds. It was hard to sleep during this. I laid there watching the nurse as she slowly and tenderly peeled away the old bandages. I found myself flooded with compassion, sadness, and humility as I watched. I acknowledged I did not even have *near* the worst of things. In fact, it was hard not to feel guilty lying there with such a miniscule problem. I felt like I should have been up helping these two.

Finally catching a glimpse of their burns, I began to pray for these two men. I begged the Lord to show His love to them right there. I told the Lord that I knew He had spared them for a reason. I begged that He would capitalize on this window of opportunity to make Himself known to them. I couldn't speak their language, but I knew He transcended such constraints.

I finally rested before sunlight started to shine through the small windows. Somehow, the Lord multiplied my sleep. My doctor greeted me and inquired of my progress. It was determined that the current course of action was taking effect on the infection. He insisted I stay one more day to follow up on the intestinal aspect. My heart sank.

Shortly after the doctor left and I came to terms with the inevitability of staying for yet another day, my thoughts went to wishing I had my Bible with me. Later my roommate and fellow pilot walked through the ICW doors. He brought my toiletries—and, yes, my *Bible*. Half asleep, I motioned to my forehead as if to signal, "You read my mind." He smiled and left me to rest.

Later in the day I began to talk with my other ward mate, a United States soldier. We enjoyed one another's company and had a great time as we attempted to converse with the two Arab men, one of whom spoke limited English. We began to realize the gravity of what they had been through.

They had been part of a convoy. An Improvised Explosive Device had struck a fuel truck in that group injuring a multitude of innocent workers and bystanders. The older of the two men lost three of his friends. Nine others, including both of them, were burned. The two of them were in good condition by comparison.

The afternoon wore on and patients were beginning to be released. The staff moved the burn victims across the hall. Before long, the soldier and I were also situated across the hall for the remainder of our stay. I soon found myself overwhelmed with what my eyes beheld in this larger ward. A local teenage boy had both legs amputated just above the knees. Another young boy had blast wounds to his torso region and inner thigh. I found it difficult to process all that I was witnessing.

As the daylight dimmed on another day in the ICW, I attempted more sleep. Again I found myself abruptly stirred by the commotion as the hospital staff nursed all those injured. Later into the night and early morning I found myself filled with sorrow and compassion as I heard the tear-filled cries and fearful screams from the thirteen year old as he anticipated the pain from the changing of his dressings. Even now the images remain stamped in my memories. I knew then as I know now that the Lord was big enough to have a purpose in each of their lives. Best of all, His ability to perform this did not depend on anyone figuring out the ordeal.

I had just dozed when I was shaken by the boisterous moaning of the older burn victim. He had gotten out of bed, which struck me as rather strange. He normally was not allowed to walk due to the burns. It occurred to me that he was sleepwalking because he was not responding to any of the now *very* alert medical personnel. He continued to yell out one of his lost companion's names. Through-out his torment the staff tried to wake him so they could understand what was happening.

Then, after five minutes, he awoke as if jolted back to life. In that instant I saw the horror through his eyes. The past had become the present.

Coming to terms with his surroundings, he realized what he had just been dreaming. Immediately he broke into uncontrollable sobs.

My heart *ripped* open as I shared his tears. What I did know in those moments arrested my spirit in comfort. Just as my heart had been filled with sorrow, I realized Christ, too, was saddened. War is an unfortunate reality in a sinful world ruled by a fallen angel who thought he could do better than God.

Wrapped in the Father's peace I fell asleep, as I felt *and* heard the chilled antibiotics pumped into my system. Soon, as the morning before, my eyes awakened me to the sunlight flooding the room. Shortly, around eight o'clock, the doctor returned to assess my condition. The prognosis was good. I was progressing better and would be released in a few hours.

Before he left I wanted to ask him about the culprit *and* impact of my ailments. He agreed he had a moment. I asked him, "I am certain my company is going to seek advisement as to whether they should allow me to return to this project on future rotations. Can you tell me what caused these two problems, and are they going to be something I might expect every time I come to Iraq?"

In so many words he replied, "CDIF was caused by the penicillin that you took for sinusitis. This is rare, but it can happen. Anyone who takes antibiotics is at risk of such a reaction. You're at risk just as much as I am." Days before I became ill I had developed a sinus infection and had been given penicillin to wipe it out. If I understood the doctor properly, when I consumed that antibiotic series, it swept through my system so violently and thoroughly that the remaining good bacteria began doing me harm.

The doctor continued, "Your epididymitis was probably caused by dehydration. It is common here in theater among people, especially the young guys your age. I see this along with kidney stones. Both are common. What I can tell you is it's not you," as he motioned toward my body and stomach. "I don't see any reason why you cannot perform your duties here. It's just the luck of the draw that you had these illnesses." I thanked him for his encouragement and time.

If it is true there is a purpose behind every event God permits, the "luck of the draw" had nothing to do with my illness. Evidence from my life had by now affirmed that fact. I believe the Lord ordained this to my perspective. He *needed* me to experience humanity in its most basic form to accomplish this.

ONE WORD SURFACES: *GRACE*

My thoughts returned to a day five months earlier. It was the last day at my brother's house. I had told the Lord I would be obedient to go to Iraq if His desires had been nothing more than changing my perception of life by instructing me about its brevity as seen through the eyes of death. If I learned this, I would take that knowledge back home. The prayer met the Father's will—and He answered.

Where did I see death through all of it? I did not need to see an actual deceased person to understand. Death passed by *all* these Arab men. Their wounds substantiated that conclusion. There was an element more convincing. It is a sobering piece of information I have not expressed about the man whose rekindled nightmare of losing his friend brought him to uncontrollable tears. Upon coming to grips with reality, he *immediately* looked at me. I *saw* the pain of death from that horrific day through his tear-stained eyes. There lingers no question in my mind I had seen death.

I grasped what it meant to be human. I saw war wounds. It had not been some two-dimensional theatrical series of pictures. These were real people in *real* pain. I heard their cries, smelled their wounds. I *needed* to sense these things to understand how God made all mankind to be and feel. He did not stop there either. He went through this with me so I could describe the depth of His love and compassion for others.

Through it all, I saw the endearing Father's grace and mercy to me. I saw it through the medical staff. More than that, I saw it poured out on these two particular men who suffered terrible burns. Somehow, as if miraculously, they found ways to laugh and carry on conversations with those around them. How was it possible? The Father let me vividly observe there was only *one* ultimate reason. It was His grace. God had spared them for some purpose. It had not been their time to depart the earth. God's sovereignty provided *every one* of us hope that day.

God *showered me* in His grace as I applied the lessons stemming from this glimpse into the brevity of life. As a believer in Christ possessing eternal security, how much more peaceably satisfied should *I* be in such a painful, chaotic, fallen world? How much more thankful ought I be for life and breath? Perspective changes *everything*.

This experience had humbled me. I recognized how careful I need to be with complaints about day in and day out struggles. Are they really so bad? Life is good the bulk of the time. Actually, with the eternal God leading my steps, life is good *all* the time. I should never grumble.

I needed to reform my perspectives. This had to have been the thrust of what He had been trying to show me. The true blessing was the Lord's tenderness and love through the instruction. I never perceived any harsh correction. He only wanted to remind me to remain grateful for everything He gives me—health, opportunities, and life itself.

NAVY DIAGNOSIS ANSWERED

God had another angle of my life to clarify. He prearranged to resolve the remnant, nagging confusion surrounding my dismissal from the Navy through this latest illness.

Prior to being taken to the combat hospital that last day of January, the flight surgeon and I searched for causes and remedies. In these initial stages, and considering my issues were originating in the abdominal area again, I wondered if there had finally been a relapse. I had decided it was prudent, wise, and thorough to mention my being found NPQ in the Navy based on the official diagnosis of IBS.

He was not stirred. He found it hard to believe the Navy had come to a proper conclusion in their diagnosis of IBS. He said IBS was most often something that individuals deal with for the majority of their lives, not intermittingly over the course of a few weeks. What encompassing and lasting relief these words were to me.

The flight surgeon went on to confess there *was* a side of IBS that was sometimes driven by anxiety. So, he asked about the intensity of my work. I remarked it had been quite the event being the first team on site tasked with the responsibility to stand the contract up. Though, I had been in theater for nearly three months without a shadow of my former symptoms. My answer affirmed his reservation in proceeding down the road of IBS. He never pursued the prospect further.

Time allowed him the unbiased opportunity to consider another possibility. Several of the Navy doctors had supposed the onset of IBS might have been tied to the rapid change of diet. Certainly, I had experienced that upon entering Officer Candidate School. I had been in a life-long routine of partaking in high doses of milk products. The Navy had cut that out of my training diet. After I shared this, the flight surgeon *readily* agreed the *sole factor of a changed diet could have been adequate to have been the culprit* instigating the symptoms that led to my discharge.

The combat surgeon at the hospital reinforced this two days later. Not only in the Navy, but now in Iraq, doctor after doctor remarked how mentally *and* physically capable I was. The evidence appeared irrefutable. My malady in the Navy could be *attributed* to a military component, but not *caused* by the holistic military environment. It likely had been the diet change and little else.

This would continue to be fortified in the years following. I would be *instructed* on more than one occasion to engage in several flights that would place me in situations of abnormal stress and tension, even to risking my *life*. Aside from the predictable symptoms associated with renegade medication or commonplace illnesses, these ill effects never occurred again. For certain, they *never* again came close to such extremes of pain or incapacitation. Most notably, they *never once* resurrected themselves under the stresses surrounding work and intense flying.

Whatever the case, the Lord had allowed such a diagnosis, correct or not. He had permitted that set of circumstances to direct me down the path He had planned for me. I found it emboldening and encouraging knowing that I probably could have, no, *absolutely would have* been able to handle the Navy if He had chosen to have me there.

The Father had securely settled my wonderings. Anything I ever had done or would ever do was and would always be possible in His strength. Just as Philippians 4:13 promises, "I can do everything through Him who gives me strength." I witnessed first-hand the Lord performing the incredible while in the combat hospital. A medical aide was having difficulty drawing a blood sample from me. I prayed for the Lord to help him, and in that *very* instant he had success. No doubt my verbal credit to the Lord afterward impacted this staff member. It was wondrously rewarding to see God in action by touching lives, healing my past, *and* answering my prayer with such immediacy.

A Chaplain's Message

While attending the base chapel service the Sunday morning following my release from the hospital, nothing was more consuming to my heart than my prayers for those suffering nationals. I was struck speechless when I learned the chaplain also had observed the aftermath of the mass casualty event.

He believed the best message to preach following an experience of this magnitude was Jesus Christ's love, lived out through our lives. It was as simple as that. My heart began to melt again and become filled with sorrow, compassion, and love for those who had been injured in the explosion. Visual images flooded my mind.

The chaplain then went on to say that through prayer God transforms our hearts and teaches us to love through compassion. I finally understood through my life encounter I *had* become like the Father. Christ lived this example, and so had I. I had been in the hospital praying for those men. I had learned how to love on an entirely new level.

Through that chaplain's message, the Father reinforced *all* of His instruction and grace surrounding the events in the hospital. He expounded upon them, confirmed them, and aligned them with His Word. Not only did I have experience, but I had Scripture to back it up.

This holistic experience granted me the ability to see the Father in new ways all the while knowing He had always been right there with me. This truth is a wonderful treasure to possess, even if it has to be associated with struggle or personally difficult moments.

MOVING TOWARD HOME

It was February 7, 2007. I was weeks from going home. On that day's flight, I crossed the threshold of one thousand hours of flight experience. I had operated and flown the entire flight. It had been my fifth time to do so since arriving in Iraq. As the last to depart, I wormed my way through the tight-quartered aircraft. As I stepped out onto the air stair door I heard the words, "Present Arms," as our three prior-military aircrew raised their M4 rifles and saluted. It was an honoring moment of camaraderie and an amusing surprise.

Surrounding me were my colleagues who appeared to have been enjoying our time together. I had nothing impressive to offer. Something else must have been contributing to their willingness to be around me. One reason came to my mind. It was not me they wanted to be around, it was the loving Father. Christ was living through me. All I had been doing in the preceding months was sharing God's history of intimate interaction with me as I strove to be a reflection of the Lord Jesus Christ's love and character. I had been demonstrating His peace and hope that guide my steps. Through this behavior He launched His ministry through my life. I had prayed for this before ever stepping foot in the sand. God had been answering. I did not see it at the time. I would only come to realize it after my return home.

My time in Iraq eventually came to an end. My inaugural endeavor in this part of the world had proven exciting. I learned many things and was alternately humbled or emboldened in my faith more times than I could count.

It had been a lot to inhale in such a short time. Perhaps this is why I had barely noticed the Lord at work in the lives of my companions. Before leaving I prayed that all of these lessons would congeal once I arrived home. I desired to become bolder for the cross, more determined in my pursuit of Him, and more eager to return on future rotations.

February rolled into March. Hardly surprising, the Father fulfilled my request. The events, lessons, and stressors of my four months in Iraq began to take shape. I began to sort through everything that had taken place and making sense of it all. Likewise, it was not until a couple weeks after returning to the sweet land I called home that I seized the spiritual responsibilities before me.

It was remarkable how being in that region affected the soul. I am sure it was in part due to the unseen risk to one's survival. Knowing the Lord had given me a respite from my human concern of being shot out of the sky or, of dying, provided relief. Though, I noted something else contributing to these feelings. Perhaps of more truth was that the spiritual emptiness I at times perceived had produced a by-product of hopelessness leading to fear. While sorting through that complex set of emotions, I began to appreciate the freedom of the land where I am blessed to live. I was able to openly and without constraint worship the Father and His Son, Jesus Christ, whom I love more *every* day.

SHARING WHAT I KNOW

In that reflection my burden toward the Church in America and my fellow believers grew in passion and resolve. Looking back at my time in Afghanistan on what *I* had been picturing as the Lord's ministerial direction, I became astounded. Too often what I framed as His path for me played out differently. I had believed that any ministry or broad sharing of His love with others would occur somewhere in the future. I had begun to think it would take place after I attained formal teaching in Scripture. I had the incorrect notion I would only then be adequately equipped to take on such important tasks.

After two weeks of putting the pieces of my journey together, the Father made it plain that His ministry through my life had begun. He had continued to endow me with the same passions and burdens that formed upon my heart through the Navy and Afghanistan. It was as if the Father was asking, "Peter, why the need to postpone sharing your testimonies of My living interactions through your life?" I knew His correction was valid. What I had learned and experienced through my relationship with Christ had been His teaching and presence.

Who was I to choose whether to withhold or reveal the truth of who He *is*? It was His story. I did not have His permission to wait until some later point in time when I saw fit or when I felt I was properly trained to convey the truth. I was not to even be concerned with when and where. He alone would be responsible for the details. The *joyful* expectation found in that excites me.

I knew I was to take my knowledge, experience, and relationship with Christ and tell it to those God placed before me.

I once thought that my time in the United States Navy would become a thing of the past. True, it always will be a mile-marker. Was it something integral to my witness, or ministry? The Lord was speaking one audible word of truth to me after I returned from Iraq. That morsel of truth was: *there was* no *way to remove my past in the Navy from my testimony.* He had thoroughly crafted and incorporated it into my life story. His hand of orchestration and divine omniscience was so obvious. In the end, my testimony *does* nothing but bring glory to Him.

I still find this truth at work. My story is a beautiful painting of being in the Father's will. He does not erase my past, *or* leave my experiences back there as milestones. Instead, He integrates every angle of my past to enable me to make sense of my future and give credit to His arrangement of my life.

My goal is to live a life empowered by my hope in Christ. He is its *only* source. So, I was to be willingly ready to share that incomprehensible hope with everyone. So it was, with *all* of these truths cemented in my heart, His ministry through my life had taken form.

Twenty-six

SECOND AND THIRD ROTATIONS: PATIENCE AND BLESSING

After a fleeting two months at home, it was time to start toward my next rotation to Iraq. It was surreal to conceive the reality of a return, especially so quickly. It was as if I still could not quite grasp that I had willingly set foot in harm's way. I held onto the Lord's clear direction and purposes. If it hadn't been for His continued sustaining, I do not think I could have been as enthusiastic in the face of reengaging the dangers and soul-pounding impacts that were now familiar.

This rotation brought additional duties. I had become comfortable in the aircraft and with the operational tempo. So, I was assigned flight-crew scheduling, company daily reports, and day-to-day communications with the military unit we were supporting. The military required duties mounted for the task force as we transitioned into the blisteringly hot summer. I became deeply involved in bringing our new pilots up to speed on how to conduct our missions. Even though it was rewarding, *all* of this mandated more time. I often felt I was struggling to breathe. At the end of the rotation this fast-paced routine found me exhausted. While handing off my duties as I neared the final days of my second round, I noticed, sadly, how frayed I had become. We would all tear down walls to get the mission accomplished, but it can often take a toll.

PATIENCE

My patience had been eroding. Tasks that might have come naturally for some proved more stressful for my perfectionistic personality. I was in a test of my patience on a level of which I had yet not experienced in my life. The Lord knew my inner heart lacked the measure of patience He desired me to possess, and it had approached a level I was capable of seeing.

With what felt like not an ounce of fuel left in my reserve tanks, I began my second long-legged journey back home. I had now spent over six months in Iraq. So, I was savoring every quiet moment as an ordinary passenger on each flight. The last of my two domestic Southwest Airlines flights would resume after the brief stop in St. Louis. One short flight, and I'd be home in Dallas. I had spent more than seventeen hours in airplane seats. The passenger exchange in St. Louis afforded me the usual opportunity to change places onboard. I chose a window seat. My flesh was saying, "You deserve this seat. You've been traveling a long time. Don't feel bad about trying to squeeze every last drop of enjoyment out of this trip."

Everyone was seated and even the seat next to me was empty. Then, just before the door was closed a man in his twenties rushed onboard. With him was his pregnant wife. The empty seat next to me and one other middle seat were the last on this 737. Worse, they were separated by several rows. Now *His Spirit* was saying to my heart, "Peter, you should offer to move to the middle seat farther back and allow this couple to sit together."

I chose *not* to. It didn't take long before I sensed the Father's loving reprimand. It was a miserable flight to Dallas. The majority of that time I spent in confession to the Lord for my selfishness, as well as prayer as to how I might salvage the situation.

Would I be granted the opportunity to move once it was allowed on this abnormally turbulent flight? Not a chance. We had been instructed to remain in our seats for nearly the entire flight, spare *maybe* five minutes. Seemingly out of options I then started to consider how I might apologize to this husband sitting next to me, and I wanted to be able to heartedly express it in such a way that it did not come across as "secularly stereotypical" Christian behavior. Christ's reputation was on the line. I cared *nothing* of my own by this point. It already had been squandered.

It took me all the way until we landed for me to gain the gumption to ask for this man's forgiveness. I turned to him and apologized for my negligence to act on what I felt I should have done when he and his wife walked onboard. Before I could even finish that sentence, he calmly interjected, "Oh, don't give it another thought. It was a short flight anyway." I was relieved and encouraged by God's mercy.

Why was it that I had found myself so filled with impatience and selfishness? Whether it had been anything done externally (like yell or throw a punch) or simply in my thoughts, it was no less of a significant flaw in my heart. When Scripture talks about having the fruits of patience and selfless love, I never noticed it saying anything about them only being visible. My heart needed repairing by someone I thankfully found ready—my incomprehensibly patient Father.

This moment aboard the aircraft reminded me who I was, and I was *not* God. My task, and *always* a hard one for me, is to remain patient upon the Lord's gentle, meticulous shaping. My inability to do that can flow into impatience with myself. My seemingly inherent quest for speedy, personal perfection in my deployment duties had contributed to that impatient nature. I am ultimately an imperfect child—and the Father knows that.

I still had far to go in my walk with Christ. The Lord gave me the eyes to see and identify my failure. In this way I might avoid a failure the next time by listening to His Spirit's leading and then reacting appropriately. The Father will empower me through His Spirit, as He promises. The overwhelming peace this time was knowing His unconditional love sustained me. The foundation of our relationship had not been shaken.

BLESSING

My patience was in the fires of maturation, and it was being tested. My trust in the Lord and His sovereignty had also been growing. Several weeks preceding my departure from Iraq I applied this expanding trust.

Luke was soon to be winged in the United States Navy. I passionately desired to have the privilege of continuing to celebrate with him during his appointment as Naval Aviator. There was, however, a possible snag. I was slated to become captain in the King Air 200. My upgrade flight training was likely going to fall within the same window. I passionately prayed the Father would enable me to be there *for* Luke. He knew my heart. I believed He would honor such a request, and I left it at that.

More than a month after leaving it to the Lord's discretion, I found out Luke would be graduating August 31, 2007, one week after I returned from my company's upgrade training. God graciously fulfilled my request and affirmed my trust.

I made it to Luke's winging ceremony. David, who had been there for his commissioning, joined us. Kurt, another mutual friend, also came. Many in Luke's family expected the event to be difficult for me. To my surprise, it wasn't.

As he had done two years before, Luke approached me after his ceremony to express his thanks that I had come and shared in his momentous triumph. The night before I departed Kingsville, as two brothers in Christ, we prayed for the Lord's governance, spiritual fortitude, and blessing to fall upon one another's future. This unity liberated me. It undergirded God's spiritual and emotional restoration of that period of my life. The Father *had* mended my Navy past. The Spirit of the Lord had empowered me to press forward in peace.

I felt only pure enjoyment during the weekend with Luke, his family, and our friends. The loving Father was *so* good in the way He folded His many purposes in each of our lives. It had also been a reprieve for me. I was a week from embarking on my third tour to Iraq. After only fifty-one days home, it was time to leave again.

LIFE IN WARTIME

My time in Iraq had been and was normally rather uneventful. The strict measures and policies the military and our company set forth for the conduct of our intelligence missions sought to make certain it remained that way. Sure, we had our exciting days. I recall looking down at the ground out of my cockpit window seeing the tracer fire from the ground warfare. Perhaps it was sometimes the caliber of anti-aircraft artillery. We knew some of these weaponry units existed. Surface-to-air missile threats were also always on the forefront of our minds. At one time I was onboard a flight when one of our aircrew calmly remarked he thought he had observed a smoke trail beneath our wing. It's anyone's guess if it was, and if it had even been aimed at us.

There were some exciting days, especially in these first deployments. Fighting and threats remained tense. But, in our particular missions, it was business as usual. As contractors, we never took part in hostile activities. Though, the military deemed our task crucially important. I cannot recount how many honorable former and retired military members have reinforced the magnitude of what we were doing. We were there to save lives through our support of them. Yet, we didn't always realize the positive impact of our work. Sometimes we simply weren't where we were needed most. On all occasions, however, our duty was the mission. Time didn't allow focus on much else.

This was the problem. Every day was the same. It wasn't any better being on the ground. We were never allowed to leave the base except to conduct missions. So, there was no interaction with the local people like infantry members would experience. Our days were comprised of duties, eating, and sleeping.

There was not much to look at either. Sure, Iraq had its beauty, especially in the north and northeastern part of the country. The river valleys were a lush green, the skies a deep blue. But, the expanse of brown that incessantly blew across the land held little appeal. It wreaked havoc on our sinuses, and daily it deposited a fresh layer of powdery dust over everything.

DOUBLE BLESSING

I felt like I was caught in an endless cycle. I had reached a point at which I needed renewed focus on the mission. I appreciated the spiritual, ministerial, and financial goals of being in Iraq, but I desperately wanted to know on a tangible level that I was also fighting for something valuable. I specifically asked the Lord to grant me that mental resolve. I desired to step into the aircraft with a newfound eagerness. I yearned to have a fulfilling sense of honor and duty. I wanted it to go far beyond just a job of earning income to pay off college debt. My heart was craving meaning in what I had been and *was* doing—a sense of deeper purpose.

Originally, I wanted to be a part of saving lives, whether of civilians or soldiers. Yet, over the repeated months of flying in Iraq, the missions became procedural, systematic, and uneventful. The mission was critical. I had simply begun to lose my focus. This was the real impetus behind my seeking after the Father's affirmation. I needed to know I was meant to be here—that I belonged.

Then an early November day dawned. On the first mission flight I played an integral role in saving human life. Later in the day I spoke by phone with the United States Marine ground unit we had been supporting. We were both vocally appreciative and ecstatic. I had the privilege of joining forces with our crew, project team, and military counterparts to help saves lives. I never learned for certain if our information prevented the loss of life. But, I *knew* had we not acted on it, had we not been there, it *could* have meant death for someone.

This unprecedented achievement validated the objective behind what we did each and every day. Knowing one or even more lives might have been saved was indescribable. That day became significant for me. I had *never* felt more honored and blessed. I could not have fathomed a better means to reengage me in the fight for human life and freedom. The God of the Universe answered my heart's crying prayer. The encouragement and motivation that materialized was refreshing and far-reaching. Once again I had no cause for arrogance. The glory was all His.

This third rotation to Iraq was jam-packed with divine emboldening. As the next calendar year launched, I saw God use many people to empower me through words. On one occasion, Luke told me how my work was service just as much as his. Though our interaction in the years to follow would become infrequent, there remained camaraderie in the knowledge we supported each other in service to our country, freedom, liberty, and our brotherhood in Christ.

Most importantly, however, God orchestrated His design during those months to grant me an awesome sense of duty and honor. He blessed me to be part of something that mattered to lives here on earth. The providential hand of my Father satisfied what I longed for since the beginning days of entering the military.

Twenty-seven

CONVINCED
BY SCRIPTURE

Before I would leave Iraq for the third time, the Lord had in store for me another proclamation of His grasp on my life. The interactions I had with Christ within the events of the United States Navy had made His presence in me visible and convincing. Then, as the gravity of death came to the forefront prior to my first tour to Iraq, He assured me once more that I was His child. That time, however, He did so by enabling me to engage His Word and identify with fellow believers. This third resounding moment of declaration found the Father capitalizing on the time I spent in intensive, soul-searching engagement of His Word. These three occasions would combine to form an unbreakable triad of truth that would spur me to walk in His strength and trust in His promises.

Just days before I was set to return home for the 2007 Thanksgiving holiday, I was sitting on my bed in my dusty Iraq room. I decided to examine a book one of my colleagues had given me to read. It was titled *The Joy of Loving* and contained excerpts from Mother Teresa. One quote of hers that stood out was from James 2:14. I had read this passage before, but for some reason it stood out to me this time. It speaks about the relationship between a believer's faith and earthly deeds. It seemed to contradict what Paul said on the subject.

Over the next hour and a half, I sought to discover and resolve what appeared through my human eyes to be discrepancies between

James and Paul. Paul claimed salvation was by faith through grace alone. Ephesians 2:8-9 declares, "For it is by grace you have been saved, through faith—and this not from yourselves, it is the gift of God—not by works, so that no one can boast."

The Gospel of John undergirded this in describing God's gift through His Son as free. "For God so loved the world that He gave His one and only Son, that whoever believes in Him shall not perish but have eternal life." (John 3:16). Faith for believing seemed to be the key, and was in fact upon which I had founded my previous understandings of my salvation.

Yet James said works were somehow involved. If, as I had come to believe, works were inadequate to save me, what purpose did they serve? I started by searching the Greek definitions of the words Paul and James used. I discovered grace meant the same throughout. I found, though, that the works Paul and James discussed were different. Paul referenced the works of the Israelite people, whereas James had been talking about works that are supposed to flow out of a believer in Christ. They would provide evidence of the faith and salvation of the believer.

I began to retell in my mind how short I came in my holy, obedient commitment to God. Had all my works been nothing more than human attempts? If not, where was the proof these came from a changed life? I began to wonder upon what *I* had been basing my salvation. I reflected on how God had formerly spoken and dealt with me through His Spirit. I wanted scriptural truth to back up those experiences.

I searched deeper in His Word. In all the cross-referencing of passages, I read Romans 2:4, "Or do you show contempt for the riches of His kindness, tolerance and patience, not realizing that God's kindness leads you toward repentance?" This didn't help the matter. It would seem possible that all my experiences could have been God's goodness to draw me to Him in repentance. What if my lack of obedience had become contemptible in His eyes?

I was *not* ready to give up. After all, I *had* to resolve this angst. I remembered the passages from Romans 10:9, 13, "That if you confess with your mouth, 'Jesus is Lord,' and believe in your heart that God raised Him from the dead, you will be saved. . . . for, 'Everyone who calls on the name of the Lord will be saved.'" Then, with great comfort I recalled the Gospels were laden with Christ's promises that by belief in Him we would be saved.

I had to also admit that Christ with the Father seemed so close to me by this point of my life that it was as if they had become a life-long immediate family member. I couldn't perceive how it was possible to move forward in this life if severed from the hope I found in an invisible Lord.

Yet, I still could not manage to come to peace with the appearance of inconsistencies between James 2:14 and Romans 2:4, and all the numerous passages that speak of salvation by faith alone.

I became helplessly overwhelmed in spirit and body. I was confused, and frustrated that I was. I had been straining so hard that my physical frame was about to give out. I was driven into some of the most sincere prayer I had ever voiced to my loving Father. It was *so* real that I once more felt as though I had left the dimensions of this world and entered into the realm of His throne room. I passionately yearned to know how to rectify faith and works with salvation. It was critical to know this not for myself alone, but for those who found themselves in my shoes. The intensity of my prayer and conversation with the Lord Almighty dug to such physically straining depths that my brow began to pain me.

I somehow managed to comprehend that I might have returned to confronting direct attack from the Adversary. In greater adamant persistence I beseeched the Lord to grant me resolution. I *needed* Him to assure me of my salvation, but this time with respect to His Holy Word. I no longer wanted to rely on my experiences, prayers, theology, or human logic. Neither did I want to be moored through means of someone else's teaching, including biblical commentators.

I was *longing* for His personal, intimate answer as explained entirely from the source. I wanted *Him!*

After I had finished passionately praying, I probed further into Scripture passages I'd learned over the years. Recently, I had read 1 John. I seemed to remember reading somewhere within it about how we might know we were saved. I was *certain* it was somewhere in 1 John. I never found the passage. I opted to leave the matter in His capable hands instead. As it was I had to get some rest because I had an early mission flight.

I quickly fell asleep. Morning came all too soon. I had not been shown anything during the night. This started my day in ongoing restlessness. I was going to have to wait patiently for God's plan to materialize in His time.

I continued to ponder His Word. As I did, I was brought back to one, undying truth. I could not deny that I believed in God, and it was a belief residing in my heart *and* mind. He, His actions, and His power had begun to flow from my mouth daily. Romans 10:9 was solidly engaged. But what about James?

After lunch I had a few moments before our second mission to weed through personal emails. One of them was a biblical devotional. It had come in the day before, but I had not opened it. I noticed the title—it had to do with assurance of salvation. I couldn't believe my eyes. There was the very key verse I had been seeking the previous night: 1 John 5:13, "I write these things to you who believe in the name of the Son of God so that you may know that you have eternal life."

He had heard my heart's plea. He had given me His truth by means of His Word. Truly, I cleaved to the Son of God, Jesus Christ. Accordingly, I trusted in what it then proclaimed: *I had eternal life!* My interactions with Him, my fundamental understanding of biblical truths, and my closeness to the Lord were all screaming at me, "You're accounted for, you're Mine."

Yet this truth did not resolve the gap between faith and works.

I knew I had to first believe works were useless to attain eternal life if I were to share this biblical truth with others. There was only one thing left to do. I would for a second time have to wait for the Lord's answer. In the meantime, I would rest in what His Word had clearly proclaimed regarding salvation through belief. After all, I *did* believe Scripture could not and did not contradict itself in the core basics of its message. If it did, that would make God a liar. Thus, I knew there was something my finite mind was missing.

Days passed. John 6:40 had come to reaffirm the source of my salvation: "For my Father's will is that everyone who looks to the Son and believes in Him shall have eternal life, and I will raise him up at that last day." With the most crucial matter settled in my heart, I journeyed back to the States.

I shared with my parents all the events that had transpired. It was through this, twelve days after I had set eyes on the passage from James, the Lord granted the latter half of my request. My dad pointed out that those who did not believe in Christ are capable of doing good works. The difference is works performed from human motivation and effort would never reconcile the person before God. Only when they are accomplished through the purity of Christ's empowerment and love can an individual be holy and their works presentable to Him.

It seemed this truth already had been implanted in me. I realized I had drawn that same understanding after working through the passage in James nearly a year earlier. It had been masked by my fierce night of internal struggle. The works James referenced are an outflow of a believer's faith. They are material witness to what exists. They are my sense of belonging.

Other Scripture confirms this truth. In Matthew 7:15-23, Christ tells through a parable that a good tree is incapable of bearing bad fruit. Likewise, a bad tree cannot bear good fruit. If Christ is my source and I am the tree, His good fruit will grow and be evident through my actions.

God's peace soothingly permeated my heart through this renewed knowledge in His Word. Scripture was clear. Scripture agreed. God had heard my passionate cries to Him again, and once more *He* was due the credit.

Twenty-eight

Fourth Rotation to Iraq: Foretaste

Nearly as soon as I returned to Iraq for my fourth rotation, my spiritual focus, fortitude, energy, and determination in the operational tasks began to wane. After two months, I began handing off many of my administrative duties to my replacements. Unnerved by weariness and afraid it might lead to impatience, I prayed, asking God to renew my hope and vigor.

The loving Father gave His answer immediately, but I almost missed it. I expressed to my roommate the areas that I felt had been lacking patience. He reminded me that in my second and third rotations I had become impatient as I passed down operational knowledge to incoming personnel. He reminded me how disappointed I had been that even my vocal inflections bore evidence of my lack of Christ-like character. Now I was on my fourth rotation and weeks away from departure. Already buried in fatigue and *more* than ready to get to the States, I was no longer becoming exasperated or impatient in my pass downs. In fact, I could not recollect one moment of annoyance this time.

The Lord was at work within me. He was transforming my character. The proof had been staring me in the face. God granted me a renewed sense of hope knowing even this flaw *was* being mended. The first evidence of His work was that I noticed these character flaws because I walked closer with Him. The second evidence was

His work in making my actions more like His. What is more, the Father gave me the energy to cling to Him through the spiritual struggles overseas. The Father was deep in the process of reforming His child.

The Lord did not stop there with His encouragement. April had barely begun and I was hours shy of my 300th day serving in Operation Iraqi Freedom. Again, in a more convincing way, the team and I had the privilege in aiding the saving of lives on the ground. The magnitude of this triumph crossed the lines of definition.

How humbling of an answer from the Lord was this? I had nothing to do with getting to play an integral role in this assignment. All I had done was follow where He led. Frankly, I was fascinated and awestruck with love toward God. Truly, I was and *am* a blessed man.

Then on May 3, 2008, days from my return to Texas, came another momentous event—the fulfillment of His long-standing promise. My parents' final loan for my schooling was repaid. In three years with Dynamic Aviation God removed all of my and my parents' loans. Iraq served His purposes as the majority of the six-figure repayment occurred in less than twelve months of deployments. It was so much more than being free from debt. There was no misunderstood leading to LeTourneau. None of us were hallucinating when we sensed the Lord's reassuring words being spoken to us through His Spirit that the debt would be repaid in His time and His way. The fact the loans were satisfied was a testament to His personal reality, His mighty power, His faithfulness to do *exactly* as He promised.

I must put to rest any notion of my taking credit for repayment. I did not initiate the idea of LeTourneau or Iraq (the bookends to this story), and coincidence falls short in explaining the perfection by which events unfolded, as my journals recorded. From the day I previewed LeTourneau the Father lovingly beckoned me to follow His footsteps and trust in His capability to fulfill this promise. As He met financial needs along the way, that trust transformed into a calm assurance. Using the intimate encounters of college, the Navy, and Iraq, He established a rapport with me. My simple task was to follow and trust. He provided everything else.

The Lord was the one to orchestrate the steps that led to my going to Iraq. He had inspired my direction to Dynamic Aviation through immediate answer to prayer. He had responded to my open-handed seeking over the idea of going to Iraq. I entered the company's ISR department the day it was formed. I was permitted to deploy as a first officer on a contract requesting all captains because of the experience I had gained in Afghanistan, another idea not my own. After my second deployment I became captain ahead of the company's increase to flight experience minimums, allowing me to achieve loan payoff more quickly.

I pursued the goal of going to Iraq *after* the Father pointed me to it. It was more than being at the right place at the right time. Divine placement was His plan. There was *too* much inexplicable timing. The scope and consequence of each of those events vividly assures me He decisively met His mark.

Perhaps it is believable that God directed my paths. But, did He have anything to do with my physical efforts that ultimately allowed me to obtain the wages necessary to so rapidly settle my debt? Could I take credit for at least that portion of involvement? My spirit cautions otherwise. In just a few more years I would learn the Scriptural truth behind that argument. The Lord had given strict warning to the Israelites not to forget His involvement in even the menial tasks of life. Deuteronomy 8:18 cautioned, "But remember the Lord your God, for it is He who gives you the ability to produce wealth, and so confirms His covenant, which He swore to your forefathers, as it is today." Some translations phrase it as God giving the *power* to produce wealth, or the *power* to be successful. Surely, this principle attribute of God transcends all people groups. Even in the attainment of the funds I had no bragging rights. The Father had granted me the health, brain capacity, courage, and power to do it.

All I had right to possess in paying off the loans was to be filled with joy that I had the privilege to share in the Lord's involvement to accomplish something amazing. The Father directed my steps. His faithfulness proved true through His presence, authenticating Scripture's declaration that God is not a liar. He bolstered my trust.

As my college friends would attest, I often expressed angst over the mounting debt. Admittedly, it was hard to make it a practice to trust Him. Though by never forgetting His promise, it became easier with time.

The loans were paid in full, but I still owed tens of thousands of dollars to my parents for their contribution. Not until I'd returned every cent would I consider His promise fulfilled. That might appear easy to accomplish through a few more Iraq rotations. It would not be as straightforward as that. *Trust* was going to prove essential.

Twenty-nine

FIFTH AND SIXTH ROTATIONS TO IRAQ: FULFILLMENT AND INVIGORATION

After a five-week road trip to friends' weddings and visits to friends and family, summer 2008 launched a packed next four months of State-side work for my department. Fall morphed into winter and the New Year. As January gave way to February, it was time to begin thinking about my fifth rotation. To prepare for that, I needed to obtain my medical certificate from the FAA and attend deployment training at Fort Benning, Ga.

Before I could take a step in this direction my anticipated tour and my future as a pilot came into question. On March 3 I was smacked with unsteadiness. It was as if I was in a thick fog and my sense of physical balance was thrown off. If the reason is never found and corrected, this can lead to a loss of a pilot's flight medical. That ends one's ability to fly an aircraft permanently.

I had never experienced this in my life. Perhaps I had come as far as the Father had intended me to serve in Iraq. Maybe it was His time to vividly move me on to something else. If the Lord desired to draw my flight career to a sudden and unexpected close this would be the way to do it. All I *did* know was that I had to be truthful with the FAA.

I felt helpless to do *anything* about it. I bathed the situation in prayer. I would have to trust the Father's proven love and hands to be capable to follow through. I relinquished all my longings and desires toward any future in flying. I acknowledged He had given it to me, and He had every right to take it away. Regardless of whether I would ever fly again or do something else for the remainder of my life, I was quietly thankful for life itself. He knew my future.

Meanwhile, I elected to retain my scheduled pre-deployment training slot at Fort Benning. I was grateful I did as answers were waiting. On March 10 I had to divulge to the Army medical doctors what had been happening. They issued a notice of delayed deployment. That is, until a few days later when a doctor pronounced I was suffering from severe hay fever. I had allergies? I'd never had allergies before. The dryness and dustiness of Iraq could have been the culprit. Even though the diagnosis caught me off guard, it made sense. In any case, it was good news. The Army cleared me to deploy.

My slated tour date never materialized. It was March 19, and I was still at home. Since returning from Fort Benning I was not seeing the symptoms subside. I was still unsteady. Then I started to experience feverish chills and headaches. I chose to seek additional medical attention.

I decided to go to the medical clinic I normally attended for pre-deployment physicals. I had a chronic sinus infection in addition to my allergies. The doctor appeased my anxiousness by requesting a blood workup and scheduling me for an MRI. They came back negative for anything abnormal. Everything was as he had expected. He referred me to an ear, nose, and throat specialist.

He flatly remarked I had *no* symptoms, vertigo or otherwise, that could be addressed by his area of expertise. This news was *most* reassuring. He advised I see an allergist.

Feeling remarkably better and having secured the most critical answers to my suffering, I was in a position to obtain my renewed

FAA medical and deploy to Iraq. I had by now lost a month and was well overdue for my tour. Feeling the pressure to keep my obligations to my company as expeditiously as I could, I emailed the suggested allergist to affirm nothing struck him with cause for alarm. He, too, agreed allergic inflammation was the correct determination. Because my complaints were mild and transient, it did not seem critical enough to further postpone my deployment to Iraq. What a relief.

Peacefully trusting the Lord, I made an appointment to see my FAA examiner. On April 10 I walked into his office. He reviewed the papers, asked a few questions, gave me the routine physical, and deemed me fit. He issued my second class FAA medical, and with *no restrictions*. He had no concern whatsoever. In truth, he was pleased with my preparation of all the evidentiary paperwork. As soon as I arrived at my car in the examiner office's parking lot, I called my coordinating manager to relay the news. We were ecstatic.

God's peace swarmed my soul, showing me I was still supposed to fly while reassuring me of my safety as I would return to Iraq. My immediate steps had been approved. Through these events God had again shown me the danger in taking for granted my life or my expectations. It *can* all change at the snap of a finger. I learned that I had to *always* trust implicitly in the plans *He* had for my life. Only then would I be able to rest knowing that life's grief would never move me.

I was unaware how deep my trust in the Father had grown through this experience until all the events played out. Over the Easter weekend I shared with my mother and brother another observation from this trying period. My approach to prayer had taken to new form. I did not feel the pressing need to voice my every concern. I trusted He knew and I found rest leaving any answers to the prayers in His hands. This unconditional trust had filled me with a peace that wherever I landed in life I could rest easy knowing it was the best place to be—under His headship. I had found a resolute sense of trust in Him.

Back to the Sandbox

It was time, though, to get mentally and emotionally focused on heading back to the sandbox. On April 23 I was on an airliner heading overseas. God had great things in store for me this tour. Little did I know that He was going to prove to me precisely how He was safeguarding my existence.

During a mission that summer, the gravity of death came near. While in my assigned airspace over one of Iraq's larger cities, I made a turn back toward the east. Suddenly, the aircraft's traffic alert system announced that an aircraft was less than one-half mile away. I turned in time to see an F/A-16 in a sharp, ninety degree climbing turn. A midair collision had been split seconds away. By the time I could have disconnected autopilot, it would have been over. This extreme closure rate combined with his straying into our airspace is why I seriously doubt he was "looking us over" in fun. Had I turned left two seconds earlier, he and I would have been on an uncorrectable collision course.

I was convinced the Lord carried through on His promise that day to keep me safe. I, along with my crew, had not been killed. I had no evasive action at my disposal by the time we obtained a visual; *all* of our lives could have ended.

I was exceedingly more than thankful to the Father in whom I had placed my trust. He had proven His love and care for me and for those who had been in *my* care and responsibility as Aircraft Commander. My love and gratitude runs all the deeper today. As I did then, I thank the Heavenly Father for His watchful eye that kept me safe from my frail human limitations. He supplied us all with the hedge of protection we desperately, but unknowingly, needed.

To the Last Penny

Surpassingly amazing is what the Father did at the conclusion of that fifth tour in August 2009. In the span of that one rotation, God finally and completely fulfilled His promise to one day fully reconcile my school loans. He did not stop at enabling me to earn the funds to repay *only* the loans. He moved me through this rotation's prelude of trial to repay every cent of my school *and* car loans, and every cent my parents paid. Roughly $150,000 of indebtedness.

The impeccable timing of the repayment made God's hand unmistakable. A month prior to this moment, my dad lost his job of fourteen years as a result of the economy. The five-figure remaining balance I paid back to my parents covered what was left on their home mortgage. My parents no longer had to be concerned with the burden of that monthly payment.

Equally astonishing is that when I began repaying them a year earlier, I detected what I believed to be God's Spirit urging. I perceived He wanted me to express to my parents the importance of putting all the repaid monies toward their house. I sensed some life event coming, perhaps some kind of an economic crisis, that would make it absolutely vital to remove their house loan. Then, *just* before I was to cut them their last check my dad became unemployed.

It *was* His Spirit from whom I felt the sense of urgency. I didn't have any solid proof, yet I obeyed and relayed the direction to my parents. Only later was the accuracy of this clear direction confirmed. I *truly was* getting to know my Father's voice.

The profoundness of seeing His promise come to fruition became evident a year later. In the years preceding this repayment, some told me I had misread God's guarantee as I stepped into my LeTourneau education. They said that throughout Scripture God was opposed to carrying debt. Somehow I had known better, but I was unable to put my finger on it. I *did* know it was dangerous to attempt to put God in a box when trying to explain things beyond our grasp. Then, during a conversation with my father in 2010, the Lord revealed to me how to articulate the truth of His infinite perspective.

Consider this. You go to a luxurious sit-down restaurant and place an order. You receive your meal. Though you have not paid for it, the fact you ordered and received the food promises the restaurant you intend to pay for the meal. After you've eaten, you grant a form of payment. There could be several hours of time lapsing between the order and payment. But, was it ever considered a debt? It would not be viewed as such because the intent *and* capability always existed to pay for the meal.

God had placed a similar order in my situation. The difference was the time that passed *seemed* longer through the limited lens of my humanity. In God's concept of time, the interval between His promise and the fulfillment were practically instantaneous. As His Word proclaims in Psalm fifty, verse ten, God owns the cattle on a thousand hills. He already had the cash when He commanded I enter LeTourneau University. It is amazing that He accomplished His promise in only five years.

I had learned how to trust Him. I had learned to view things from *His* perspective.

INVIGORATION

My life became an ebb and flow of struggles and disappointment intermingled with joys and encouragement. As I prepared to head to Iraq in mid-November 2009, this tour would be no different. By the start of this sixth rotation I had spent nearly a year and a quarter in the country's blowing sands. I was running low on steam. My spiritual vigor was in worse shape. Despite the Father's involvement through the elimination of debt several months prior, I noted what seemed like rebellious attitudes toward Christ forming in my heart. I had no idea from where they came. Not knowing their origin made them like a continual gnawing, festering wound. I disliked such thoughts and feelings. I knew where they could lead. I wanted them gone.

The time to depart the States drew close and these perplexing emotions began to compound. The last thing I wanted to do would be to deploy with a spiritual cloudiness. The week before I was scheduled to leave I began to target my prayer on two fronts. I did not know if there was some unresolved or unconfessed sin that was breaking fellowship. I asked that He identify, convict where necessary, and remove any associated internal conflicts. I also realized my recent proximity to the Lord could have spurred Satan to attack me. I acknowledged, though, that he had to obtain approval from God to "sift me like wheat." With that as a possibility, I asked that the Lord would grant a reprieve from any such attack and enable me to have a time of refreshing and regeneration.

Had so many amazing wonders taken place in the recent months that I found myself spiritually and physically tapped out and vulnerable to the Adversary? I pulled my parents into discussion over what I had been experiencing. As they drove me to the airport, we were able to dialogue once more.

My parents had much wisdom. They shared truth from God's Word. It was instruction I already knew in my spirit to be true. I needed to remember to rely upon the Father to know my heart and address any and everything that needed to be sorted out. Together they shared the biblical life experiences of a couple devout figures. My mind was refreshed by the unsettling events surrounding Elijah's denouncement of Baal as well as the many passionate moments of David, like in Psalm 138. In all instances, God was present to preserve them.

My dad said that if the Lord led me into the work I was doing which was in a sometimes spiritually lonely place, then I needed to remember to focus my attentions on the One Who placed me there. Instead of allowing myself to feed on circumstances that might lend to feeling discouraged, I needed to trust His ability to provide my spiritual sustenance.

The Father *would* hear *and* answer. He already had begun. I could not yet see the Lord had a far-reaching and perfect design. In a matter of weeks He would turn my mourning into a rotation full of emboldening and gracious blessing. Any confusion, sadness, or disappointment, He would transform into ceaseless joy. This process would carry on throughout my deployment and my return home.

The afternoon I stepped aboard the first flight back the Lord began meeting me at the point of my need through an edifying conversation with a newfound believer sitting next to me. The Lord held my heart captive as I watched Him reawaken my memories of our connection and my passionate love for Him. All of the spiritual milestones proving His faithfulness and the encounters where I felt Him being closer to me than a brother He restored to my memory. I began to reflect on those moments where my personal worship of Him fed an atmosphere of rewarding intimacy. I did and *do* possess a wholehearted longing to be near to my Heavenly Father. *He* had been and *is* my ultimate strength and peace. Surely, these were to be a reminder of my *true* heart's desire.

As my mother remarked during my final phone conversation preceding my international leg, "The Lord has a stronger grip on you than you have on Him." My responsibility was to trust Him.

And so I voiced to my loving Father this prayer:

May I, oh merciful Father, never leave this point of understanding only to travel this misery again. Might I leave this point in a renewed comprehension of who You are and what You offer in provision for me. I pray my life be changed and emboldened to live my life as You desire it to be lived every day, while remembering my humanness and relying on Your capabilities alone. Only in this will I be refreshed and truly transformed. Only when I give my entire being to You will I be genuinely and permanently changed. May I be a proper reflection and disciple of You. According to Your will and Word may this come to pass. Amen.

JOY

I leaped into this tour with that prayer on my heart. To my marveling, the Lord would persist to offer me joy as He revealed to me how deep my affections for Him were. Christmas Eve arrived. It was my second time away from family in the season I had grown to appreciate. While I attended a candlelight service, the chaplain explained how one could recognize an appropriate view of Christmas. It is about God's Son—Jesus Christ. I will have taken hold of the *true* value of Christmas when I gladly choose to celebrate Christ and the meaning behind His coming to earth.

His message presented me with a gift that warm night. The Father granted me a glimpse into my heart. He gave me the opportunity to see I *did* identify with the real meaning of Christmas. No doubt this had been made possible through the absence of the familiar. The special times with family and friends at home would not happen this year. I did not get to see the radiance of a lit Christmas tree and all the other seasonal trimmings. Yet, none of that mattered. Rather, I found a deeply-rooted contentedness in my heart. A celebratory remembrance of Jesus overtook me as I enjoyed simply being with the Lord in His house. I savored the fellowship with other believers in worship of the King. What Christ meant to me was entirely satisfying and it empowered my walk with Him.

Struggles persisted as the calendar turned to 2010, but the Lord's encouragement would weather the storms. It was at times a spiritually and even relationally lonely existence being locked in a country that was a third of the way around the world. Nevertheless, my love for the Lord had grown as an outflow of my heart of gratitude for His immense love as well as eternal desires and provisions. His hope shone through all of it. If for the moment, my joy was complete. This was and *is* all to the glory of God!

A GRATEFUL HEART

In my renewed enthusiasm I made sure I expressed my deep appreciation and love for the part my parents played in facilitating and mentoring that spiritual growth. Although words couldn't express the sentiment, I wrote to them, "The encouragement that comes from being connected with not just other believers, but other believers of the same flesh and blood . . . that is just an appreciation that I will never be able to adequately put into words."

After I sent that message of love I was nearly brought to my knees. I began to express my deepest gratitude to the Lord for His sacrifice on my behalf. Words seemed insufficient as I attempted to communicate to Him how consuming was His peace evolving from the understanding of His truth. My heart was filled with awe over this God in whom I had chosen to place all of my being.

My emotion began to well up in tearful joy. Who was I to have been recognized and pursued by a forbearing, Almighty God? There had never been another time in my memory in which I had been so emotionally moved over the simple *joy* of being His child. Sensing His love outweighed *any* sorrowful times born in confession of my sin. I tasted the richness of His Kingdom and my Lord and Father filled me with an indescribable hope and peace.

The Lord's care and love continued to usher me through to the end of my sixth tour in Iraq. On as positive a note as it had begun it also came to a shining close. A week prior to my departure I began to behold His divine touch. I had chosen to exit theater to Kuwait via military transport. I made a two-legged reservation and was approved. In itself, this was a blessing. Normally, there had not been such ease in being assigned a standby seat as a contractor.

If there was ever one thing that would disrupt getting on an outbound flight it would be weather. A significant system was slated to hit the day before my departure from Iraq. With it would usually be an accompanying dust storm wreaking havoc on Air Force flight itineraries. Jokes of being stuck filled the hours and days preceding the storm. However, I already had a quiet assurance.

Friday came, the day before I was supposed to leave. So powerful was the storm that it created an unusual, all-day rain. Not only had it rained at our base, but across the entire theater. It rained *so* much throughout the country that it suppressed any dust from forming. Instead of being an insufferable dust event when the winds did eventually pick up, it ended up being nothing more than a harmlessly cool, strong wind. Any concerns about getting out were erased.

That night I had to return to the small, one-room terminal to check in as verification I still intended to take my reserved flight. To my amazement, the operations personnel informed me that there were four *direct* flights to Kuwait. It didn't make sense. Weeks before they had told me direct flights to Kuwait were no longer being conducted. While that was true, they were doing them this time. I was intrigued. I was told I could check again in the morning at which time I could place my name on the list for the direct flight, if I chose.

Saturday morning I returned to the passenger terminal and inquired about the status of the direct flight. There was one flight scheduled to leave at the same time as the one for which I had acquired a reservation. But, this one was for R&R personnel only and was not open to me. There were two more C-130 flights a few hours later than my reserved flight. I asked his opinion. If I decided to keep my two-legged reservation I might likely make that flight. However, if I kept it I would lengthen my journey to Kuwait. On the other hand, if I chose to hop on one of the two direct flights I would forfeit my reservation and only be allowed to fly standby. Obviously, the operations clerk said he could not tell me what to do, but the direct option would be a given for him.

It was without a doubt a risky proposal. Determined that the Lord was behind the affairs of my travels I cancelled my two sure reservations and signed up as a standby for the flight straight to Kuwait. Somehow I just knew it was the best decision. It was as if God's signature was written all across my path.

I decided to nap for what was now an extended wait. I went to sleep on the cold, metal benches of the passenger terminal. Before long I was awakened by commotion. The flight I had reserved had been cancelled. It is no surprise, then, when I say it was at that moment I found it *not* so odd to have given up what had been a sure set of flights in exchange for a chance direct flight.

I *did* get on the direct flight to Kuwait a few hours later. I must underscore how much of a blessing it was to have gotten a slot on this flight. A direct flight eliminated one or more stops. Stops increase the likelihood of delays and may also mean being on an even older fleet of maintenance-hungry aircraft. *Any* stop for *any* reason brings with it potentially negative outcomes.

It was time to board. Smiling, I noted this C-130 was from Dyess Air Force Base not far from my Texas home. It felt as though home had come to get me. In what seemed to be an unusually short flight, we arrived in Kuwait without event.

Family Reunion in Kuwait

Since I arrived sooner than expected, I was able to begin processing my visa earlier. At most the turnaround would be twenty-four hours. This would make it possible to depart on an earlier United flight to Washington, D.C. In checking the passenger loads I discovered the flight leaving the night prior to the one on which I was scheduled was only one-third full. Would it be possible to get on a quieter, roomier flight out of Kuwait? For the duration of Sunday and Monday I wrote emails, made phone calls to my managers, and continued checking the status of all the United flights.

But, wait. There was more in the Lord's storehouse of grace. While on the C-130 flight to Kuwait, it dawned on me that my brother's wife, Andrea, was slated to be coming into Afghanistan around the same time I was heading out. I knew she was going through Fort Benning's CRC course the prior week. If she was on schedule she would also have to pass through the same transient base where I now was. The odds of running across one person in a sea of hundreds to thousands were remote. I subconsciously concluded it was unlikely I would run into my sister-in-law.

I *should have* known better. Once more the Lord wanted to prove to me He was the God of the impossible. Sunday afternoon I was sitting in the waiting area for my opportunity to get on the computers and check my flight status. I took note of those who walked up to use the computers or phones. One female coming to sign up for the computers captured my attention. She looked a lot like Andrea. *Nah, it couldn't be her.* A few seconds later I looked at her again, this time taking note of the nametape. It read, "Sampson." I said out loud, "*ANDREA?*" Sure enough it *was* she. I got up and with looks of sheer surprise and mutually outstretched arms we embraced.

We ended up eating dinner together that night and the following night. It was a blessed time as we had what seemed like limitless moments to catch up. Monday night came too quickly. Truly, a fantastic meeting such as that could *not* have been *arranged* any better.

The Father's hand had been pouring out blessing upon my journey home. I found myself enamored by the flood of His personal touches. It was as if I were being treated like royalty. Every one of my steps He made smooth.

I also gained spiritual perspective. I realized how closely my trust in Him, when trading my reserved flight for an uncertain one, paralleled what it means to come to Jesus Christ. I exchange the certainty of what I know in my human realm for something that cannot be physically sensed. His visible and exacting handiwork behind my transit home can be explained by nothing other than blessing and love dispensed by the hand of the Lord God Almighty.

These travels had been the whipped cream and maraschino cherry atop what had already been a spectacular ice cream sundae. Without a doubt, the trip and the rotation had been blessing from every direction. Oh, and did I mention that I *did* end up being able to get out on an earlier flight from Kuwait and thereby get home a day earlier than expected?

How satisfying it was and is to acquire every last good thing, whether in possession or by word, from a Lord and Father who knows how to meet every need, passion, and longing. *Every* moment of my deployment had come by His divine appointment. They were all good and served His purpose of reminding me I was His loved son.

Thirty

TRUST IN HIS
PROMISE AND PRESENCE

From the mountaintops of LeTourneau and the United States Navy to the valleys of personal discouragement and disappointing spiritual character, the Father orchestrated my life events to proclaim me His loved child and brother with Christ. In a decade He staked His claim on me through three distinct instances along with the added support of many more quiet affirmations. These formed a firm foundation of truth. The intimacy of my relationship with Christ grew ever more personal with each expression of His love toward me. The bounds of my love for Him grew even more.

My belief, faith, hope, and trust had reached an initial zenith on the trek to spiritual maturity and connection to the Father. He had walked with me through the journeys of life reassuring me during the ascent that He had a firm grip on me. He promised I had been saved, but it was now my turn to reciprocate in resolute avowal of my trust in that promise. It was time for me to continue the climb with an even greater measure of empowering through His Spirit and take hold of *more* spectacular views along the way.

On Easter 2010 my pastor posed the familiar question, "Do you only believe in God? Or, do you believe in your heart? Remember, even Satan believes *and* knows God." What did it mean to believe in the heart? I had come to learn that it meant placing my full trust in His capability, and *only* His capability to save. It meant relying upon

Him. It meant surrendering my control to Him. So, why did the pastor's question reengage a spiritual unsettledness? I had answered these in previous wrestling and encounters with God. Why was I coming back to the old, habitual struggle?

The questions *had* been answered. It was time for me to place my own stake of implicit trust. For the remainder of that Easter Sunday I dug deep within my heart to find out if I had truly trusted Him. This persisted into Monday morning while seeking the Father.

Why was I back here questioning the same things once more? My time with Him turned into a passionate plea for His answer. Recognized from times past, I noted I was on course for destructive sin if I continued to allow embittered feelings toward the Father to follow.

I acknowledged this was a problem. I *cried* out to the Lord. "*Show* me who You are. *Show* me whether my trust is adequate. You've done *so* much for me, *why* am I having these feelings of desiring to do things on my own? Something isn't right, Lord. *Search* me and *reveal* to me today what I need to see, *please*." I instinctively knew He wanted me to take hold of His faith and continue the climb up the narrow trail in front of Him, one so steep that to lose my balance was detrimental. I needed to know that the Father was with me not only holding me but ready and able to catch me.

WRESTLING

I prayed this just after I finished reading the Scripture assigned to that day's *Our Daily Bread*. By His omniscience, it *was* before I had read the devotional itself. No sooner had I begun to read it that I knew the Lord was answering. The first sentence spoke of a Scottish pastor, Robert Murray McCheyne, who was sometimes troubled with a seeming coldness of heart toward the things of God. He learned that giving praise to the Lord was the solution. I identified with that notion. Nonetheless, these feelings rooted in frustration grew worse the more I delved into analyzing my heart.

Throughout the rest of that Monday I persisted in ongoing conversation with the Father. I wrestled with Him, and I was wearied in the fight. Every moment when I would think it was resolved, another unsettling question would be suggested. Then, I heard a message on the radio about what Easter means. It gave the refrain that being saved meant the only way I will ever be accepted in the holy presence of God will be as I'm covered by Christ's atonement.

I believed that to be true. This next thought rushed to my mind in response, *If I am viewed as Christ, then what importance am I? Do I just become a number? What benefit is it to me to simply be "connected" to Him?* The day pressed on. What had already become a weary fight leaving me battered grew *more* tiresome.

In the background throughout that day the Lord was quietly and lovingly reminding me of my experiences with Him. Then, that Monday night during men's Bible study, we worked through the last part of Philippians 3. It affirmed the understanding I'd held all day.

Trust. Specifically, trusting God for salvation is a daily, renewing decision. I am unable to discern the existence of such trust in a vacuum. I had been having an issue because I so often attempt to quantify my trust in Him by some physical, tangible, empirical evidence. Granted, those times were no less important to remember. However, they would leave me wanting. As the Father pointed out to me earlier, I need to reference *other* times in my life where I adequately and substantially placed my trust in Him.

The most vivid example was while in the Naval Hospital in Pensacola, I had found myself stripped of *everything* I knew. Still, I discovered myself being content. If all that was to remain out of this life would be just the Father and me, then I would be satisfied. Then I recalled of how just the week before this struggle I had sought His counsel after my company requested I take on new, challenging flight assignments. He was the first person to whom I went.

The Lord graciously answered my passionate cry by revealing

that my trust had been and *is* there. The disappointing reality was that I had been oblivious as a result of my narrow field of view. I went home from that night's Bible study recharged and refocused.

RENEWED DECISION

Much to my chagrin I was not done wrestling with the Lord, even though I began that Tuesday morning in praise over what He had shown me. I found myself instead asking, *So, I have been trusting; but, what about now? What am I supposed to make out of these feelings of cynicism to Your sovereign control in my life? Why have I felt dissatisfied by the thought of being covered in Christ?*

The Lord spared nothing to hear and console my cries early that Tuesday. I did not like the notion that being united with Christ meant I then amounted to nothing. It was not that I had a problem admitting that by myself I was nothing before God. I would be the first to confess that. What I *really* wanted was to be known by Him. I desired the individuality of relationship. I did not want to simply be connected. I wanted to matter. I wanted to count for something for His sake in this life and in the next. What was confounding about these very thoughts was that none of them even made historically factual sense. Had not *every one* of these desires been permeating my life?

Those notions had been *nothing* but a lie from Satan and I needed to resist. I was being assaulted—sifted like wheat as Christ said to Peter. Jesus said in Luke 22:31-32a, "Simon, Simon, Satan has asked to sift you as wheat. But I have prayed for you, Simon, that your faith may not fail." Not only had my life been filled with testimony of personal interactions with the Father, but He reminded me of all the times in His Word and during Jesus' life in which God had been shown to be nothing *but* personal. For starters, He used Adam in naming the animals. More personal yet is when Jesus desired to have a connection with Peter, James, and John in the garden. He was longing for relationship and unity. I already knew He desired to use me as a part of His plan. As the Apostle Paul laid out in 2 Corinthians, I was an *ambassador* of the Lord Jesus Christ.

That was precisely what I yearned to possess. I wanted *that* kind of relationship with Christ and the Father. I wanted to be united in purpose and cause—something greater than myself. Why would I want to control my own affairs? Letting the Lord Almighty lead my life had meant nothing but great contentment, satisfaction, and purpose. Certainly, there *was* much to gain from being united with Christ.

I found myself that Tuesday morning at the point of renewed decision. Was I trusting Him or just believing in His existence? I believe I had *more than enough* evidence to persuade me that my trust had been placed in Him. In being united with Christ, did I lose my individuality, purpose, or intimate relationship? Emphatically, *no*. I had greater purpose in being joined in Christ. I saw too much evidence that things were better than I could conceive when I gave my control to Him. In being united with Christ did I become a puppet on a string? I did not believe so nor did I see such a notion in Scripture. Jesus, as God, did not have to lower Himself to washing the disciples' feet. Instead, *that* was relationship. Yet, it was also purpose for the disciples to go and do likewise. They had an individual and collective mission. They counted—they mattered. So do I.

In heartfelt and biblical conclusion, I prayed, "Lord, in the clarity and sanity of my mind and heart, I ask that You yet again take complete control over my life. Show me that I am Yours. I realize I *must* surrender. Show me *how* to surrender. I trust You to keep me safe. Don't *ever* let me go!" That has *become* my consistent, albeit sometimes unspoken, prayer of my heart ever since. I saw then as clearly as I see now that He loves me and the best answer to my life is found only in Him. It was immaterial if my flesh ever desired the contrary.

That is the reason renewing of the mind is so important and why the apostle Paul reminded the Galatians that the sinful nature and His Spirit are in endless conflict with one another. I had come to realize I had been warring in my soul in some part due to Satan's use of depraved thinking. I had learned what Satan's lies looked like. Assuredly, that fight *is* never over. Though it may not always be the cause of my struggle, spiritual warfare *is* nevertheless real. I was going to have to learn how to fight it.

The Father continued to quench my passionate thirst that morning. My usual devotional explained that abiding in Christ meant seeking Him in every circumstance and trial. In a quote attributed only to Christiansen, the excerpt read, "He fully understands my soul's deep longing, and He whispers softly, 'Thou art Mine.'" It could not have proven more fitting to my heart's wrestling.

Then, I opened my devotional for our church's building program. Each day the devotional had a prayer by one of our members. The topic and prayer for that Tuesday was surrender. "Lord, I take my hands off my life; it is no longer mine. Forgive me for thinking I can do it my own way. Please take charge of the task and of me. With all my heart I trust You. I'm sorry for taking control. You are the one who can see around the curve, over the mountain, and will lead me accordingly. I yield to what, where, and when You tell me to do and to go. Not I, but Christ! In His name I pray. Amen." I was further encouraged when another excerpt reinforced that as trusting is not a onetime event, surrendering has to be learned.

Nothing better reflected *exactly* where I had been those couple of days. I recorded one last prayer in the journal for that day to summarize where our relationship had arrived. In deep love and affection I told the loving Father:

Lord Jesus, even now bring to me a rest in my soul and a peace in my heart knowing I am Yours. I consciously trust You to be fully capable to deliver me from my sinfulness; I surrender my control knowing then Your best *and* the best I could imagine are ahead of me; and, I concede that such surrender does not render me as a nameless existence but rather envelopes me in fully intimate and loving relationship and fellowship with You. It is the same as You describe in such places as John 17 and Psalm 139. Thank You for having never left me and for being my Great Helper as I've wrestled with Your Truth. Thank You for patiently loving me.

I moved forward fully trusting in Him. I relied on the fact He is faithful to do as He promised and usher me into eternal, unadulterated relationship with Him. His Holy Spirit was a down-payment of that promise. Why had I become so sure? It was because I *firmly* knew it was His nature. There was no longer any rational fear of falling off the edge during the precipitous ascent up that spiritual mountain. I *knew* He had a *strong* grip on me and would *never* let me fall. The Father's gift of trust and empowerment through His Spirit assured I only had higher and more glorious peaks to reach— and the view was going to be *breathtaking* with my life-Friend by my side.

Thirty-one

CONNECTION EQUALS COMMUNICATION

Being connected to the Father meant unfettered access to Him at any time. Though I had applied such power in the past, I became witness to its boundless limits. I came to grasp the *real* empowerment when my personal legacy of communication combined with unspoken trust. One example came months later.

In May 2010 Dynamic Aviation received a requisition to provide aerial support for the BP Oil Spill that had occurred weeks before. Our company had to act swiftly to accommodate the immediate need. They acquired pilots and mechanics from every segment of the company. Anyone available went to help. Since I was home and had been upgraded as captain in the smaller King Air 90 I served on two occasions.

I knew our combined efforts were helping keep matters under control for the benefit of others. It also was fun. I spent eighty hours inspecting the expanse of waters. Sometimes our assignments would take us 130 miles from shore near our operations center in Kiln, Miss. That was intimidating at first. Ultimately, this became some of the most enjoyable flying I had done since flight training at LeTourneau.

Eventually, though, the fun and exhilaration ended. The oil well was sealed and remnants of oil became near impossible to find. It was time to pack it up. Early Friday morning, July, 23, 2010, I received a phone call in my hotel room in Gulfport. Four of our aircraft were set to depart back to our home base in Virginia. I was tasked with taking our spare King Air. My First Officer, Rachel Ballou, was an intern contracted to fly for the operation. I also had onboard another intern, Nathan Moses, an office administrator providing overwatch of daily flights. Lastly, Peter Bjorkman, a seasoned mechanic, joined the crew.

We knew the day was coming, but we did not dream it was coming with so little warning. Bringing the trip together took logistical preparation. Safety was of paramount importance. Before leaving the hotel I called my mother to ask for prayer, that safety and clear thinking be the anchors for all the personnel, particularly those heading home that day. We piled in our vehicles and left the hotel bound for the Stennis Airport. After the half hour commute, it was show time.

Having flown with Rachel on two spotter flights, I was confident in her competence to fly the airplane. I also knew her opportunity of flying the King Air was over now that we had wrapped up operations. So, I happily appointed her to fly back to Virginia. Piled into the sweltering aircraft cabin and cockpit we commenced our flight. With little air traffic delay we made our way to nine thousand feet. The flight rewarded us all with a smooth and pleasant inauguration to our sunny trip.

New Point of View

It was nice to sit back, relax, and enjoy the views, but the quiet flight didn't last long. Roughly half an hour into our flight, Houston Center notified us that there was a Military Operations Area ahead. We would have to either descend to seven thousand or be vectored to the east. I chose the former so our course would not have to be altered. Air Traffic Control acknowledged my intent and stated he would call our descent in a few minutes. That was easy enough. Our trek across Mississippi and Alabama continued. In front of us were a few billowing clouds, so I cautioned Nathan and Pete, who were playing chess on a laptop, that we might encounter a little turbulence ahead.

Before we would penetrate the cloud, Houston Center came back to give instructions for our descent. I grabbed my pen and paper and began to jot down his instructions. Rachel having overheard the directions poised herself to begin the descent. As I was in the middle of reading back ATC's instructions, Rachel began to pull the power back while initiating the gradual let down. No sooner had she moved the engine levers and while I was still completing my sentence on the radio, we felt a moderate shudder reverberate through the frame of the aircraft. Rachel and I looked at each other in befuddlement.

I was in shock. My right hand engine auto ignition had engaged from its armed status. I glanced out at the right engine. By all appearances everything seemed to be running normally. I could see the propeller turning as usual, and there were no flames, smoke, or oil coming from the engine or its housing. There had been no additional noises or vibrations since the initial shudder. Neither was there any visible damage. I had no alarms or other warning lights alerting me to any problems.

Among the several anomalies I *did* notice my right engine showed a temperature glancing the top of the redline limit for normal operations and its revolutions had rolled back to near idle. I asked Rachel how the aircraft was handling. She remarked that she had to put in a little left rudder to keep it straight. Unquestionably, this indicated that the aircraft was responding to the dissimilar thrusts being put out by the two engines. On all accounts from my past simulated training for engine failures, I had never seen anything like this before. I was convinced something was wrong.

The one thing a pilot would *never* want to do in an aircraft at *any* time, much less in an emergency, would be to act rashly. In my case, the last thing I wanted was to take what *might* have been a perfectly operational engine and shut it down only to then exasperate the *real* problem. Having analyzed the engine indications and conducted our visual checks, we came to the consensus that the right engine was failing to produce the power it was designed to put out. With minimal delay, it was time to shut it down.

By this stage I had assumed control of the aircraft. I proceeded to draw from my years of practicing such an event. With each movement of an engine lever or switch, Rachel and I would confirm that it corresponded to the correct engine. It was *critical* to ensure things were accomplished right the first time. The engine was secured and the situation was under control. We proceeded to declare an emergency with our friendly Houston Center controller. Immediately, we received priority handling.

I requested Rachel resume the flying while maintaining safe airspeed, altitude, and course as much as possible. I carefully but expeditiously ran the entire emergency checklist while she hand flew the ill aircraft. I continued working with ATC and discussed with them the possible alternates. I ensured Rachel had a constant awareness of everything.

I decided it best to proceed straight to a small, country strip in Monroeville, Ala. I notified Houston Center of my decision; we were forty miles to the west. Before long, it was time to begin the task of getting on the ground. I asked Rachel to begin our descent. I would take over ten miles out and conduct the landing. She agreed.

Nathan and Pete had been feeling rather left out by this point. What they thought was a few bumps from a couple billowing clouds turned out to be more than they had bargained for. I turned around and advised that they buckle and prepare for landing. Rachel and I cinched ourselves down. The *real* business of the day was only beginning.

Nearing the Monroe County Airport, I was handed off to Atlanta Center and then our destination frequency. I requested approach flaps, followed with the gear as we turned to our final stretch. As Rachel selected the down position with the gear handle, we *both* instantly knew something was *very* wrong. The customary sound of the gear motor and the deceleration as a result of the gear entering the air stream were absent. I began thinking, *Are you serious? A second malfunction on top of the engine? Can't I just land the airplane already? Lord, please allow the gear to go down.*

I asked Rachel to give a glance across the circuit-breaker panels to see if any of them had popped. She said there had not been any. As she had done so, I also arrested my descent and increased my left engine's thrust. In my mind I had begun to prepare for a climb to a higher altitude in anticipation of a manual gear extension.

Unfortunately, it was so hot and muggy that the performance of my remaining engine was not going to grant me the rate of climb I would have hoped. I decided I would take what altitude I could get, circle over the airport and sparsely populated area, and be ready to break the gear extension procedure off at any moment if it became necessary. I would land in whatever controlled state I ended up. I was about to institute my thoughts when the *welcome* sounds and feelings returned. The gear finally engaged and indicated down in place.

By the time the gear decided to cooperate, I noticed I was nearly over the threshold of the runway and I was still at the higher altitude. I briefly considered breaking off for a downwind to final for the opposite direction runway. Though, my options should anything else unexpected occur would present a more grim outcome than remaining in the location I was and spiral down to retake the final approach. Disappointed and wearied, I told Rachel that I would make a 360 degree left descending turn while keeping it reasonably tight. I would thereafter realign with the runway. While I did so, Rachel addressed the landing checks.

Time passed second by second as the four of us *tried* to be patient and wait for the sight of the runway once more. Piercing through a few more pockets of warm, southern air, I *finally* reacquired the extended line to the runway. As if nothing were inhibiting the aircraft, we landed *firmly* and safely on the solid runway surface as any other normal, two-engine flight of the past. Ready to stop right in the middle of the runway, shut the aircraft down, and get out, I pressed on to taxi it off to the parking area near the field office.

After making a few phone calls to my company, we were informed that one of the aircraft crew that had preceded us in the transit home had been notified and were on their way back to pick us up. In the meantime, we should relax and unwind. We swapped stories of what we had all been thinking and feeling. We even mustered a few laughs over the lack of enthusiasm of having to fly more just to get home. Our mercy flight finally arrived. As Nathan was marshaling it in, I put my arm over his shoulder and said, "Thanks."

Putting his arm over my shoulder he said, "You did a good job." With what I am certain was a smirk of knowing otherwise, I pointed to the sky and stated that I was convinced the Lord had been *entirely* involved in protecting all of us.

Leaving the other aircraft behind, we took off as one happy family and continued our journey to Virginia. The flight back proved relaxing and fun. I don't think I had ever been as contented in my life to be a passenger. We played some cards, chatted some more, and even joked and teased one another. Pete even commented that he wished he had just taken a Greyhound bus home. After our first fuel stop, I joked with him again. "Don't you wish you would have just driven the aircraft tug home?"

He smiled and laughed.

Several times Nathan commented how he was so glad he had ended up not being assigned to one of the other three aircraft flying back to Virginia because, he "would have missed all the fun and memories." I understood. I felt the same way.

Here we were, four young adults having come through an eye-opening, life-threatening experience. The camaraderie was inevitable. Our friendship grew stronger, our bonds tighter, and our faith united. The spectacular airborne views of rainbows, sunset lit clouds, and distant thunderstorm lightning topped the day off.

At last there it was—the first significant airborne emergency of my flying history. The engine failure was unlike anything I could have imagined. The cockpit can go from calm to intense in an instant. How did I keep my head? I did not even notice that I had. I felt as though I had been all over the place in trying to handle a myriad of tasks.

In it all, I sensed a calming peace that afforded me the clarity and preparation to work through the emergencies. How can there be an environment of confusion and, yet, calmness and collectiveness coexisting in the same space? Again, it is when the Lord is present. For several months, the Father had been ready to answer a prayer and be deeply involved in the events of that day.

Statistically, a pilot eventually accumulates enough aeronautical exposure that the possibilities for something to go wrong finally intersect with the pilot in some significant emergency. Shortly after my return from Iraq that spring, I sensed my day would surely be around the corner. I brought my concern before the loving Father. He had shown I would never lack His help. "Lord, I am not sure how I will deal with an engine failure or other emergency if it ever does occur. I ask that if and when that day does come, would You please prepare me for it? Would You grant me the clarity of mind and focus and the recollection of my training to ready me for such a time? Prepare me in *advance*." The Lord knew and heard me.

Before we took off from the Mississippi airport, I had taken note that our aircraft had not been flown in nearly three months. I briefly considered something could go wrong, but it was an unfounded apprehension. Each airplane was well maintained, and I was no more likely to encounter an undesirable event in our aircraft than in any other. As soon as I had given thought to the prospect, I laid it back to rest in the recesses of my mind. That's why I found it easy to sit back, relax, and soak in the beauty of the many billowing white clouds that filled the blue sky once we reached cruising altitude.

Here is the amazing part from that day. Seemingly out of the blue, fifteen minutes prior to the engine malfunction, an alarming notion of an impending, serious emergency pierced my aimless thoughts. Undoubtedly, this was His Spirit. Sitting there in my seat during cruise I began to converse with the Lord. I humbly petitioned Him, "How horrible would it be to encounter an engine failure or *any* emergency on this flight. Here I've got two interns and a mechanic onboard. Not that I would wish it happen to any other group or person, but I *really* don't want to have to deal with an emergency *today*. So, Lord, I just ask that You please give us a safe flight all the way to Virginia."

Can you see how in that very prayer God had answered my cry from earlier in the year? Through my concerns, thoughts, and prayers shortly into the flight that Friday the Father made me cognizant of what was impending. Once it did happen I was restrained in a moment of disbelief. I had been *so* alerted to the undesired possibility that I had been caught in its surreal grips.

The Lord did not stop by only answering my prayer for warning. Once Rachel and I did realize the culprit, He rushed His clarity of mind and focus. He prepared and engaged me to deal with it. As I had asked, my years of flight training and procedures came flooding back in habitual action. He enabled me to use them to calmly work through each emergency as it unfolded. In my feeble frame I could not comprehend how I was capable to process everything.

Was I nervous? Was I shaking, particularly after stepping off the airplane? Of course. Who wouldn't? What I *hadn't* expected but joyfully embraced was the Lord's indescribable peace coursing my physical veins. Throughout it remained evident. I knew nothing was outside His awareness. Nowhere else can one derive such a powerful, controlling force to the point of invoking limitless peace. It can only come from the God of the Universe. He was the Controller over my life and all of our lives. He *had* answered my prayers. Here was yet another personal, vivid example of His attentiveness to me.

Not only had the Father alerted me that Friday, but He had prepared me the preceding April when I received my upgrade training in the King Air 90. As was customary, I had been given a simulated engine failure. Through a course of disappointing decisions, I had discovered how difficult a physical task maneuvering the aircraft could be in the configuration in which I had decided to operate it. It was doable, but I saw it required every ounce of finesse for me to put the aircraft where I wanted it. My choices that day of training had formed a unique muscle memory that was applied when I did have the emergency. The feel and physical finesse were almost identical to that of which I had practiced.

One remaining thought occurred to me while on the flight to Virginia—how fragile my life is. My days are numbered and only the King knows the final date. Soon after the engine malfunction happened, I understood that I was the one humanly accountable for the other three lives onboard. Though the Lord was ultimately responsible, in the physical realm they needed me to fly them safely to the ground. Such an immense charge ushers powerful and humbling thoughts. If I had not known to sink my reliance and dependence upon the sufficiency of the Lord Jesus Christ, it would have become an unbearable obligation. Praise Him for His power, and may the Father's name be forever praised for His sovereign protection.

I believe there is only one formula that enables a person to know the future, and that is if the Lord reveals it. Clearly, having been connected to Him granted me unfettered and *immediate* communication to Him when I most needed it. I rested even more assured that He was continuing to preserve and watch over my life for some purpose—if nothing else but to know Him better.

Thirty-two

SEVENTH ROTATION TO IRAQ: POWER

Part of my deployment preparation for my seventh tour to Iraq entailed traveling to California. I would be on a different contract this time, so I needed to brush up on a platform I had not flown in two years. Professional expertise grew, but spiritual growth outpaced it. I spent my free time continuing to review my journal material for inclusion in this book.

In reviewing the occasions God's hand had been at work, the familiar inclination toward embittered feelings reared its face. This time it tried to persuade me to disbelieve and disinherit all that the Lord had done in my past. I now knew that I could not always trust my feelings. I sensed this was another attack. I also understood I had to act immediately as Christ instructed me through His Word. Without delay, I entreated the Lord to remove *Satan* from my presence. I proclaimed, as the book of James states, that the Adversary had *no* business messing with me. Through the blood of Jesus Christ, I resisted him and instructed him to leave me alone. I knew what I needed to do then was to trust in God's Word and His promises, and I needed to hold strong to what He had surely done in my past.

I proceeded to read a portion of a journal from November 2007. There I saw how I fervently prayed for Him to assure me of salvation through His Word. A smile rippled across my face. I not only harkened back to that event, but the cynicism I felt moments before left me. I sensed pleasure in recalling what He did for me in *both* instances.

I became all the more ecstatic knowing I *was* doing the correct thing by relying on His Word. I did need to be ready to tell Satan to depart if I sensed him starting to attack. How easy it would be to stray if not for His steady hand. I recognized that day as I do now that His grace and mercy are my shelter. I thank Him for that and for persistently granting me *everything* I need.

By the Saturday after Thanksgiving, I was off to Iraq one more time. I was around a different team, yet I felt I'd never left. My tours had begun to grate on me. The Lord addressed this as soon as I arrived. He surrounded me on every side with an unusual number of Christians. They supported and undergirded me in my faith walk. We all upheld one another.

Christmas morphed into the new year. The Lord kept me spiritually satiated and protected throughout my tour as He brought new focus, new understandings, and new light to ways He was working in my life.

The Father revealed one aspect of my spiritual character that had been transformed by His Holy Spirit. As memories of my childhood flooded my mind, I recalled how passive-aggressiveness used to control my outward behavior. If I did not get my way or felt wronged, I would sulk all day trying to draw sympathy. If someone did eventually ask me a question, I would either not answer out of spite, or I would answer in such a way that they would catch on that they had mistreated me. I remember how miserable I would feel in acting out such behavior. Instead of seeking reconciliation, I would rub it in with pathetic hopes of making the other person feel worse.

This is no way for a child of the King to behave. The Father was revealing to me that this *had* changed. I *still* cannot remember the last time such behavior evidenced itself. To the contrary, I remember times where I have confronted a person if I have felt ill-treated. Where did my former ways go? I cannot even *track* a string of events where those behaviors waned or disappeared. What I *do* detect is that they are rarely if ever there any longer.

Another area of my life that saw change during my rotations to Iraq relates to attending chapel services. In past tours, if I had missed *one* Sunday of chapel due to being required on a mission, I would see significant deterioration in my attitude, my patience, and my over-all demeanor. Thankfully, this seventh tour was revealing something different. Due to a work schedule shift, I missed another Sunday of worship. To my delight, I noticed how the Lord provided everything I needed to get through to the next Sunday. I was ready and hungry for renewing, but I hadn't noticed a sign of lacking patience. What had changed? Outside spending more quality time reading God's Word and searching both His heart and mine, any subsequent character change *must have* occurred inside me.

These were a few of the aspects the Lord brought to my encour-aged awareness. I had nothing to do with changing my character. It was *all* God. I simply cannot reason my way into justifying such transformation by anything or anyone else. Part of me says Satan would love for me to believe otherwise so I will not find strength in knowing that the Lord has His hand of redemption on my life.

Did I just grow older and become miraculously transmuted? I find the opposite supposition to be true as I reflect on what Scrip-ture says about the fallen state of human nature, and as I observe the world. Left to me there persists one singular thing to which my fleshly nature defaults—itself. There was only one written code in my soul and bodily members before I came to Christ—sin. I knew nothing different. There was no reference point to anything more substantive.

I am convinced core character change came through being con-nected to the Source—Christ. Only as He has filled me with His love and revealed to me His desire for something better in my life could I have even had a remote *chance*, a remote *hope* of defaulting to something better. As Scripture states, without Christ and the Holy

Spirit, it would have appeared to me as nothing but foolishness.

In that conclusion I find hope. Why? I see the Lord has not only grabbed hold of my life, but most importantly, He *knows* me personally. He has changed me. I cannot fathom the pain of hearing Him say to me, "I never knew you." Praise and glory to His name that I will never have to hear that.

I could tell many other events from which I could draw confidence in my position and security in Him. Seeing these aspects of my core being transformed over the years offers me all the more concrete evidence to convince me of what is true.

Through the weeks that remained of that seventh and final rotation to Iraq, Christ poured encouragement into my heart and filled it to overflowing. Eventually, I headed home to Texas. I was grateful for everything He had done to grow and mature me spiritually in the past, in the present, and in the future. The loving and gracious Father even allowed me to serve people and country from our first to our last task force in Iraq in that process. How perfect His timing.

The years since college were wrought with trials, struggles, rewards, and encouragement. I watched as the Lord took what appeared to me to be a flailing relationship with Christ and transform it into a strong anchor of trust, hope, and peace while underway on the tossing seas of life, even those yet to come. He had His greater purposes as surely as He *still* does.

Thirty-three

TRUST IN LIVING COLOR

The Father's immense love is incomprehensible. It is indescribable. It is eternal. The apostle Paul expressed this succinctly, "so that Christ may dwell in your hearts through faith. And I pray that you, being rooted and established in love, may have power, together with all the saints, to grasp how wide and long and high and deep is the love of Christ, and to know this love that surpasses knowledge—that you may be filled to the measure of all the fullness of God." (Eph. 3:17-19). Only He can grant us the ability to understand His love.

What the everlasting Father's love *did* to me is unmistakable. It revolutionized my whole being. I praise Him because my cravings for intimate connection are met through the Lord Jesus. My life has become an eager anticipation for each new interactive encounter with the One Who knows me better than I do. Only He can satisfy my hunger. Only He can quench my thirst.

The Father's timely communication, direct answers to prayer, and affirmations of belonging are my stones of remembrance. They remind me of God's consistently loving and eternal faithfulness. I find myself having nowhere else to turn but to Him in every moment of my life, and I am thankful I do not stand alone. Simon Peter answered him, "Lord, to whom shall we go? You have the words of eternal life" (John 6:68).

Trust is the defining marker of God's transformation of me and my character. It is the new lens through which I view life. Trust is at the core of how I have changed. The best illustration of this difference is how He broadened my foundation of trust.

This process took time. It also required a difficult adjustment on my part. Looking back, I see how many questions I repeated time and again. Though the Lord's voice stays the same, it has quieted in recent years. He hasn't left, nor has He changed. I truly believe that. But, this less frequent and obvious closeness sometimes sends me back to wondering again whether I am His possession. Recently, though, a chain of events that challenged me to trust helped me put this into perspective and gain clarity.

This reality would bring me to a fresh understanding founded upon a legacy of Christ's followers, tied to the human parallel of a father and child. The Father's love never fades, but by definition it seeks out my best. This means it does not coddle me. His love assures me of my belonging so I might be empowered to stand and engage the world. Because I am God's son, His heritage and identity passes on to me.

Yet, I can never experience the fullness of life with God if I never act on it. The Father's love mandates I leave the safe haven of the nest and soar. I relish the intimacy I have enjoyed with the Father. Fear of losing that combined with doubts of my value and adequacy could disallow my taking flight courageously. So, He has *pushed* me out of the nest for my own good. I do not like feeling uncertainty, but the push is necessary if my faith is to be perfected and I am to reflect my Father.

The Father showed me I have no reason to be uneasy in this process. I already possess everything I need to bring Him glory as I soar in His strength. He patiently and lovingly granted me a means to fight through my personal doubts. Forming this marvelous history of my walk with Jesus revealed to my heart that I *am* ready to become more. I want my spiritual maturity to expand. I *want* to move beyond these repetitive struggles so I can become everything the Father designed me to be. If the Lord is going to shine through me to the world, I must fly because of my trust in Who He has proven Himself to be. I have to apply what I have been taught by the promises of His Word and rely in who I am in Him as His heir.

What in my formative years was a longing for the Lord's touch and closeness has grown into a maturing walk of faith.

PRESSED TO TRUST

The launching pad that would bring the answers to what I now understand came in summer 2012. I had resumed deployments. Since the company was no longer in Iraq, I went to Afghanistan. Quietness permeated this rotation. Then, two weeks before I would return to the States, our base came under attack by rockets while I was on an afternoon flight. First it was two. In short succession there was a third. My co-captain and I were stunned as each additional attack was announced over the airport frequency. It became so bad that field operations were suspended in suspicion of further attacks. This was serious.

We had to decide where to land, quickly. Rockets continued to bombard the base. There was an alternate airport, but air traffic was already being rerouted there. That could further delay us and we were getting low on fuel. We agreed to return to our home airport. We were committed. There was not enough fuel remaining to allow for a change of mind.

I remember my hand shaking on our aircraft's glare shield as we headed inbound. I could not help but reflect on the gravity of what had been my decision as aircraft commander. My choice could result in the death of crew members under my care. It was a familiar weight of responsibility harkening back to the near midair collision in Iraq, but this time I had moments to mull over it. I recall how concerned I was for the sake of the others. I felt helpless. I had no control over our lives, and I knew it. What if I had chosen poorly?

I had no other alternative but to pour out to my sovereign Father a desperate prayer. I later learned my co-captain had as well. Even while I maneuvered the aircraft on an eerily quiet short final to the runway, I was *crying* out to the Lord. I asked that He protect us and get us to a safe stopping point so we could egress to the bunkers.

We landed safely. Seconds after engine shutdown and after seven hits to the airfield, the ordeal was over. The Lord kept us all from harm. I may never know the "could have been" scenario, but Almighty God chose to hold out His shielding hand. Praise and glory is God's.

The experience didn't hit me until the following morning. While I communicated with the Lord, my stifled emotions broke into a stream of tears. I was relieved. I was filled with joyful satisfaction knowing I possessed a solid connection with a real God, Savior, and Friend. He had granted me wisdom. I had sought His help, and my trust revealed He was *my* soul's firm foundation.

A Revisited Struggle, Different Results

The loving Father showed me so many aspects of His character throughout my journey. It then becomes a wonder why I repeatedly flailed in my faith. Why could I not rid myself of the recurrent, bewildering feelings of cynicism and dissatisfaction toward Christ? Rather than moving forward in strength I seemed imprisoned by shame for doubting Him. Of all people, I should have the *least* cause to struggle in grasping God's tangible reality.

As 2013 approached I again felt spiritually lost in a dry and barren wilderness, though I could not nail down what had precipitated it. The absence of what I normally sensed as the power and immensity of the Lord was palpable. This latest struggle lasted from December into February. It was as if someone walked by and kicked over my lifetime's tower of spiritual building blocks. However, the Lord was restacking the good blocks on a broader footing. It was a necessary part of my faith journey. It was time to engage all I had learned.

Other than the promises found in His Word, the Father remained silent. I am convinced He heard me as I was forced to test my heart and navigate the familiar skies. I could ask all the questions I wanted, but it became *my* responsibility to grab hold of each promise if I were to stay aloft.

I began to rehearse God's promises and what each meant to me. I am sorely destitute without Christ (Rom. 3:10-12). No one *but* Jesus is capable to redeem me from my corruption. The solution was straightforward. All that was required was to believe in God's Son—to cling to Him in the trust He provides. When Jesus was asked in John 6:28-29 what the works of God entailed, He replied it was to believe in the Son God had sent. In verse 40 it was repeated. It was the Father's will that if I looked to the Son and believed in Him I would have eternal life. If I put my trust in Him I would never be put to shame, according to Romans 10:11, Hebrews 7:25, and 1 John 5:13.

Adding to these promises was the remembrance that Jesus calls me His *friend. He loves me.* Jesus wishes me to be with Him in eternity. He desires to reside in me so we might be *one in unity.* These words of hope from Jesus as relayed in John 15:13-16 and 17:20-24 make it obvious I matter to Him *so* much that He wants to be connected with me. More than a friend, I am a *brother of Jesus.* I am God's *son* (1 John 3:1)! The Father's love for me as His child conforms me to the likeness of my firstborn Brother (Rom. 8:28-30; Heb. 2:11). What an immense sense of belonging.

This work of coming into the family was not dependent on my assistance. Paul emphasizes in 1 Thessalonians 5:24 that God will be faithful to complete the task. In the process I have the rights of an heir (Gal. 4:4-7). As His heir *I possess His Spirit.* Without Him I would not be able to discern the ultimate value of clinging to God's Son (1 Cor. 2:11-12) nor be capable to confess Jesus Christ as Lord (Rom. 10:9-10).

God's intent for all this is to prepare and enable me to *share* in the glory of Jesus Christ. In 2 Thessalonians 2:14, the phrase "that you may gain the glory of our Lord Jesus Christ" (NASB), literally means *to the gaining of*. Can you imagine partaking in the glory of an Almighty God?

I admit I am separated by thousands of years from the life of Jesus. This is where faith comes in. Hundreds of years of prophecy were fulfilled in Christ. I am preceded by generations of disciples and apostles who walked with Him. They were eyewitnesses to His resurrection (1 Cor. 15:1-8). Therefore, I can believe they hold authority to authenticate the life, testimonies, and promises of Jesus. By this means I can believe Christ's death as foretold in Isaiah 53:6 granted Him all the rights to declare me pure before the Father.

Then there was the truth that my life has been blessed when lived the Father's way. The wisdom presented throughout God's Word alongside the words of Jesus, validate God's reality. The more I considered this argument, the more convinced I became to believe in Him. Even if I were to suppose the Bible were nothing more than a historical record of each writer's observation of the world, I would arrive at no different conclusion. It would not diminish the proposition that the God of the Bible is the one, true God. Everything I observe aligns with the God they precisely pinpointed. Scripture proven true means I have no sweat in this life when I rely on His principles and strength.

The Lord *is* powerful. He *is* provider of all that is required. *He is* intimately personal in my life. What reason would there be not to believe in someone like Jesus who offers this degree of love, peace, joy, and hope that transcends my current existence? I *want* Him to hold me eternally. This spiritual struggle presented me no other conclusion.

Many of these closing arguments by God were familiar while some were new discoveries. This time, however, these uneasy spiritual moments aroused a different response. I had not found myself begging the Father's presence as a prerequisite to action. I sensed an underlying peace. How?

I recognized the Adversary's three-year-old provocation of his same lies. Satan's goal amid the Father's quietness was to curb my progress by causing me to question my worth. I discerned the threat had the Adversary's signature. I would not permit these nagging questions of my identity to linger.

I knew what to do this time. I *needed* to focus on the Father and cling to His promises. I needed to reflect on all He had provided me eternally and throughout my human existence. I needed to *believe* He would carry me through in His time and His way. I arrived at renewed resolve:

> Lord Jesus, I can sense the battle between the Adversary and the flesh telling me You don't exist and not to believe in You. Still, my spirit and heart strongly *yearn* to believe in someone like You and believe You exist if it were only because of the immense hope for the future and provision for the present that You provide. . . . If that means I have to persist in faith, then I choose to do so. Your message remains the only one befitting of my confidence. Jesus, I feel as though in my flesh I am a ship at sea that is listing and adrift. . . . I need You to patch the holes in my hull and make me straight so I can set sail on a path leading directly to You. I thank You, in faith, for offering an eternal solution for my heart and life that does not doom me to the seas forever.

The Father *never* left my side. In the quiet I heard His calm voice speaking reassuring words of love through the fog, "Be still, My child. You may not understand what is going on right now, but you will. Continue professing and believing in faith while trusting that I *am* the only one who can save you." He reminded me not to forget the times He had felt so close. My past encounters had been milestones along the path of our solid Father/child relationship.

In the end I made a choice to trust God for my salvation and worth. My faith survived the trial and grew stronger. I was getting it through my thick skull that God was authentically present in *every* moment. He was providing the protection and strength.

I could have allowed my flesh to act on the cynicism from a spiritually exhausting conflict. Instead, His Spirit enabled my heart to revere the Father in the face of His silence. To my surprise, a mature fear and awe prevented me from responding negatively.

In Good Company

Fatigue from those two months brought on an unassociated struggle, but God used it, as well. One night I was faced with what I am convinced was the Adversary's invitation to give in to my wearied flesh. So strong was its lure that my soul was being offered the alternative ease of denying what I have believed of Christ, even disowning Christ Himself.

Later that evening I took my usual shower. I had become distraught for having *allowed* such a distasteful temptation to enter my mind. I asked the Lord, "Why, if I have committed my life to You, would I even *think* of forsaking You?" *Instantly* His Spirit reminded me of Christ's temptation in the desert, recorded in Matthew 4. "Again, the devil took him to a very high mountain and showed him all the kingdoms of the world and their splendor. 'All this I will give you,' he said, 'if you will bow down and worship me.'" What was Satan asking Christ to do but disown His Father?

Under the falling water I gave a whimper. Smiling, my eyes watered as *joy* flooded my heart. *I wasn't alone in my temptation.* Jesus had endured the identical temptation—to deny the Father. My heart was filled with immense contentedness in this unprecedented moment. I had *shared* in Christ's suffering (Rom. 8:17). This intimate connection was unimaginable. *I could identify with Jesus, and He could identify with me.* I had experienced sweet encounters in the past, yet I don't believe I have *ever* been able to identify with Him as precisely.

CALLED AS AN AMBASSADOR

In the weeks that followed the Father underscored my worth. He reminded me I am His ambassador (2 Cor. 5:17-21). Here on earth I am *God's* representative. There is value in that purpose. To think I mean nothing to the Lord *is* a lie from Satan. God does not want me to be an aimless asset among heavenly mementos. He wants me *united* with Him so I can serve as His ambassador. I had to cling to its truth.

I have since come to a striking parallel between this life and my eternal purpose. A ship by nature does not command its own direction, yet it serves a crucial purpose. It conveys people from one point to another. Without it, people would be standing on the shore without a hope. As God's son, I am like that vessel. I am God's ambassador—His mouthpiece. He is using me to carry people to His message of love. I serve a unique purpose—to transport His precious cargo.

Unlike the ship, though, I can receive the intangibles of love from the Father while appreciating my significance in the process of bearing the light of Jesus Christ. I am more than a material vessel discarded once its purpose is no longer needed. The Father's love and longing for interpersonal fellowship and intimate relationship will endure. God doesn't *need* my help. Jesus could have continued His work on earth. I believe His absence in physical form most clearly indicates He wants to *specifically* use me (John 14:12).

When I understand my purpose and value from the *Father's* perspective, the barriers of pride and worthlessness fall away, my ability to receive God's love grows, and my desire to be the extension of that love takes firm hold. I am grateful *not* to be an inanimate ship but a person with whom the Lord can relate and use.

ANSWERS WHY

It was not until recently that the reason for these reemerging struggles became evident. I wanted to persist delighting in the Father's routinely intimate contact and the security found there. However, once He showed me everything I need to fly, it became necessary for Him to give me a push out of the nest.

He had to do this in increasing measure because I was not leaping out on my own. I find this akin to my childhood temperament with the emotional trepidation I felt when tasked with jumping from a diving board into deep waters. I was high up and alone. I had to choose to spring off. I *despise* those feelings. In the same way I believe my embittered emotion portrayed amid these necessary spiritual moments when I *thought* the Father had left was because I was desperately searching only to find silence. My response was to pout with a frown and sulk with arms crossed as if to say, "You don't care about me. I *can't* be Your son." In reality, the Father hadn't departed, but wanted to watch me *soar*.

Satan attacks me at my points of weakness and susceptibility. He knows my human responses, particularly as it relates to my *longing* to feel the closeness of a Father and Savior whom I have grown to love. It only makes sense that the Adversary would tempt me with doubts of this eternal connection, controlling me through feelings of fear and uncertainty. Because I enjoy His company, I want to *know* I have a place in the Father's heart.

There will be more tests like these for me. There will be times I feel I am aboard a ship being tossed at sea amid an irrepressible fog in search of safe harbor. There may be moments tempting me to entertain sour thoughts. I may beg Jesus to calm the storm. Perhaps I will ask Him to believe for me when I am spiritually weary. There will be occasions I won't understand why I am journeying with a silent Companion. Yet each instance will serve to mature me and make me more like my brother, Jesus. I will have to choose to believe by faith alone. I have to remember my feelings do *not* represent the truth of His promises.

Faith is all I can offer the Lord Jesus, but He's definitely worth my investment. I want to believe in One Who thinks of me highly enough to love me so much. I proclaim in joyful contentedness that I principally desire to follow such a Savior were I *never* to understand it all. *Lord, to whom shall I go?* I *want* to hope in a God Who by nature encompasses everything I seek—from love to eternal life. He also knows I eagerly desire the reward in believing *without* seeing. This means I must be patient with my growth in Jesus Christ as He perfects my faith (Hebrews 12). I *do believe*—by a *clinging faith and trust*. Standing behind the eyewitnesses of Christ's life, my confidence is well placed.

Anyone who says trust is easy would be sorely mistaken. The struggle can also be rewarding and emboldening. James 1:2-4 says, "Consider it pure joy, my brothers, whenever you face trials of many kinds, because you know that the testing of your faith develops perseverance. Perseverance must finish its work so that you may be mature and complete, not lacking anything." I *should* be thankful when I am tested because it is evidence the Father *has* kept me safe. How wonderful it *is* to be a child of One Who is marvelously attuned to who I am and knows exactly how many swells I can handle.

The hidden benefit to journeying through these new and uncertain explorations is capturing a glimpse of what my life could be like every day apart from even the whispering voice of the Father. Without Him I would *never* encounter His calming, transcending peace and joy. I would never be able to look behind me and see Him eagerly standing there, granting my heart the ability to trust He will *forever* usher me to His greatest. In this quietness I have been given the eyes to see that I know He *is* the only real God.

The fatherly silence some days reemerges. His omnipresent love endures, though, always directing me. The hope is that by knowing the Father here on earth, I will know Him better in eternity.

A WILLING TRUST

The Father *has* matured my faith, and my trust *hasn't* been misplaced. My responses to uncertainty these days are different. I find

I do not become anxious like I once did in the quietness of His leading. When it seems my prayer or seeking of His direction is unanswered, I am discovering I am content to trust that He will send it in due time. Our history of meaningful interaction has made me more assured He knows what is best for me. The joy of being in this satisfying relationship with Jesus is becoming my sole heart's desire. I am finding I have peace waiting on Him. I confess I have yet to be perfected in this, but it is becoming who I am.

I am noticing this calm trust coloring my approach to the day-to-day unknowns and decisions. I find when I relinquish my finances to God I discover more blessing. Several years ago I sensed His leading toward flying a different aircraft in our company. But, instead of jumping to conclusions, I was content to remain still. The imminent call for a training date served as the impetus for me to complete the writing of this testimony (a purpose greater than I could have imagined).

This same trust is the security and peace I take with me as I continue to deploy overseas. It is my guide as I sense the Lord encouraging me to pursue a career shift to the airlines. I have taken steps in this belief by spending five figures training to be capable of doing so. He has given me the belief that it will allow me to better engage His desired ministry. I believe this book is at least part of the purpose for directing my heart toward ministry as He did in 2005. Mission aviation was His tool to get me to a place where I could see His plan.

I am grateful I have always been granted the direction I've needed *at the moment I need it*. I *am* increasingly resting in trust and eagerly anticipating the Father's intimate touch—the confidence I will see His hand again in the future as it fits His grander plan. Trusting in His faithfulness is what will keep me steadfast.

Trust also has enabled me to love others differently. The Father's love has been patient but correcting. I have placed my stock in its goodness, granting me the power to share the same unconditional love to those around me. My love for my family and my friendships from college continue to flourish. But, I see where this love now extends time and again to new people He places in my path, people who soon become new friends.

There is no question trust transforms. There is no better reason to trust Him.

Thirty-four

LIFE AND SPIRITUAL VICTORY IN CHRIST

My deepest yearning is that by testifying of the miraculous, fulfilling, and empowering work of the Lord Jesus Christ through my life, I could attest of God's surpassing greatness to the world. The story of how I have benefited through this arduous journey should not be kept to myself.

I have been blessed to behold the *mighty* power of the Father's sovereignty ushering me through this life. This is more than my witnessing His hand orchestrating one life event at a time. It has become ever apparent that each separate encounter with Him has specific contribution to the bigger, more glorious artistry of His grander painting of perfecting me as His son. I have seen how *every* aspect has purpose. What I might have perceived as times of spiritual weakness actually did nothing but propel me toward strength, peace, and assurance. *Every* minute affair has been expertly intertwined to complete His masterful object of grace. Who am I to have deserved such a grandiose story of love?

The Father staked His claim on me by showing me His presence all along the way, and without His ceaseless love I would have never known His recognizably personal touch, the point of reference to my deepest, most pressing needs. In increasing measure He filled me with peace and contentment through my relationship with Christ. In turn, I came to the point of rendering to Him more than my belief. Out of reciprocated love, I chose to love and follow Him. I kept seeking Him. He kept answering in endless love, proving He knows me. I placed my *unwavering* trust in His declarations, eternal and unchanging promise, and power to translate me to Himself. His affirmation of my faith and trust spurred me toward Him.

The closer I come to Christ as He persistently draws me to Himself, the more my faith and trust changes me. I have *never* been the same. My life here on earth has become unstoppable. Questions are disappearing. Trust is becoming easier. My belief is becoming firmer. The resolve that my faith is vibrant and living is becoming stronger. I have learned how to love and forgive as He has loved and forgiven me. The power to fend off spiritual attack is being realized through His Spirit. *This* is victory!

I cannot begin to adequately express the sense of belonging in knowing the Father loves me *so* much to have transcended space and time to patiently perfect me into His pronouncement of glory. Not only has He initiated everything, but His success has never been dependent on me. Neither my failure to listen nor my sin, though serious to Him, *ever did* or *ever does* mean the undoing of His plan. He remembers I am but dust. What rest this has given my soul.

I have come to know the Father as being *much* more than one to give up on His child out of frustration. So, I have gained greater assurance that He will *never* let me go. He will *finish* His work. He has invested too much of Himself not to complete it. As His Word declares His character in Philippians 1:6, the Almighty Lord will carry on to completion what He begins.

Every chasm of my spiritual, physical, mental, and emotional being has been touched through these years. But I have learned that for God to work and to see those positive impacts, I *must* remain open and pliable to His will. It was when I tucked my toes behind the Father's heels that I discovered fulfilling joy and pleasure in everything I did. *Never* was life boring. *Never* was it lacking anything. Only when I surrendered my wants, my passions, *and* my failures did He mold and shape me into *His* image—and *what* a beautiful resemblance to possess.

My Hope for You, Reader

This relationship has not been an easy road, but the benefits have been wild. This and much more is what I long for you, dear reader, to glean. The enormous reach a relationship in Christ provides is the most profound truth I could pray enourages every life that reads this. Being connected to Him offers *immeasurably* more than one could ever imagine. He is ready to help in the day-to-day trials and struggles; but, the loving Father wants *much* more. He wants to bring us into *His* purposes so we can discover who He is and how magnificent He is. More than the most passionate pursuit of a human relationship, He wants a relationship with us on a level beyond what we can fathom. He offers a contentment and peace that transcends this life. He *loves* us to an extreme we have yet to taste.

I hear the Father's quiet and loving lips saying, "Peter, when you cannot grasp how wide and long and high and deep My power, love, control, and existence stretches, simply rest in those smaller glimpses of Me that you *can* comprehend." In those instances of unattainable knowledge, I must rest and trust in the moments He and I have communed in relationship *so intense* that He drew me into His presence. Whether I felt His love and intimacy in the nearness of fellowship or through the inexplicable precision of His personal answers to my seeking, my heart responded back in zealous love. Therefore, I must take hold of the peace that proclaims He is real, the rest that He hears and knows me personally, and the assurance of His presence in my life. This is the depth of His love and connection He longs for each of us to experience.

I can appreciate it being a challenge to surrender control to a God Who is unseen. That is why faith and trust are paramount. *That* is also where His grace is found. In fact, the more intimately near the Father draws me, the more clearly I see that He is unfathomable.

It is as the Psalmist David so eloquently penned in Psalm 144:3 when he pronounced, "O Lord, what is man that You care for him, the son of man that You think of him?" Earlier, in Psalm 8:4, he echoed the same strain, "what is man that you are mindful of him, the son of man that you care for him?"

None of us will ever fully understand the infinite, inconceivable God as long as we are restrained to perceive Him through our human mind. I still have trouble comprehending the reality of God. Yet, it is through this lack of knowledge that He is all the more glorified when we believe and put our lives in His hands.

I find peace as I think of the many believers of Jesus' day who have preceded me who also had difficulty grasping the enormity of who God is as manifested in Christ. The apostle Peter believed in Jesus so passionately that he was ready to follow Him to death. Then, in the next moment Peter denied he had *ever* known Him. Despite Christ having told His followers He would be killed and still rise to life, it was only *after* the promise was completely fulfilled that they believed Scripture and the words Jesus had declared to them. Even Peter wondered what had happened when he saw the empty tomb. Had Peter taken hold of God's reality? Why would *any* of Jesus' followers have been afraid after His death and burial if they unequivocally believed Christ was who He said He was?

It stands to reason those who continually walked and talked with the *tangible, physical* form of God in Christ, nonetheless fell short in comprehending the sheer magnitude and supernatural character that comprises the eternal and everlasting God of the Universe. The simple fact we cannot understand the infinite limits of time and space in which God exists pronounces we do not and cannot fully grasp hold of who He is.

My spirit rests in the knowledge He *knows* my weak and finite existence better than I ever will this side of eternity. Until I see the Lord Jesus face to face, I know He realizes and accounts for my inherently weak human frame and the fact I cannot fully comprehend Him or understand His ways. How does that not speak to His patience and forbearance? In those moments I must avoid trying to figure Him out and resist being led into disbelief. Then I must rest in the ways He has been present in my life on a level I *can* understand and appreciate. Just as it was for the apostles and believers of Jesus' day after He was raised from the grave, so, too, my belief and faith in Him will become more resolute and unshaken.

So can yours.

Parting Perspective

A relationship with a God this alive has made my journey worth the trials. Progressively handing over every aspect of my life to the control of the Father has resulted in my good. I have unfettered access to God the Father through His Son. I can communicate and tap into His power through His Spirit. This has taken my life and approach to this world to new, unseen heights, enabling me to effectively engage it. Because I have the Holy Spirit I am able to relate and understand who God is and the magnitude of what He offers me in Christ. It is this gradual but genuine transformation that has assured me I am His loved child.

My heart is warmed even more as I recall the truth of Ephesians 5:18 that was reinforced by my pastor. The *filling of the Spirit* is a continual, recurring process. I am encouraged to know that, as with the apostle Paul and the host of believers past and present, I am not limited to one powerful experience with God's Spirit after the point I came to know Him. He has come to dwell powerfully within my life.

To the Father's glory, my holistic history of encounters with Him *have* greatly benefited the relationship I enjoy with Him through Christ. What a blessing it is to be connected to an unbeatably personal Savior and Lord! *Nothing* in this life can or ever will match this invisible but authentic reality. Perhaps through differing ways, all these treasures of relationship, security, and purpose are equally available to every person.

Bottom line, my spiritual growth in my walk with Christ will never be complete this side of eternity. *That* truth offers me true joy, fulfillment, peace, and immense hope. *There* is where perspective finds root. My prayer is for you to experience Christ in similar relationship and to take courage as you appreciate the richness of that journey.

Thank You, Father, for weaving such a complex yet perfect story through my life! Everything points to You. I am so thankful You are able to tell Your story through me, and that there is much remaining to be told. I do look forward to embarking on the ascent up the mountain of spiritual maturity where I will one day reach the glorious peak and be connected to You in pure and endless relationship. I cherish and look forward in anticipation of sharing that breathtaking view with You, my true life Friend, by my side. It is all because of You. I **love** You, Lord Jesus!

—Peter

Acknowledgements

Herein is my life as it has been defined by my Savior, my Friend—the Lord Jesus Christ. To Him be all glory, praise, and honor. My prayer is that those who read this testimony and journey of my life—from college, to the United States Navy, to the Middle East, Asia, and beyond—will be encouraged, emboldened, and empowered to experience a similarly loving and fulfilling relationship with the Father and Creator.

I give foremost thanks to the Lord for continually rescuing me out of a world of hurt and darkness to one day usher me into His presence, and for initiating and deepening my loving knowledge of Him. Oh, how I eagerly await His *embrace*. What you read in these pages was *His* story lived out through my life. The Father is also the one to be credited for His amazing authorship. He organized my thoughts and guided the writing.

I also give thanks to my parents, Thomas and Patricia Hoewisch, who have not just been my guardians, but have become my beloved and wise mentors along my spiritual journey. I love you both *very* much. Thank you for your patience and enduring love. Thank you for always motivating me to find, establish, and nurture my *own* relationship with Christ. You have tirelessly inspired me in becoming the best reflective image of our Lord and Savior, Jesus. Even in the writing of this book you stood by my side in patience and quietness because you knew it was an "assignment from headquarters." I know our mutual Father has a fitting reward for all your sacrifices throughout the years.

To my brothers, Mark and Matthew, I send words of love and appreciation. I know each of you are aware how deep this same love extends to you. It was not an easy thing dealing with me as the youngest brother. You have become more than family, and *definitely* more than brothers. You have become my friends. Likewise, both of you have never stopped loving me and have been by my side as I maneuvered through the many rapids that shaped my life.

I would be remiss not to recognize how much all of my family has meant, including the heritage of those I never met or was too young to know before their departure from this earth. Heidi, my sister, my heart aches to have known you for at least an instant, but I look forward to spending an eternity catching up. My grandparents, Mr. and Mrs. Hans Hoewisch and Mr. and Mrs. Leonard Overway; my extended family, Andrea, Cynthia, Ian, Evan, Steven, Jenny, Lee, and Faye; to my uncles and aunts, Roger, Gene and Marion, Dorothy and Wayne, Stan and Ethel, Aug and Mary, Tim and Becky, Ellen and Wayne, Cheryl and Bill, together with my cousins and all your families.

Speaking of family, there are more friends than I can number who have been used by the sovereign Lord to mold and shape me into the man He desired. I must acknowledge some who shared in my most intimate hurts and struggles: Tim, Adam, Micah, Jason, Nathanael, Luke, Kurt, Glenn, David, Bo, Scott. I thank each of you and the stalwart, faithful women in your lives for your persistent love and encouragement.

To my peers throughout the years who have become close friends, the family of my friends, my parents' friends who welcomed me into their lives, the staff of LeTourneau University who mentored me, my extended church family, to the *innumerable* peers and management at Dynamic Aviation, you have all become like a second family. To Senior Chief Cleaves, Mr. Gauthier, Mr. James, and all those with whom I formed a rapport during the Navy, I must express my gratitude.

Family and friends continue to be a consistent blessing in my life, but some very crucial people have been used by God to bless me in this project. I must acknowledge the tireless work of my developmental, primary editor. Julie-Allyson Ieron, I thank you for the countless hours and patience expended helping me craft this work into something God-honoring. I have learned much through your encouraging edits. I also thank Carrie Thompson, Madison Wasinger, Katherine Lloyd, and Dave Sheets for your time, guidance, patience, and encouragement. I thank all the staff of Christian Writer's Guild, Believer's Press, Bethany Press, designers, and crafters who have made this a reality. I also extend my deepest thanks to my family, friends, and all who have given incalculable time and support through advice and insight to this enduring, immense project.

Whether mentioned by name or quietly in my heart, I pray you each know you *did* have a memorable and lasting impression because of what you poured into my life. This has warmed the Lord's heart. The Father will never forget. You *all* hold a special place in my heart. I am a blessed man to have been touched and impacted by *so* many. From the fullness of my heart, *thank you*.

May the praises of our Lord and Father
ring out for all to hear as **His** *story is told.*

Endnotes

1   Rick Warren, "Seeing Life from God's View," in *The Purpose-Driven Life*. (Grand Rapids, Mich.: Zondervan, 2002), 43.

2   "Aviation Selection Test Battery (ASTB)," U. S. Navy, accessed March 25, 2014, www.usnavy.vt.edu/documents/astboverview.pdf

3   "U.S. Naval Flight Surgeon's Manual Third Edition 1991," Naval Aerospace Medical Institute, accessed June 12, 2014, http://www.operationalmedicine.org/TextbookFiles/FlightSurgeonsManual.pdf (page 315)

DISCLAIMER

PERSPECTIVE-A flight to victory through relationship with a living Savior [the "book"] is a true story of specific life events from material recorded and written by Peter Hoewisch [the "author"] and all rights thereto are now owned by Insightful Perspectives LLC [the "owner"]. The author's primary source for information and recollection was his papers, journals, and correspondence. Supporting details of locations, people, and events were accurate at the time they were recorded in the good faith efforts and memories of the author. This book is written for the spiritual inspiration and encouragement of all readers. While a reader may discover or apply a similar approach to life through this book, it is not intended nor is it to be construed as a manual for living or to be duplicated as advice, whether in specific or general. There are no warranties, guarantees, or promises, written or implied, offered in or that extend beyond this book for the betterment of anyone. Intangible insights and positive, individual conclusions are the only benefits meant for the reader and for the good of the public and humanities. This book is the sole expression of the author, and not necessarily that of any other person. Neither the publisher providing publishing services, the owner, the author, nor any entity or person [the "group"] are liable for any physical, psychological, emotional, financial, or other damages resulting from any application or loss of time in the use of this book's material. You are responsible for your own choices, actions, and results. Neither is the group responsible for unintentional inaccuracies, were they to exist, or for similarities to other locations, people, or events. By purchasing, owning, or reading this book, you, the reader, accept the book as is, with all faults, and release the author, the owner, the publisher, this book, and all entities affiliated with this work of art from any and all claims, demands, liability, and/or financial remuneration, culpability, or restitution arising from the use of this book. Only where applicable and according to the terms and conditions of the owner, the reseller(s), and/or other applicable laws and regulations, rejection of these Disclaimer terms after purchase may allow but limit responsibility to a maximum of a refund of the book's purchase price. By purchasing and/or reading this book, you accede to the nature of this book being a personal story, written for your personal enrichment and edification.

www.ingramcontent.com/pod-product-compliance
Lightning Source LLC
Chambersburg PA
CBHW051545030726
47592CB00001B/137